THE OXFORD HISTORY OF MUSIC
VOL. V

THE VIENNESE PERIOD

THE OXFORD
HISTORY OF MUSIC

VOL. V

THE VIENNESE PERIOD

BY

W. H. HADOW

Second Edition

NEW YORK
COOPER SQUARE PUBLISHERS, INC.
1973

Revised edition Published 1931 by Oxford University Press
Reprinted by Permission of Oxford University Press
Published 1973 by Cooper Square Publishers, Inc.
59 Fourth Avenue, New York, New York 10003
International Standard Book Number 0-8154-0473-5
Library of Congress Catalog Card Number 72-97075

Printed in the United States of America

DEDICATED TO

M. L. H.

PREFACE

THE object of this volume is to sketch the history of Musical Composition from the time of C. P. E. Bach to that of Schubert. The field is so wide and the need of selection so obvious that it may be serviceable to explain in a few words the method which is here adopted and the principal topics which are here discussed.

Two causes, apart from the force of personal genius, affected the history of Music during the latter part of the eighteenth century: first, the change in social and aesthetic conditions; second, the increase of skill in vocalization and in the manufacture and use of most instruments. Accordingly, the first chapter briefly indicates the general level of taste, and the effect for good and ill of patronage, during the period in question; the second touches upon the structure of instruments and the careers of virtuosi. The latter of these invades some of the ground already covered in vol. iv. I regret this for many reasons, among others because Mr. Fuller Maitland's account is of wider range than mine: indeed, if mine had not been already finished, when his volume appeared, it would probably be here represented by a set of references. And though the standpoint from which it is written seems sufficiently distinct to justify its retention, I would ask all readers who find it insufficient, to supplement it from Mr. Fuller Maitland's treatment of 'the Orchestra,' 'the Keyed-instruments,' and 'the Rise of Virtuosity.'

From chapter iii onwards this volume deals exclusively with the history of composition. For its plan three possible alternatives presented themselves : (1) to follow the century decade by decade, keeping abreast the work done in the different forms by different composers ; (2) to take each country as a unit, and narrate its particular record in successive detail ; (3) to divide on the basis of the musical forms themselves, and to trace the development of each separately. The special character of the period indicated that the last of these was the most advisable, and though it has the disadvantage of covering the century four times, I feel sure that it is clearer than either of the others. For the convenience of the reader it may be well to append here the dates of the chief composers whose works are mentioned.

A. The pioneers :—

    C. P. E. Bach, 1714–88 : first two volumes of sonatas, 1742 and 1744.

    Gluck, 1714–87 : began his reform of opera with *Orfeo*, 1762.

B. Italian composers, first period :—

    Jommelli, 1714–74; Traetta, 1727–79; Piccinni, 1728–1800; Sarti, 1729–1802; Sacchini, 1734–86.

C. Composers of the Viennese School :—

    Haydn, 1732–1809 : maturest compositions between 1780 and 1802.

    Mozart, 1756–91 : maturest compositions between 1780 and 1791.

    Beethoven, 1770–1827 : invited to Vienna by Haydn, 1792.

    Schubert, 1797–1828 : *Erlkönig* (Op. 1), written in the winter of 1815–6.

D. Italian composers : second period :—

    Paisiello, 1741–1816; Boccherini, 1743–1805; Salieri, 1750–1825; Cherubini, 1760–1842; Spontini, 1774–1851.

E. Contemporary French composers [1]:—

Gossec, 1734–1829; Grétry, 1741–1813; Méhul, 1763–1817; Lesueur, 1763–1837; Boieldieu, 1774–1834.

F. Transition to the Romantic period:—

Spohr, 1784–1859: first violin-concerto written in 1802.

[Weber, 1786–1826: *Der Freischütz*, produced at Berlin, 1821.]

[Rossini, 1792–1868: first appearance in Vienna, 1822.]

The main problems with which this volume is concerned are those of the actual growth and progress of the musical forms, and of the manner in which the style of the great composers was affected by their own maturing experience and by the work of their predecessors and contemporaries. Among other points may be specified the influence of C. P. E. Bach upon Haydn, the place of the folk-song in classical composition, the part played by Gluck in the history of opera, the gradual divergence of sonata, symphony, and quartet, the interrelation of Haydn and Mozart, the character of Beethoven's third period, the debt owed by German song to the national movement in German poetry. All these deserve, and some have elsewhere received, a more elaborate treatment than can be accorded within the limits of a single volume : my principal endeavour has been to present a straightforward narrative of the facts, so grouped and emphasized as to show their historical connexion, and illustrated in such terms of comment and criticism as the occasion seemed to require.

[1] Auber (1782–1871) belongs to the next period.

CONTENTS

CHAPTER   PAGE

I. ON THE GENERAL CONDITION OF TASTE IN THE EIGHTEENTH CENTURY . . . 1

II. INSTRUMENTS AND VIRTUOSI. . . . 19

III. THE CONFLICT OF STYLES 57

IV. GLUCK AND THE REFORM OF THE OPERA . 85

V. THE OPERA FROM MOZART TO WEBER . 105

VI. ORATORIO AND CHURCH MUSIC . . . 142

VII. THE INSTRUMENTAL FORMS.
C. P. E. BACH AND THE GROWTH OF THE SONATA 183

VIII. THE INSTRUMENTAL FORMS (*continued*).
THE EARLY SYMPHONIES AND QUARTETS OF HAYDN 206

IX. THE INSTRUMENTAL FORMS (*continued*).
HAYDN AND MOZART 231

X. THE INSTRUMENTAL FORMS (*continued*).
BEETHOVEN 268

XI. THE INSTRUMENTAL FORMS (*continued*).
SCHUBERT AND THE LATER CONTEMPORARIES OF BEETHOVEN 304

XII. SONG 324

INDEX 345

THE VIENNESE PERIOD

CHAPTER I

ON THE GENERAL CONDITION OF TASTE IN THE EIGHTEENTH CENTURY

AMONG the many paradoxes which lie along the surface of the eighteenth century there is none more remarkable than its combination of lavish display with an almost barbarous discomfort. Wealth was abundant, and on occasion could be freely expended: at no time since the Roman Empire was pageantry more magnificent or ostentation more profuse; and yet men, who had at their command everything that money could buy, were content to lack pleasures which we take for granted, and to endure hardships which we should assuredly regard as intolerable. In most European capitals the streets were narrow, filthy, and ill-paved, lighted by a few feeble cressets, protected by a few feeble watchmen, the nightly scenes of disturbance and riot which you could scarce hope to traverse without a guard. Through country districts the high roads lay thick in dust and neglect; scored with deep ruts, or strewn with boulders, amid which your carriage tumbled and jolted until at evening it brought you to some wretched inn where you were expected to furnish your own bedding and provisions. Mr. Clarke, writing from Madrid in 1761, mentions that the houses are built with dry walls, 'lime being very dear and scarce,' that house-rent is exorbitant, and that 'if you want glass windows you must put them in yourself.' 'There is,' he adds, 'no such thing in Madrid as a tavern or a coffee-house, and only one news-

paper.' Paris under Louis XV was little better: visitors
like Walpole and Franklin, natives like Mercier, have left
us equally unpleasing records of dirt, noise, confusion, and
shameless robbery[1]: while Vienna, though 'fed from the
Imperial kitchen,' and, we may almost add, lodged under
the Imperial roof, appears to have been no less wanting in
the bare essentials of amenity and refinement. Yet the
splendours of the Escurial rivalled those of Versailles: the
banquets at Schönbrunn were served upon solid gold, and
the extravagance of dress ranged from Prince Esterhazy in
'a gala-robe sewn with jewels' to Michael Kelly the actor
with his gold-embroidered coat, his two watches, his lace
ruffles, and his 'diamond ring on each little finger[2].'

Of this curious contrast three possible explanations may
be offered. In the first place money was spent not only
for the pleasure that it purchased but for the social position
that it implied. The days of the rich *roturier* had not yet
come: wealth was still an inherited privilege of nobility, and
its display served mainly to adorn the blazon of the sixteen
quarterings. The strongest motive principle of the age was
the pride of birth. Lady Mary Wortley Montagu gives an
amusing picture of two Austrian countesses whose chairs met
one night at a street corner, and who sat till two in the
morning because neither would be the first to give way: the
intercourse of the great families was regulated by strict order
of precedence, and hedged about with the most thorny and
uncompromising etiquette. It became therefore a point of
honour that a noble should emulate his equals and outshine
his inferiors; that at all hazards he should live brilliantly in

---

[1] See De Broc, *La France sous l'ancien régime*, ii. 174–187. For a companion
picture from Thuringia, see Lewes's *Life of Goethe*, Bk. IV. ch. i. 'Weimar in the
eighteenth century.'

[2] See M. Kelly, *Reminiscences*, i. 249. For the magnificence of ladies' court
dress the reader may consult *Le Livre-journal de Madame Éloffe* (quoted entire in
vol. i. of De Reiset's *Modes et usages au temps de Marie-Antoinette*) and Lady
Mary Wortley Montagu's letters from Vienna.

public; that he should sit at the top of the fashion and maintain such state and dignity as befitted his rank. A notable
instance may be found in one of the small German courts.
The temperament of the country, the exigencies of the time,
the example of the great king, all combined to foster the
military spirit: every potentate had his army, from Oldenburg
to Hohenzollern; and among them (a pathetic figure) reigned
the Graf von Limburg-Styrum, starving his revenues to raise
a Hussar-corps of which the full fighting-strength amounted
to a colonel, six officers, and two privates. It is little wonder
that roads were ill-kept, towns ill-lighted, and dwelling-rooms
ill-furnished, when the chief object of human existence was
to make a brave show on state occasions.

Secondly, there went with this a certain homeliness of
manner, rising at its best into simplicity, at its worst sinking
into vulgarity and coarseness. The elaborate ceremonial of
the age was mainly a matter of public exhibition, put on
with the diamonds and the gold embroidery, returned with
them to the wardrobe or the tiring-room. Maria Theresa,
stateliest of empresses on the throne, was in private careless and unceremonious, often slovenly in attire, speaking
by preference the broadest and most colloquial Viennese.
Joseph II used to dine off 'boiled bacon and water with
a single glass of Tokay,' and to spend his afternoon wandering
about the streets, 'one pocket full of gold pieces for the
poor, the other full of chocolate-drops for himself.' Nor
were the hobbies of royalty less significant. Our own 'Farmer
George' is no isolated exception; Charles III of Spain was
a turner, Louis XVI a locksmith, while the Hapsburgs, as
an audacious bandmaster ventured to tell one of them, would
certainly have made their mark as professional musicians.

At the same time this unconstrained ease of life had its
darker side. Speech ventured on a freedom which surpasses
our utmost limits, habits were often indelicate and pleasures
gross. Frederick at Sans-Souci, Karl August at Weimar, were

both fond of rough practical joking; the behaviour of Kaunitz, the famous Austrian chancellor, would not now be tolerated at a village ordinary; and in the little Salon of the Hermitage, to which only the inner circle of diplomacy was admitted, an official notice imposed a fine of ten kopecks for 'scowling, lying, and using abusive language [1].' It was but natural that the tone set by the court should be echoed and re-echoed through society at large. If Serene Highnesses were unmannerly, no better could be expected of their subjects. If patrician amusements were often coarse and cruel, it was not for the humble plebeian to improve upon them. Spain kept up her auto-da-fé till the mid-century; France, though more civilized than her contemporaries, often mistook the accidents for the essentials of civilization; while in London criminals were still drawn and quartered before a gaping crowd, the national sportsmanship found its outlet in the cock-pit and the prize-ring, and our banquets may be estimated by the tavern-bill of a dinner for seven persons, which, with no costly dish, swells by sheer bulk to a total of eighty pounds [2].

In the third place there was a remarkable instability among all matters of judgement and opinion. The Age of Reason made frequent lapses into extreme superstition and credulity: the most practical of centuries often wasted its money on schemes beside which those of Laputa were commonplace. Nothing was too absurd for a sceptical generation to believe: Cagliostro carried his impostures from court to court; Paganini was compelled to produce a certificate that he was of mortal parentage; Harlequin, in London, gathered a thronging crowd by the public announcement that he would creep into a quart bottle. Nor is the literary taste of the time less fertile in contrasts. The France of Voltaire took Crébillon for a genius; the England of Gray and Johnson accepted Douglas as a tragedy and Ossian as a classic: throughout Europe the

[1] See Waliszewski, *Catharine II*, p. 516.
[2] See G. W. E. Russell, *Collections and Recollections*, ch. vii. It is dated 1751.

standard fluctuated with every breath of fashion and fell before every impact of caprice. Even in Germany, where the progress of literature was most continuous, it seems to have spread but slowly through the prejudices and preoccupations of the social life: elsewhere the haphazard and uncertain verdict indicated a temper that cared but little for any questions of principle or system.

Here, then, we have a background for the musical history of the period: a society brilliant, light, artificial, sumptuous in ceremonial, lavish in expenditure, 'presenting,' as Ruskin says, 'a celestial appearance,' and claiming in return the right of unlimited amusement: a Church which appeared to have outlived its Creed and forgotten its duties; its lower offices ranking with the peasant or the lackey, its higher given up to principalities and powers: a *bourgeoisie* solid, coarse, ill-educated, but sound at heart, beginning, as the century waned, to feel its strength and prepare for its coming democracy. It is impossible to over-estimate the importance to music of the social and political changes which culminated in the decade of Revolution. They meant that the old régime had been tried and found wanting; that the standard of taste was no longer an aristocratic privilege; that the doors of the salon should be thrown open, and that art should emerge into a larger and more liberal atmosphere. A couple of generations separated Georg von Reutter from Beethoven, each in his time regarded as the greatest of Viennese composers, and in this one fact we may find the artistic record of the age.

Before we trace the development which this change implies, it may be well to modify an over-statement commonly accepted among musical historians. We are told that between J. S. Bach and Haydn there spread a dreary and unprofitable desert, in which men had strayed from the wonted paths and had not yet found others; an inglorious period of darkness, dimly illuminated by the talents of Carl Philipp Emanuel, but otherwise lost in silence and old night. 'At the particular time

at which E. Bach lived,' says Dr. Maczewski[1], 'there were
no great men. The gigantic days of Handel and J. S. Bach
were exchanged for a time of peruke and powder, when the
highest ideal was neatness, smoothness, and elegance. Depth,
force, originality were gone, and taste was the most important
word in all things.' As here presented this remark can only
lead to error and misconception. The so-called 'Zopf' period
is not an interval between J. S. Bach and Haydn; the former
died in 1750, and the latter's first known compositions were
produced in 1751; it overlapped with a wide margin the work
of both generations, it flourished before the Matthäus Passion,
it lingered after the Salomon Symphonies. That Dr. Maczewski has correctly described the general taste of the mid-
century is unquestionably true; but he has impaired the value
of his description by a false attribution of causes. When
J. S. Bach died there was no reaction against his methods, for
they had never exercised any influence in his lifetime. He was
famous as a brilliant player, as a learned contrapuntist, as the
father of an amiable and talented son, but no one, not even
Frederick the Great, had any idea that there was a difference
between his music and that of Graun or Hasse. His choral
works were absolutely unknown, granted a single hearing
before the good people of Leipsic, and then consigned to
dust and oblivion until Mendelssohn discovered them eighty
years later. A few of his instrumental compositions were
engraved, the *Wohltemperirtes Klavier* was sometimes used
as a textbook for students: but apart from these his writings
were treated with as little respect as the commentaries of
a schoolman or the dissertations of a university professor.
Indirectly, he influenced the art through his sons, of whom
two at least were taught by him to stem the shallow tide of
Italian music; directly, he exerted no real authority till the
time of Beethoven, and very little till that of Mendelssohn
and Schumann.

[1] Grove's *Dictionary* (first edition), i. 113.

At the beginning of our period aesthetic judgement was controversial rather than critical. It cannot be doubted that there was a widespread desire for musical enjoyment, that emulation was keen and party spirit vigorous; but opinion, on some points punctilious and exacting, maintained on others a callous indifference which we find it very difficult to comprehend. Pagin the violinist was hissed in Paris for daring to 'play in the Italian style'; but the same audience that condemned him listened with complacence to an opera in which the orchestra was loud and strident, in which the conductor 'made a noise like a man chopping wood,' and in which the quality of the singing had become so proverbial that Traetta, wishing to express the shriek of a despairing heroine, left the note blank in his score, and wrote above the line 'un urlo francese'—a French howl. No doubt Italy was more sensitive; at least it had some feeling for quality of tone, and 'a nice strain of virtuosity': but even in Italy the verdict was often a mere matter of popular clamour and caprice. Take, for instance, the Roman opera-house, at that time the highest school in which a musician could graduate. The first part of the performance usually went for nothing, since the audience made so much disturbance that even the orchestra was inaudible. Then, when quiet was established, the abbés took their seats in the front row, a lighted taper in one hand, a book of the play in the other, and uttered loud and sarcastic cries of 'Bravo bestia' if an actor missed or altered a word. No allowance was made for circumstances: the soprano who showed signs of nervousness, the tenor who was out of voice from a cold, were driven off the stage by a torrent of street abuse. The composer, who presided for the first three nights at the harpsichord, had to thank fortune for his reception. In 1749 Jommelli brought out his *Ricimero*, and the audience boarded the stage and carried him round the theatre in triumph. Next year he produced his first version of *Armida*, and was obliged to fly for his life

through a back door. So far as we can tell there was very
little to choose between the two works; but in the interval
he had applied for the directorship of the Papal Choir, and
the Roman public disapproved of his youthful presumption.
Nor had the composer any serious chance of appealing to
posterity by publication. To print an orchestral score was
difficult in France and England, more difficult in Germany,
and in Italy almost impossible. 'There is no such thing as
a music shop in the country,' says Dr. Burney, writing from
Venice in 1770. 'Musical compositions are so short-lived,
such is the rage for novelty, that for the few copies wanted
it is not worth while to be at the expense of engraving.'

A more remarkable instance yet remains. The Mannheim
Orchestra, conducted by Stamitz for the Elector Palatine,
was unhesitatingly accepted as the finest in Europe. To
gain a place in its ranks was an object of strenuous ambition,
to attend its concerts was a rare and distinguished privilege.
'It was here,' says Dr. Burney, 'that Stamitz, stimulated by
Jommelli, first surpassed the bounds of common opera overtures, which had hitherto only served in the theatre as a kind
of court cryer. It was here that the *crescendo* and *diminuendo*
had birth, and the *piano* (which was before chiefly used as
an echo, with which it was generally synonymous) as well as
the *forte* were found to be musical colours, which had their
shades as much as red and blue in painting.' He then adds
a qualification of which both the substance and the tone are
equally interesting. 'I found, however, an imperfection in
this band, common to all others that I have ever heard, but
which I was in hopes would be removed by men so attentive
and so able: the defect I mean is the want of truth in the
wind instruments. I know it is natural to these instruments
to be out of tune, but some of that art and diligence, which
the great performers have manifested in vanquishing difficulties
of other kinds, would surely be well employed in correcting
this leaven which so much sours and corrupts all harmony.

This was too plainly the case to-night with the bassoons and hautbois, which were rather too sharp at the beginning, and continued growing sharper to the end of the opera[1].' This defect was still apparent when Mozart visited Mannheim in 1778, but it seems to have been ignored or disregarded by other visitors, such, for instance, as Reichardt and Marpurg. Perhaps they were overwhelmed at hearing soft passages which were not intended for the purpose of a mechanical echo; or felt a touch of reverential awe in the place where *crescendo* and *diminuendo* had their birth. Or it may be that they anticipated Grétry's criticism of the Swedish ambassador: 'Il chantoit naturellement faux, mais il chantoit faux avec tant de grâce et d'expression qu'on avoit encore du plaisir à l'entendre[2].'

In the reception of chamber-music toleration was superseded by indifference. Viotti, summoned to play before Marie Antoinette, after three vain attempts to break the conversation, put up his violin, and walked out of the hall. Giornovichi, engaged for a drawing-room concert in London, found himself powerless to attract the attention of his audience, and, with perfect impunity, substituted the air 'J'ai du bon tabac' for the concerto which was announced in his name. At the English embassy in Berlin, a roguish director performed the same piece, under different titles, the whole evening through, and was complimented at the end on the diversity of his programme. Nor are such incidents at all rare or exceptional; they occur so frequently that they soon cease to arouse wonder or excite comment. The only marvel is that any artist should have stooped to endure such usage, and have risked the pillory for so precarious and uncertain a reward.

Finally, composition itself was infected by the prevalent

---

[1] Burney, *Present State of Music in Germany* (1772), pp. 95–97. Dittersdorf (*Autobiography*, ch. xiii) gives an even worse account of the orchestra at Venice.
[2] Grétry, *Essais sur la musique*, ii. 402.

taste for lightness and frivolity. Society wanted to be amused, and cared little for the propriety of the entertainment: at no time in the history of civilization has art been treated with a less degree of truth or reverence. We need do no more than allude to the farce seen by Lady Mary Wortley Montagu at Vienna, and the Passion-Play witnessed by Mr. Clarke at Madrid; but, gross and extreme as were these examples, music lagged but little behind in the race for degradation. Grand Opera interspersed its tragedy with incongruous scenes of pantomime and burlesque; Oratorios were presented with comic intermezzi; even the services of the Church were often powerless to resist the prevalent fashion. 'We have had two new Misereres this week,' says the Abbate Ortes, writing from Venice, 'one by Galuppi, one by Sacchini. They were both strings of arias, jigs, balletti, and other movements which would be just as suitable to a Te Deum as to a Miserere[1].' Observe that there is no tone of irony in this criticism; only a regret that the jigs and balletti were not sufficiently distinctive to separate confession from the rest of worship.

It seems incredible that any true artistic work can have been done under such conditions. Yet in the thirty years which followed the death of J. S. Bach, the years to which all these incidents belong, and of which they are all in a measure typical, there is no lack of noble and conspicuous achievement. To this despised period belong the most mature sonatas of Philipp Emanuel Bach, and of his brother Wilhelm Friedemann, all of the best operas of Gluck, some forty of Haydn's symphonies and a like number of his quartets, over three hundred and fifty compositions of Mozart, including the Haffner Serenade, the Paris Symphony and *Idomeneo,* Boccherini's early chamber-works, Grétry's early operas, and, among lesser lights, many of the most characteristic scores of Piccinni, Hasse, Sarti, Sacchini, and Paisiello. If a com-

[1] Letter to Hasse (April 18, 1772) quoted in Wiel's *I teatri musicali veneziani del settecento.*

poser of our own time were called upon to write for an orchestra which played habitually out of tune, and to submit his work to an audience which might be prejudiced or inattentive; if he knew that his success or failure would depend on a turn of the wheel—a chance accident to a singer, a chance rumour from the street, a hazard of victory between conflicting parties—we can imagine the terms in which he would decline the invitation. But it must be remembered that in the third quarter of the eighteenth century there were no better materials attainable, and that genius is forced to express itself through the best medium that it has at command. Besides, the case was not altogether hopeless. The controversies which agitated Paris from the 'Guerre des Bouffons' to the *Iphigénie* at least proclaimed a war from which the conquest of a kingdom might ultimately ensue. The love of virtuosity which filled Italy and England prepared the way for a more artistic temper which might one day attain to the love of music itself. For a time, indeed, there was little to be expected from the popular verdict: it was still regulated by an artificial code and an unthinking fashion. But at worst there were always a few good citizens to maintain the cause of truth and equity, and their number gradually increased as the years wore on.

Meanwhile, art turned for a livelihood to the munificence of wealthy patrons. In every capital, from Madrid to St. Petersburg, there were court-appointments of varying dignity and position: in most countries aristocracy followed the royal practice, and established a private orchestra as an essential part of its retinue [1]. The system appears to have depended but little on any question of personal taste. Frederick the Great, an enthusiastic amateur and a flute-player of some eminence, was not more cordial in patronage

[1] 'This elegant and agreeable luxury, which falls within the compass of a very large fortune, is known in every country of Europe except England.' Arthur Young, à propos of the Duc d'Aguillon's private orchestra; *Journal*, Aug. 23, 1787.

than the Empress Catherine, who did not know one tune
from another, and 'could recognize no sounds except the
voices of her nine dogs': if the former encouraged native
art by supporting Graun, Quantz, and C. P. E. Bach, the
latter attempted to educate her people by successive invitations
to Galuppi, Traetta, Paisiello, Sarti, and other famous Italians.
All palace doors lay open to the musician: Hasse was maintained at Dresden by Augustus the Strong; Sarti, before
his visit to St. Petersburg, held office under Christian VII
at Copenhagen; Naumann at Stockholm received ten years'
continuous favour from Gustavus the Unlucky; Jommelli
found at Stuttgart a full compensation for the ill-usage of
his countrymen; Scarlatti and Boccherini grew old at the
Spanish court, where, for two successive reigns the singer
Farinelli acted as chief adviser. But it was in Austria that
the custom was chiefly prevalent; partly, it would seem, from
a doctrine of *noblesse oblige*, partly from a genuine love of
music which ran through every rank and grade of society.
Maria Theresa frequently sang in the operatic performances
of her private theatre [1], Joseph II played the violoncello in
its orchestra, both alike invited the most famous artists to
Vienna and rewarded them freely with offices or commissions.
The Hofkapelle had its band, the Cathedral its choir and its
four organists, the royal opera-houses of Laxenburg and
Schönbrunn welcomed every dramatic composer from Gluck
to Giuseppe Scarlatti, and gave free places to every spectator
from the archduke in the stalls to the farmer's boy in the
gallery [2]. Almost all the great Viennese families—Lichtenstein,
Lobkowitz, Auersperg, and many others—displayed the same
generosity, the same artistic appreciation, and the tone set

---

[1] The score of Reutter's *Il Palladio Conservato* contains a note saying that at
the first performance the parts were taken by Maria Theresa, the Archduchess
Maria Anna, and the Countess Texin. Such instances are numerous, especially
with Reutter's operas.

[2] See the account of the Laxenburg theatre in Michael Kelly's *Reminiscences*,
vol. i. p. 246.

vibrating from the capital spread far and wide to country houses like those of Fürnburg and Morzin, and to episcopal palaces like those of Gran, Olmütz, and Grosswardein.

The relation implied in this patronage was, for the most part, frankly that of master and servant. As a rule, genius sat below the salt, and wore a livery like the butler or the footman. No doubt the master was often genial and kindly, no doubt the gap was often lessened by the prevalent simplicity of manners; but the system in general was not well qualified to raise the dignity of art or to increase the self-respect of the artist. At best he might be admitted to the sort of friendship which a good sportsman felt for his keeper; at worst he might be dependent on the caprices of an ignorant or tyrannical despot. With the single exception of Farinelli, an exception, it may be added, which proves far too much, we have no case of real equality and only one of considerable freedom; indeed both were precluded by the conditions of the time. And even granted that examples of graciousness and condescension far outnumbered those of ill-treatment or neglect, it still remains true that the whole principle of patronage was fraught with danger to the art that it protected. Much of the music written during the mid-century is like the furniture of a Paradiesensaal: stiff, uncomfortable chairs, all gilding and damask; inlaid tables, too elegant to be of use; priceless statuettes made of sea-shells; fantastic clocks with musical boxes in the pedestal; a thousand costly trifles which could add no jot to the ease or amenity of human life. It would have been a miracle if, amid these unreal splendours, art had always maintained its sincerity unimpaired.

The effects of patronage, for good and ill, may be illustrated by the lives of two brothers, somewhat similar in gifts, greatly dissimilar in fortune. At the outset of their career there seemed but little to choose between the prospects of Joseph and Michael Haydn. For three years they sat side by side

in the choir at St. Stephen's: when the elder's voice began
to fail, the younger was chosen to succeed him as principal
soloist: if the one was the more diligent, the other showed
in early days the more promise: Michael obtained his first
official appointment while Joseph was still giving lessons at
five florins a month. Then came the parting of the ways.
In 1761 Joseph Haydn was attached to the household of
Prince Esterhazy, next year his brother was promoted from
Grosswardein to Salzburg, and thenceforward the two careers
diverged until the end. It is not, indeed, to be maintained
that the differences were due to a single cause. The elder
brother was more gifted, more temperate, far more industrious.
But something at any rate must be allowed for material surroundings, and in these the inequality of condition can hardly
be overstated. At Salzburg the grave, saintly Archbishop
Sigismund encouraged the severer forms of Church music,
but cared little for the stage or the concert-room; his successor Archbishop Hieronymus was coarse, brutal, and over-
bearing, wholly indifferent to art and letters, keeping his
band and choir as a necessary adjunct of his office, but
thwarting all serious effort by frivolous taste and arbitrary
injunction. At Esterhàz there were two theatres, a first-rate
choir, an orchestra of picked artists, and over all Prince
Nicholas Esterhazy, wise, liberal, enlightened, a skilled
amateur, a true enthusiast, who recognized from the beginning
that his new director was a genius, and gave him not only
cordial support but entire liberty of action. The result is
in the highest degree significant. Michael Haydn wrote
Church music of great strength and dignity, but in all other
forms his composition is hasty, careless, and unequal—the
work of a disappointed man. Joseph Haydn ranged freely
from opera to symphony, from symphony to quartet, and filled
every corner of the art with fresh air and sunshine. The one
found his chief opportunity of expression in the strictest and
most conservative of all styles, and has been left behind as

the representative of an outworn and obsolete method. The other, with an open choice before him, discarded the artifices of current phraseology, saturated his music with his native folk-songs, and thus infused it with a new strength and a new vitality. It is worthy of remark that the greatest composer ever fostered by a systematic patronage was the one over whose character patronage exercised the least control.

Meantime revolt was imminent, and the first blow in its cause was struck by Mozart. He too had suffered from Archbishop Hieronymus. As Concertmeister at Salzburg he had been bullied, ill-paid, subjected to insult and indignity; in 1777 a reasonable request for leave of absence had been scornfully refused; during the next four years the position had grown more and more intolerable; at last, in 1781, the storm burst. Its occasion was trivial enough. The Archbishop had carried his court to Vienna for the season; his temper, always violent, had been exasperated by a mark of imperial disfavour; in a fit of pettish rage he determined to check Mozart's triumphal progress through the capital, and sent him peremptory orders to cancel his engagements and return to Salzburg without delay. The Concertmeister, already at the end of his endurance, came to protest; was received with a torrent of uncontrolled abuse; and in white heat of anger proffered his resignation on the spot[1]. In that memorable interview the *ancien régime* of music signed its death-warrant. The revolution peacefully inaugurated by Haydn came to a sudden and abrupt climax; the old gilded idol toppled over and scattered its fragments in the dust. It must not be inferred that the influence of wealth and station passed altogether into abeyance. Beethoven was the guest of Prince Lichnowsky, the master of the Archduke Rudolph; Schubert held for six years a loose-knit appointment as music-teacher to the family of Count Johann Esterhazy. But wealth

[1] See the whole story in Mozart's letter of May 9. Jahn's *Mozart*, ch. xxii.

and station had no longer the power to prescribe, to command, to hold genius within artificial bounds. It commissioned works, but it ceased to exercise any control over their character. In a word, it paid for the dedication, and left the artist a free hand.

There is no incongruity in the fact that Mozart was the first active leader of this popular movement. Nothing is further from the truth than to regard him as a mere court-composer, a Prince Charming of the salon and the presence-chamber, a musical exquisite whose gifts can be summed up in brilliance and delicacy of form. Grant that his fertile genius and his ready command of resource often enabled him to write without the stress of great emotional impulse, yet the best of his music, and indeed almost all the work of his maturer period, is essentially human at heart, speaking always in polished phrase, but none the less speaking truths for the understanding of mankind. His dearest wish was to found a reputation on the suffrages of the people, and the favour shown to him by Joseph II seemed in his eyes a small matter beside the welcome accorded to his operas by the citizens of Prague[1].

Yet the new-won freedom was purchased at a cost of much poverty and privation. In throwing off its dependence art forewent at the same time the most certain of its material rewards, and was compelled to engage in a struggle for the bare necessaries of existence. Mozart throughout his later years was continually pressed for money : Beethoven, though somewhat better paid, was forced to accept the charity of a private subscription : Schubert, for all his lavish industry, never earned enough to keep body and soul together. It seemed, indeed, as though the composer's chances were trembling in the balance. If he approached the theatre he found himself confronted with an impresario always astute and often unscrupulous. If he tried his fortune in the concert-room, he soon discovered that profits could be swallowed by expenses. If he attempted to print his work

---

[1] See Jahn's *Mozart*, chs. xxxvi, xxxvii.

an equal disappointment awaited him, for publishers were timid and purchasers few. Now and again he might earn a handful of ducats by writing on commission, but even with Beethoven such opportunities were not of frequent occurrence, and with Schubert they were of the extremest rarity. It is little wonder if genius were sometimes tempted to regret the flesh-pots of Egypt, and to complain that it had been brought out to die in the wilderness.

None the less it was moving onwards, and we can almost count the stages of its advance. Every decade saw it increase in personal dignity, in liberty of utterance, in depth and sincerity of feeling; every decade saw it slowly winning its way across barren tracts of apathy and ignorance. No doubt progress was difficult and toilsome; there were enemies to conquer, heights to scale, hardships to endure; more than once the march was checked by open antagonism or misled by treacherous counsel. Yet the true leaders preserved their faith unbroken, and won for music not only some of the most glorious of its achievements but the enduring right of free life and free citizenship. And though public opinion lagged far behind, it was never altogether stationary. It followed with hesitating and uncertain steps, it sometimes broke into murmur or revolt, it sometimes lent its ears to that smooth and super-ficial imposture which is the worst of all traitors in the camp. But, however blind and erring, it was not disloyal at heart; its mistakes, and they were many in number, gave at least some blundering indications of vitality; little by little its judgement formed and matured under the inspiration and example of the artist. The popular verdict may have been often foolish, but ' it is better to be a fool than to be dead.'

We shall find a striking illustration if we divide into two half-centuries the period which elapsed between 1730 and 1830. The first saw all the greatest compositions of Bach, and paid no more heed to them than if they had been so many school exercises. It did not praise, or censure, or criticize; it simply ignored. The second witnessed the whole career of Beethoven, from the qualified success of *Prometheus* to the rapturous welcome which greeted the Choral Symphony. During the one, musical judgement was mainly occupied with the quarrels of theatrical parties, and work like the Matthäus-Passion or the B-minor Mass lay wholly outside its horizon. The other, with frequent lapses, began to offer some real attention to creative genius, and attempted in some measure to comprehend the value and import of the new message. And part at least of the reason is that the later generation was roused by direct appeal to a keener and more intimate sense of responsibility.

CHAPTER II

WE are warned by Matthew Arnold that we must never allow our judgement of poetry to be affected by the historic estimate. The true question is not whether such and such a poem embodies the best ideas, and displays the fullest command of resources, that could be expected at the time in which it was written, but whether it attains the high seriousness, the intrinsic beauty, the largeness, freedom, and insight which alone can satisfy the requirements of an absolute standard. As extreme instances he quotes an English critic who compares Cædmon to Milton, a French critic who places the *Chanson de Roland* on the highest epic level, and observes with a not undue severity that such misplaced enthusiasm 'can only lead to a dangerous abuse of language.' 'To Homer,' he adds, 'is rightly due such supreme praise as that which M. Vitet gives to the *Chanson de Roland*. If our words are to have any meaning, if our judgements are to have any solidity, we must not heap that supreme praise upon poetry of an order immeasurably inferior.'

In matters of literature this warning is of the greatest value and importance: in applying it to music we shall do well to guard against a possible misinterpretation. It is true that in music, as in literature, the finest artistic work is admirable apart from all conditions of time and place; that it 'belongs to the class of the very best,' whether it be wrought in the pure counterpoint of Palestrina or in the rich glowing melody of Beethoven. But it is equally true that if we are to study music intelligently we must needs give some close attention to its historical development. For in the first place it is the most continuous of the arts: it has little or no external relation: it therefore specially requires that the masters of each successive age shall take their point of departure from their predecessors. And in the second place it is peculiarly dependent on the nature and limitations of its medium, on the tone of instruments, the skill of performers, the hundred mechanical appliances through which a composer must reach his audience. To judge clavichord music from the standpoint of the pianoforte would be not less irrational than to criticize a sonata of Bach by the structural methods of Mozart. To expect that a symphony of Haydn should be scored like one of Schubert is to ignore some two generations of invention and discovery. It thus becomes imperative that before discussing the musical composition of this period we should form some preliminary acquaintance with the conditions under which it worked. We can hardly separate the thought of the time from its expression, and its expression was partly affected by causes external to the composer.

During the eighteenth century the rudiments of musical education were chiefly provided by choir schools and charitable institutions of a similar character. In the establishment and maintenance of these Italy took an unquestioned lead. There were four schools at Naples, of which the largest, Santa Maria di Loreto, numbered some 200 pupils, and the other three— Sant' Onofrio, Della pietà dei Turchini, and Dei poveri di Gesù Cristo—from 90 to 120 apiece. At Venice there were four more—the Pietà, the Mendicanti, the Incurabili, and San Giovanni e Paolo, commonly called the Ospedaletto. The buildings, as their titles imply, had originally been employed as Hospitals or Infirmaries[1]: then they were adapted for

---

[1] Conservatorio, which properly means Infirmary, was the Neapolitan name. At Venice they were called Ospedali. It is worth noting that Burney, after his visit to Italy, proposed to establish a music-school at the Foundling Hospital in London, and that the plan fell through for want of support.

Orphanages and Foundling Institutes, in which singing formed
a large part of the instruction: finally they developed into
regular colleges of music, to which pupils from every part of
Europe could be admitted.   No doubt both discipline and
method were somewhat imperfect.   Burney gives an amusing
picture of the 'common practising room' at Sant' Onofrio,
'where,' he says, 'I found a Dutch concert consisting of seven
or eight harpsichords, more than as many violins, and several
voices, all performing different things and in different keys.'
Other boys were writing in the same room, 'but it being
holiday time many were absent who usually study there
together[1].'   The only mitigation appears to have been that
the trumpets were sent outside to practise on the stairs; but
even so one can imagine the Babel that must have occupied
the room in term-time.

   Still, with all deductions, it remains true that the general
education afforded by these colleges was for a long period the
best that could be attained.   Their directorships were sought
by the most eminent Italian masters: Leo and Durante held
office in Naples; Galuppi, Sacchini, and Traetta in Venice;
Sarti, in the interval of his wanderings, reigned for nine years
over the Ospedaletto; Porpora joined the two centres by his
promotion from Sant' Onofrio to the Incurabili.   These teachers,
were famous throughout Europe for skill and learning; their
pupils included some among the greatest virtuosi of the time;
their influence extended far beyond the limits of their country,
and held in fee the whole range of the musical world.   Indeed,
for a time the only serious rivals were themselves Italian:—
the school of Palermo where Pistocchi was educated, the school
of Bologna where Bernacchi taught singing and Padre Martini
counterpoint.   Beyond the Alps there was as yet little or no
organization.   There was a conservatorium at Munich, where
Burney found the boys singing about the streets 'in order
to convince the public, at whose expense they are maintained,

---

[1] *Present State of Music in France and Italy*, p. 336.

of their proficiency in their studies,' but it was of little account beside Venice, and its most famous teacher was the Italian Ferrandini. The choir schools trained their choristers and added a few lessons on the clavier or the violin, but if we may judge from Haydn's experience at Vienna the training was for the most part careless and unsystematic. It was not until the end of the century that the nations began to claim their independence. In 1784 Gossec founded in Paris an École Royale de Chant, which, eleven years later, was developed into the present Conservatoire[1]: in 1802 Sarti, despite some opposition, carried his plans for a Russian music-school at Ekaterinoslav: Prague followed with its Conservatorium in 1811, Vienna with the Gesellschaft der Musikfreunde in 1817, London with the Royal Academy of Music in 1823. In other words, when the great Austrian composers began their career, the performers for whom they wrote had, in the majority of cases, received their first training at an Italian school.

And not only was this the case, but the advanced courses of study were also, for the most part, in the same hands. When a boy left his conservatorio with some special mark of skill or distinction, he was sent as a matter of course to complete his training with an Italian master. For a full half-century there were no teachers comparable to Porpora and Bernacchi for the voice, Geminiani, Tartini, and Somis for the violin, Vandini and Antoniotti for the violoncello, the four Besozzis for oboe and bassoon. On the keyboard alone was the supremacy of Italy seriously challenged; and we cannot read the musical memoirs of the time without seeing that the clavier was still regarded as essentially the composer's instrument, and the organ as that of the Kapellmeister. In the field of executancy there was far more honour to be gained

---

[1] The 'maîtrises,' or cathedral schools of France, were suppressed in 1791; a fact which possibly facilitated the establishment of the Conservatoire. It should be added that they were reopened, under new organization, after the Revolution was over.

from the magic strings, or the marvels and miracles of the 'bel canto'; and here the laurels belonged as of right to the land from which both alike had taken their origin.

Two collateral causes aided to spread and establish this influence. In the first place Italy was not then, as now, a single undivided kingdom, but was partitioned among many princes, foreign as well as native. Naples and Sicily belonged to Spain: a great part of Northern Italy was under Austrian rule; and in this way was opened a certain freedom of intercourse which enabled the captive land to take captive her conquerors. At the Viennese court the Italian language was more readily spoken than the German: Francis I, the husband of Maria Theresa, was Duke of Tuscany, and for some generations his family held the title with all that it implied. The large Slav population of Austria was fertile in musicians, many of whom had Italian blood in their veins, and most of whom softened their harsh patronymics with Italian syllables and terminations. Even Haydn at first wrote his Christian name Giuseppe, and the list may be extended through Tartini, Giornovichi, and several others. Had this been only deference to a passing fashion, still the fashion itself would have been significant, and as a matter of fact it was far more than this. The bond was strengthened by all the ties of intermarriage, of contiguity, of common government, and Salieri and Paisiello felt as much at home in Vienna as Scarlatti and Farinelli at Madrid. In the second place this intercourse was further maintained by operatic companies who poured from Italy in a continuous stream, and carried their voices, their language, and their method to every palace where there was a patron and to every city where there was a theatre. It was this invasion which threatened native art in England, which shook Paris with the *Guerre des Bouffons,* which overran the rest of the Continent until it was stemmed by more than one Imperial edict. The days of Keiser and German patriotism had long since passed away: Graun and Hasse wrote to Italian libretti; so did Haydn; so did Gluck up to *Alceste,* and Mozart up to the *Entführung.* In France there was yet a national party, strengthened under the directorate of Rameau, and prepared at all hazards to resist the foreigner; but its main result was a long war of criticism and controversy, in which neither side gained any very lasting advantage. And outside France it became an accepted convention that, though comedy might descend to the vernacular, yet for opera seria only one language was admissible.

Nor was it a question of libretti alone. From the same tongue was derived almost the whole current terminology of music: the name of nearly every musical form, of nearly every musical instrument; of the different registers of the voice, of the very marks of speed and expression. A few of the more learned names, such as 'fugue' and 'counterpoint,' may be traced directly to Latin: the vast majority are pure Italian in origin and use. Even in places where the native word was retained it descended as a rule to a lower rank and a more menial employment. 'Song' and 'Lied' struggled in unequal contest with the dignity of aria and cantata and canzonet: 'fiddle' and 'geige' were relegated to the country fair, and violino reigned supreme in the master's orchestra. It is little wonder, then, if Italy bulked large in the eyes of the mid-century. The grounds on which Austria was to challenge her empire lay as yet unexplored: in her own field she claimed a position little short of autocracy.

A deplorable result of this preeminence was the popularity of the male soprano: his voice preserved by an abominable practice for which Italy was alone responsible. Through the whole century he postures with his lace and his diamonds and his artificial roulades; the centre of admiring crowds, the darling of emotional enthusiasts, surfeited with incense, and intoxicated with adulation. Senesino had his portrait taken as a Roman emperor, with tearful ladies 'kissing the hem of his coat of mail.' Caffarelli sent formal complaint to Louis XV because he had been denied a royal privilege which was 'reserved for ambassadors and plenipotentiaries.' 'All the ambassadors in the world,' he said, 'would not make one Caffarelli.' But even these portents fade into insignificance beside the career of Carlo Broschi, 'detto il Farinelli,' whose praise has come down to us in Hogarth's picture. His early days won him renown and triumph from Naples to Vienna. His arrival in London paid off a debt of £19,000 on the Lincoln's Inn Theatre. On his return home, after three years, he devoted a small part of his earnings to the construction of 'a very superb mansion,' which he called by the appropriate name of England's Folly. At the end of 1736 he was summoned to Madrid, where for three-and-twenty years he combined the offices of chief singer and minister of state. Each evening he performed four songs for the solace of his royal master; and the day's leisure was occupied in corresponding with sovereigns and negotiating treaties. It should be added that he was singularly free from the jealousy and arrogance which disfigured most of his rivals. There are many stories of his generosity; there are many accounts of the modesty and kindliness with which he bore the retirement of his later life. But we are here less concerned with the manner in which he wore his laurels than with the achievements for which he won them. What light, we may ask, is thrown upon the condition of music by the fact that for half a century he was regarded as its most popular idol?

His voice was a pure mezzo-soprano, some octave and a half in extreme compass, of remarkably even quality, and so powerful that he is said to have silenced a trumpeter in full blast. By careful training under Porpora and Bernacchi he had acquired not only great flexibility but an unusual power of sustaining his notes. Beside this he was an actor of more than average ability, and a master of those rhetorical devices by which feeling can be expressed and passion simulated.

Contemporary criticism endows him with profound musicianship; but this verdict we are led to doubt when we read that
one of his most notable feats was 'to sing at sight two songs
in a new clef, and in a style to which he was unaccustomed.'
At any rate he was unquestionably the most consummate vocalist
of his time, and from him is derived in great measure that
impetus to which the 'bel canto' owed its progress in the next
generation.

Yet, when all is said and done, it was a poor triumph.
Imagine Caesar, and Alexander, and Agamemnon king of
men, piping soprano melodies on the classic stage.   Imagine
the dramatic interest held in suspense while this strange
bedizened hero swells his chest-notes and trills his divisions.
The whole thing was false and insincere, a monument of
misdirected skill and unreal artifice.   If we had nothing else
for which to thank the Austrian school, we should owe them
gratitude for having exorcised this ugly spectre, and purified
the art with wholesome air and daylight.   From the time
of their appearance the power of the male soprano began to
wane; gradually at first, as is the case with most abuses;
more surely as the years wore on, until it finally passed
into merited obscurity and oblivion.

Yet the influence of the Austrian school would have been
less effective had not the way been prepared for it by the
course and current of events.   The capacity of the male
soprano was limited partly by the compass of his voice,
partly by constitutional inability to learn fresh devices; and
the general public, which cared nothing for the ethics of the
question, came in process of time to see that the female
soprano could beat him on his own ground.   Hence followed
a steady advance in the position of women on the operatic
stage.   Cuzzoni and Faustina might vie with one another for
precedence; they both alike yielded the *pas* to Senesino and
Farinelli.   But in the next generation Regina Minghotti at
least held her own against Gizziello, and in the next Agujari

showed herself capable of feats which no man in Europe
could hope to rival. The art of vocalization had grown more
elaborate, more difficult, more exacting, and in satisfying its
requirements the lighter voice and quicker brain carried the
day. Here, for instance, is an example of the 'divisions'
with which in 1735 Farinelli aroused the enthusiasm of his
audience :—

Now we may hesitate to accept Burney's morose comment
that in 1788 such passages 'would hardly be thought sufficiently
brilliant for a third-rate singer at the opera[1],' but
at least we may agree that, except as evidence of breathing-capacity,
they do not compare for pure marvel with the
exercise which Mozart notes as having been sung in his
presence by Agujari[2] :—

[1] *History*, vol. iv. p. 413.
[2] See Mozart's letter of March 24, 1770; also Jahn's *Mozart*, i. 113. Agujari
seems to have had a compass of three octaves and a half, from C in altissimo to the
G below tenor A. See an interesting and valuable criticism in Mr. Deacon's article
on Singing: Grove, first edition, vol. iii. p. 506.

It is no answer to say that these illustrations are irrelevant, since art is essentially opposed to mere virtuosity. The point is that the eighteenth century took the keenest delight in these miracles, and readily transferred its allegiance to the Queens of Song who had fullest power to perform them. At any rate it is a step in advance that the display of pure skill should have so completely developed its resources, and still more that in so doing it should have adopted a healthier and more natural method.

Meanwhile, under stimulus of Italian example, great singers began to arise in central and western nations. Raaff, the Rhinelander, who was born in 1714 and studied under Ferrandini and Bernacchi, enjoyed for nearly half a century the reputation of being the greatest tenor in Europe; and, on retirement, left his succession to the Irishman Michael Kelly. Sophie Arnould, no less famous as an actress than as a singer, held undisputed sway over a generation of Parisian Opera, and was selected by Gluck himself for the chief part of his *Iphigénie en Aulide*. During the same period Mara, Aloysia Weber, the two Wendlings, Fischer, and a host of other artists were filling Germany with their praises, and successfully challenging the most famous of Italian virtuosi. For a time, no doubt, they had to contend with a strong force of prejudice and opposition. When Mara first asked leave to perform before Frederick the Great, he is said to have answered bluntly: 'A German singer? I should as soon expect to receive pleasure from the neighing of my horse.' But even prejudice could not long withstand this new array of talent and industry, especially when it appeared that German talent was not too proud to learn parts and attend rehearsals. At the production of *Idomeneo* in 1781 three out of the four principal vocalists were of German blood, and the fourth, Dal Prato, reduced Mozart to despair by his idleness and incompetence. Still more striking is the contrast which thirty years effected on the stage of Vienna. In 1750 every one of the chief singers at the Hofopernhaus was an Italian. In the list of 1780 there is not a single Italian name[1].

If the history of vocalization is a record of progress and advance, still more so is that of violin-playing. At the beginning of the century Corelli's music, which never rises above the third position, was regarded as the extreme climax of difficulty; and we are told that when his sonatas first came to Paris they were sung by three voices from the opera, since there was no one in the city who could play them. At the end of the century a boy named Niccolo Paganini was covering three octaves on a single string, and performing prodigies of execution the very possibility of which Corelli could never have imagined. Between these two there stretches a period of rapid and continuous development, in which Italy again takes the lead, and the other nations are content to follow.

The most important violin-school was that of Turin, founded by Giambattista Somis (1676–1763), who had been the pupil of Corelli at Rome and of Vivaldi at Venice. Of his abilities as player and composer we have little more than shadowy tradition,

[1] See Pohl's *Haydn*, i. 88; Jahn's *Mozart*, ii. 189. When Mozart visited Mannheim in 1777 almost all the operatic singers there were Germans. See Jahn, i. 373.

but there can be no doubt that he was a great teacher. Oné of his pupils, Leclair, was the first French violinist of real eminence; another, Pugnani, was the master of the famous Viotti, through whom his method passed in successive generations to Rode, Böhm, and Joachim. It would indeed be an endless task to enumerate the artists who, directly or indirectly, have derived their skill from Piedmontese training. Giardini and Chabran studied with Somis, Durand and Baillot with Viotti, Habeneck with Baillot, Alard with Habeneck, Sarasate with Alard; Hellmesberger and Ernst preceded Joachim in the school of Böhm, Straus and Rappoldi followed him. And so the genealogy spread in a roll of honour to our own time, rich in notable names and notable achievement—a record to which the whole range of musical art can hardly show a parallel.

Far less in extent, though at the time almost equal in reputation, was the Paduan school founded by Giuseppe Tartini (1692–1770). He was born at Pisano of a family which seems to have been Slavonic in origin[1], taught himself to play, against his father's wishes, and after a stormy boyhood settled down as first violin at the great Church of Sant' Antonio. His fame as performer, composer, and theorist, attracted many pupils, among whom the most eminent were Graun, who was afterwards Kapellmeister to Frederick the Great, and Nardini, 'the silver-toned,' who, on his appointment at Stuttgart, did much to raise the level of violin-playing through Southern Germany. Yet for some reason the school never struck any deep root. Benda and Salomon, Ferrari and Dittersdorf, maintained its vitality for another generation; then it was overshadowed by its western rival and put forth no more branches. This is the more remarkable since Tartini was not only a brilliant but a learned musician, and, if we may

[1] The original form of his family name was Trtić, just as that of Giorno-vichi's was Jarnović. In the following pages the usual Italian spelling will

judge by contemporary evidence, a careful and painstaking instructor. There must have been something incommunicable in his secret, some special gift of power or charm which was too intimate to be shared. Like many men of great genius, he would seem to have mainly influenced his followers by the inspiration and magnetism of his presence, and to have swayed them with a personal force which they were little able to transmit.

Among the contemporaries of Tartini and Somis may be mentioned four more Italian violinists who attained special distinction: Veracini the Florentine, whose performance at Venice first roused Tartini to emulation; Geminiani, popularly known as 'il furibondo' from his wildness and extravagance; Locatelli, a strange compound of genius and mountebank; and, last in order of time, Antonio Lolli, who was held to atone for poor musicianship by his extraordinary command over his instrument. Of these Veracini and Locatelli seem to have taken no pupils; Geminiani settled in London about 1714, and from thence to his death in 1761 was the most successful of our violin-teachers; Lolli (1730–1802) founded the tiny school of Bergamo from which sprang artists of as diverse nationality as Boucher the Frenchman, Giornovichi the Slav, and Bridgetower the English half-caste. It should be observed that all these lie outside the main current of Italian teaching, and that all alike have been charged with eccentricity and charlatanism. They were for the most part men of intemperate character, ill-balanced and feather-headed, intent on astonishing the world rather than delighting it, and to them is in great measure due the bad repute into which the word virtuoso has justly fallen. Their mastery of technique was beyond all question or dispute, but they degraded it to unworthy ends and can no longer be set in comparison with the genuine artists of Turin and Padua.

A more serious rival appeared at Mannheim. In 1745 the Bohemian J. K. Stamitz was appointed leader of the

Elector Palatine's orchestra, and soon brought it to a pitch
of renown which overtopped every other capital in Europe.
The violin-playing was especially excellent: Stamitz himself
was a violinist, and he was ably supported by Fränzl and by
Mozart's friend Cannabich. Soon the Mannheim method
became famous: Cannabich was the master of Cramer; Anton
Stamitz of Kreutzer, who in his turn taught d'Artot and
Rovelli; Eck began his career in the Mannheim band and
ended it as the teacher of Louis Spohr, through whom the
tradition has descended to Ries, David and Wilhelmj. Nor
was its influence confined to the direct relation of master and
pupil. Through the whole German-speaking world it set
a standard of high attainment, of true and artistic interpretation, which was followed by every player from Romberg at
Bonn to Schuppanzigh at Vienna.

Last in order of time came the French school, which, indeed,
can only be said to date from the last two decades of the
century. Before them France could show a few names of
great distinction—Leclair, for instance, and Gavinies, and
Barthélémon; but the real organization began when Viotti
settled at Paris in 1782. Hence her school may fairly be
regarded as an offshoot from that of Turin, a colony which
soon bade fair to rival its mother-land in dignity and importance. Among Viotti's first pupils were Cartier, Rode,
and Baillot: then came the foundation of the Conservatoire
de Musique, and the establishment of a systematic instruction
which has enabled Paris to contribute so valuable a chapter to
the history of the violin. But as compared with Italy and
Germany her art was derivative, and though she made ample
use of her opportunities we are forced to admit that the
opportunities themselves came, in the first instance, from
outside [1].

---

[1] The cosmopolitan character of this French school may be gauged from the
fact that during the latter part of the century the most famous violinists in Paris
were Viotti the Italian, Anton Stamitz the Bohemian, Kreutzer the German,

To sum up :—by the middle of the eighteenth century there were two considerable violin-schools, both Italian; by 1775 there were three, the third being Slavo-Germanic; by 1800 there was added a fourth, the French, which was in some measure dependent on the others. It now follows to consider in what respects the treatment of the violin shows actual advance and progress during this period; or, in other words, what was the precise result which these schools effected.

First came a notable extension and improvement in method of bowing, due partly to Veracini, whose earliest sonatas (Amsterdam, 1721) show a greater command of the bow than Corelli had ever required; partly to Tartini, who was especially famous in this matter, and whose *Arte dell' Arco*— a set of fifty studies in variation-form—is even now accepted as authoritative. The same two masters also developed the technique of the left hand, particularly in double-stopping and double-shakes, and we may add that it was Tartini's method of keeping these accurately in tune which led to the most important of his acoustical discoveries. The following passage from the Sonata in C major (Op. 1, No. 3), published in 1734, will show how great a change had occurred in violin-playing during the twenty years since the death of Corelli :—

Duranowski (Durand) the Pole, and the Frenchmen Cartier, Rode and Baillot. Our own so-called ' English school,' with Cooke and Linley, Dubourg, Pinto, and. Michael Festing, though less celebrated, was hardly more various. One of the chief difficulties in classification is this frequent intermixture of nationalities.

Here, however, the advance of technical ability was met by
a serious obstacle. Like most early violinists Tartini appears
to have held his instrument on the right-hand side of the
tail-piece, thus cramping the finger and limiting the attainable
compass. Hence his music very seldom rises above the third

position, and its difficulties call rather for firmness and accuracy of touch than for any extreme range or flexibility of movement. There is a well-known story that Veracini was driven out of Dresden by hearing one of his hardest concerti played without mistake by a *ripieno* violinist from the orchestra, and it is no disrespect to his greater rival if we point out that even the *Trillo* and the *Didone abbandonata* make less demand on the skill of the virtuoso than on the power of the musician. But in 1748 Geminiani published his *Art of playing the Violin*, and at one stroke revolutionized the existing practice. He recommends that the instrument be held on the left side of the tail-piece, he takes it up to the seventh position, he gives rules for the management of the arm, for the treatment of the shifts, for almost every detail by which scope can be widened and execution facilitated. It is true that his compositions were of little musical value—we may well endorse the contemporary opinion which spoke of them as 'laboured and fantastic'—but his technical experiments did good service in their kind, and at least gave opportunity and material for truer genius to employ.

It usually happens that an enlargement in the means of expression is followed by a period of pure virtuosity, and to this rule the history of the violin affords no exception. Men found that the new devices gave them a command of resource which had been hitherto impossible, and so were tempted to treat resource as an end in itself, and to waste their heritage on mere exhibition and display. Locatelli, for instance, who had in him the makings of a great musician, could degrade his art by such empty tricks as the following :—

and his bad example was adopted by Lolli, by Giornovichi, and by other players of the Bergamese school. Indeed, Lolli once offered a piteous apology for his lack of artistic feeling. 'Do you not know,' he pleaded, 'that we are all fools at Bergamo? How should I play a serious piece?'

A significant consequence was the fondness for ornaments and *fiorituri* which we find prevalent at this time. As Liszt said of the overture to *Der Freischütz*, 'This is fine music, let us see how we can improve upon it,' so the Italian violinist of 1750 considered it his prerogative, and almost his duty, to elaborate and embroider the melodies which he was set to interpret. Geminiani published a *Treatise on Good Taste* (London 1747), which is almost entirely occupied with points of decoration, and which urges, as their extreme limit, that they be not employed in such profusion as entirely to obscure the tune. Giardini, during his engagement in the opera at Naples, 'used,' as Burney tells us, 'to flourish and change passages more frequently than he ought to have done,' and gained so much reputation by the practice that at last he ventured to alter one of Jommelli's songs in the composer's presence, and was very properly beaten for his pains. It is true that the soloists were themselves composers, and had a predilection for playing their own music; it is true that, until the Austrians, they were almost the only men who wrote for the violin with real knowledge and insight; but none the less our sympathies are won by the choleric little Maestro, not

by the disrespectful performer or the tolerant and complace.1t
critic [1].

Finally, the balance swung round on the side of musicianship. Technical proficiency came to be taken more as a matter
of course, and to be used in its proper sphere as a means
towards artistic interpretation. With Giambattista Viotti
(1753–1824) the violin-playing of the eighteenth century may
be said to culminate. As soloist and teacher in Paris, as
a leader of Haydn's orchestra in London, as a composer
whose duets and concerti are still among the treasures of
musical art, he worthily maintained the traditions of his native
Piedmont, and enriched them with sound study and unfailing
genius. Even the meteoric career of Paganini has not dimmed
his lustre; we still look back on him as ' the father of modern
violin-playing '; a master of high ability, strong and dignified
in style, delicate in taste, and incapable of unworthy trick or
artifice.

The following example (from the first book of *Violin Duets*,
No. 6) will give a fair illustration of his music :—

[1] See Burney's *History*, iv. 522. In *The Present State of Music in Germany*, p. 167,
we find the axiom that ' it is not enough for a musician to execute the mere notes
which a composer has set on paper ': a rule which does not seem to have referred
solely to expressive interpretation.

The distinguishing characteristics of Italian playing were its brilliance and its power of poetic expression. To these the Germans added depth and solidity, and the French that exquisite neatness and precision which is one of their most notable artistic qualities. As soloists the Germans advanced more slowly than the French, mainly because they were longer in taking advantage of foreign inventions and discoveries, but for this they compensated by the discipline, vigour, and attack of their orchestral and concerted pieces. Thus in the time of Haydn and Mozart, and still more in that of Beethoven, there was at least one instrument which lay ready for the new music. They drew from it a melody such as had never been conceived before, but the strings had been tuned and mellowed by the hand of many generations.

The viola took, as yet, a far lower rank. Telemann wrote a few solos for it, so did one or two of the Italians; Handel gave it some independent work in *Solomon* and *Susanna*; but as a rule it was held of little account, entrusted to inferior performers, and either kept in strict subordination or totally disregarded. The early string 'sonatas' were commonly written for two violins and a bass; so were the solo parts in the Concerto Grosso, and the tenor instrument occupied a humble place among the *ripieni* of the orchestra, where it was often set to double the violins or to play, an octave higher, with the basses. Eisel in his ʻMusicus Αὐτοδίδακτος' (Erfurt, 1738) gives its extreme compass as two octaves and a note—from C below the alto stave to D above it—and though this narrow range was somewhat extended during the next thirty years, it is clear that there was no commensurate advance in skill or dignity. We read of no great viola-player until the younger Karl Stamitz (1746–1801), and even he preferred the seven-stringed viola d'amore to the simpler and more usual instrument. In a word, before Haydn it was the poor relation of the ʻquartet,' treated with an almost open disdain, set to the most menial tasks, and, if tradition be correct, often allowed without comment to absent itself from rehearsal.

For many years the violoncello was obscured by its more popular rival the viola da gamba, which, though weaker in tone, was far easier to finger, and, with its seven strings, afforded a wider compass of notes[1]. Indeed the gamba was long regarded as the solo instrument, and the 'cello maintained its position merely as a bass accompaniment to the violins. From this it was raised about the third decade of the century by the Italians Franciscello and Antoniotti; then came Berteau the Frenchman, and then two undoubted masters, Boccherini of Lucca (1743–1805), the most notable of Italian 'cello composers, and Jean Louis Duport of Paris (1749–1819), whose famous *Essai* first laid the foundation of a systematic method, and whose tone was so sweet and pure that, according to Voltaire's compliment, ʻil savait faire d'un bœuf un rossignol.' Duport established the principle of fingering by semitones, instead of tones as in the violin, and invented a scheme of bowing which

[1] There were two kinds of viola da gamba, one with six strings tuned in fourths, from D below the bass stave to D above it, the others with seven, adding an A-string below the bass D. The latter was preferred by Bach, who wrote for it some of his most effective *obbligati*. Eisel says that the best instruments were the ʻold English,' and the next best those made by Thielke of Hamburg. Among great gamba-players was C. F. Abel of Cöthen, whose memory is preserved to us by Gainsborough's portrait.

gave greater freedom to the player's right arm, and considerably improved both quality of sound and facility of execution.   He was followed by Bernhard Romberg (1767–1841), who became, in 1800, Professor at the Paris Conservatoire, and who was probably the most capable violoncellist of the century. Thenceforward the instrument assumed its proper place in the ranks of music, and though late in the field soon showed that it was able to hold its own.

A somewhat similar development may be observed in the history of the double-bass. Eisel mentions three varieties, two with six strings tuned after the manner of the viola da gamba, one with four tuned an octave below the violoncello. All these appear to have soon passed out of orchestral use, and to have been succeeded by the three-stringed and four-stringed types, tuned viol-wise, which are employed at the present day. It is possible that the more elaborate kinds survived for solos : e. g. for Haydn's contrabass concerto, which perished in the great fire at Eisenstadt, and Mozart's remarkable *obbligato*, which not even Dragonetti could have played on any sort of double-bass familiar to us [1] : but this is merely conjectural, and we may conclude that for all practical purposes the narrower range was found amply sufficient.

Three instruments which have now become obsolete deserve mention on grounds of historic interest. The theorbo was a large, many-stringed bass lute of deeper compass than our modern contrabassi, and employed, like them, to strengthen and enrich the lower registers of the orchestra. It was still to be found in the band of the Austrian Hofkapelle when, in 1740, Haydn entered St. Stephen's as a chorister, and it lasted at Berlin as late as 1755. But like all lutes it was encumbered with mechanical difficulties ; it had a variable temper, and needed constant attention ; at last musicians grew impatient with it and threw it aside. The lira da braccio was a member of the viol family, much beloved by amateurs, and in special

---

[1] See a note on this work in Professor Prout's *Orchestra*, vol. i. p. 71.

favour with Ferdinand IV of Naples, for whom Haydn wrote
five concerti and seven nocturnes. One of the concerti (composed for two lire in G major) still survives in MS. at Eisenstadt,
and is remarkable for the high range of the solo parts, which
never descend below middle E, and through most of the music
are soaring above the treble stave. A still clearer indication of
the compass in current use may be found in the MS. of the
third nocturne, where, for the opening movement, Haydn has
cancelled the names of ' lira 1 and 2 ' and has substituted those
of flute and oboe. Last comes the baryton, celebrated by the
praises of Leopold Mozart, a round-shouldered, flat-bodied viol
with seven gut strings and from nine to twenty-four sympathetic
strings of metal. Its most famous player was Prince Nicholas
Esterhazy, in whose service Haydn wrote for it no less than 175
pieces; but we can form little or no idea of its character or
usage since this vast mass of music has wholly disappeared,
except three divertimenti and a few inconsiderable fragments.
If we can judge by these it was, like the lira da braccio,
principally employed in its upper register, for, with one exception, they contain no single note that could not be reached by
a violin [1] : but the rule ' ex pede Herculem ' is an unsafe basis
for musical criticism, and we may well be content to leave the
question in obscurity.

It is little wonder that with such variety, such range, and
above all such continued exercise of skill and talent, the strings
should have long maintained a dominant place in all musical
representation. They alone, among instruments, could rival the
singing voice; they alone could surpass its marvels of execution
and challenge its power of touching the human heart. But one
of the main achievements of the Austrian school was to set the
orchestral forces on a nearer equality, and we must, therefore,
proceed to consider what levies they could raise from the allied
dependencies of brass and wood.

---

[1] According to Pohl, Haydn printed in 1781 six divertimenti with the
baryton part assigned to the flute. See Pohl's *Haydn*, vol. i. pp. 254–5.

Eisel allows the trumpet its present nominal compass of three octaves, and divides it into seven overlapping registers :— Flarter Grob, Grobstimme, Faulstimme, Mittelstimme, Principal, Andre Clarin, and Erste Clarin. Of these the lowest (Flarter Grob) was practically impossible, and the others restricted to the natural sounds of the harmonic series. Even here was a danger to be avoided, for the fourth and sixth of the scale were 'so necessarily and inevitably imperfect' that musicians were warned against using them except for passing-notes. As a rule the three higher registers alone were in habitual practice, and it is by their names that the trumpets are usually designated in the scores of the time : 'first and second clarin' for florid passages, 'principal' for basis of continuous tone. That some clarin-players attained a high degree of proficiency is clear from the *obbligati* of Handel and Bach, but they were few in number, and were little encouraged by other composers.

The horn was introduced into chamber-music by Vivaldi, and into the orchestra by Handel. At first it met with a good deal of opposition: it was described as 'coarse and vulgar,' fit for the hunting-field, but wholly unsuited to the refined and culti-vated society of oboe and violin. Hence, up to the middle of the century, it is used with comparative infrequence, and when it does appear is treated like a softer and duller trumpet, with very little distinctive character of its own. But about 1770 a Dresden player named Hampel endeavoured to improve its quality of sound by inserting a pad of cotton into the bell, found that this raised the pitch a semitone, experimented with his hand, and so discovered the series of stopped notes which have given to the instrument a virtually unbroken scale [1]. The importance of this device may be estimated if we compare Mozart's horn concerti, or Beethoven's well-known sonata,

---

[1] A few years before this a Russian named Kölbal invented a horn with valves (Amorshorn or Amorschall) for which in 1783 the young Cherubini wrote two pieces at the commission of Lord Cowper. But little use was made of this invention until the middle of the nineteenth century.

with the most brilliant of Handel's *obbligato* parts : e. g. the
the songs 'Mirth, admit me of thy crew,' in *L'Allegro*, and
'Va tacito e nascosto' in *Giulio Cesare*. The whole temper of
the instrument is altered, there are new shades of colour, new
delicacies of *timbre*, new opportunities for tact and feeling; and
although in this matter even the Austrians have been outstripped
by their successors, we can hardly overstate the distance which
they advanced upon preceding usage.

It is probable that this improvement in the horn tended
to throw the trombones into abeyance. Handel wrote for
them in *Israel* and *Saul*[1], Bach in many of his Church
Cantatas; but later they are confined to special points of
dramatic emphasis (as in Gluck's *Orfeo* and *Alceste*, Haydn's
Tobias, Mozart's *Don Juan*, *Zauberflöte*, and *Requiem*), until
Beethoven restored them in the fifth symphony. There were
five at the Viennese Hofkapelle in 1740, there were none
among the Mannheim orchestra of 1777 : in a word they
seem to have been gradually ousted by a growing love for
softness of tone and evenness of texture.

Of the wood-wind family three members may be dismissed
in a few words. The flute, freely used by Bach and Handel,
was a favourite solo instrument from the time of Quantz and
his pupil Frederick the Great: and there is no evidence of
any important change in its construction from about 1720,
when it superseded the flageolet, to Boehm's inventions in
1832. According to Eisel its compass was two octaves, from
D below the treble stave, but it must have been capable of
a higher range, since Handel writes for it up to F *in alt*.
Equally uneventful were the careers of oboe and bassoon, to
which, at the mid-century, was entrusted the chief place in
the wind-forces of the orchestra. They were made celebrated
by many eminent soloists, by the Besozzis of Parma, by Johann

---

[1] Mr. W. H. Stone has recalled the fact that the *obbligato* to 'The Trumpet
shall sound' in the *Messiah* was originally written for a small alto trombone. See
Grove, vol. iv. p. 176. Trombones were never used in opera until Gluck's *Orfeo*.

Fischer of Freiburg, by Parke of London: but throughout this period they remained virtually unchanged, and the revolution in their treatment, which is one of the chief marks of Viennese orchestration, was not affected by any question of skill or mechanism. Two deeper-toned varieties of oboe may be mentioned, the oboe d'amore, which gradually dropped out of use, and the oboe di caccia which, by Haydn's time, had developed into the corno inglese: apart from these there is no point in the character of the instrument which requires either comment or elucidation.

A far more interesting problem is raised by the history of the clarinet. It was invented by Denner of Nuremberg in 1690; its first appearance in any known score is dated 1757 when the Belgian Gossec introduced it into the accompaniment of two songs written for Sophie Arnould's début[1]. For over sixty years it remained totally neglected by the great composers: its very name seems to have been unknown to Handel and Bach; it was but sparingly employed by Gluck and Haydn; until Mozart there was no one who fully realized its value. Yet we know that during all this time it was existent, for Eisel in 1738 gives a complete account of it, mentions its chalumeau register[2] by name, and even asserts that 'virtuosi' could add five or six notes to its usual compass. The difficulty is incontestable. Here are virtuosi, but apparently no pieces for them to play. Here is an instrument which we should probably rank next to the violin for beauty and expression, and through half a century no master deems it worthy of a place in his orchestra.

The true explanation would seem to be that in early days the clarinet did not possess that full reedy tone which is now its principal charm, but was rather hard and brilliant, like the trumpet, from which its name is derived. Eisel speaks of it as

---

[1] W. F. Bach wrote a sestet for two horns, clarinet, violin, viola, and violoncello; but we have no means of knowing the year of its composition, except that it was probably before 1767. See Bitter, vol. ii. p. 260.

[2] The chalumeau is the lowest clarinet register, named from an obsolete reed instrument, which appeared for the last time in Gluck's *Alceste*.

'trumpet-like,' Burney remarks its presence in regimental
bands, the Versailles Theatre, which was one of the first to
adopt it, contained, according to Lacroix [1], no brass instruments
except horns.   There is no improbability in this assimilation of
timbres.   The cornetto, a rough wooden pipe encased in leather,
was employed by Bach and Gluck to reinforce the clarin, and
the bass cornetto, or serpent, is the direct ancestor of our
modern ophicleide.   Hence it is probable that during this half
century the clarinet was regarded as a kind of trumpet, thinner
in sound, though more flexible in range, that it was accepted as
an understudy, and even, at Versailles, as a substitute.   Having
thus little character or vocation of its own it was set to play
trumpet-music [2], much in the fashion of our modern cornet à
pistons, and we may note that for many years after its promotion to the orchestra its part was commonly written among
those of the brass instruments, not among those of the wood-
wind.   However, by course of experience its voice grew sweeter
and more mellow; it came to be better constructed and better
played: at Mannheim it once for all assumed its true place,
and taught Mozart the lesson which he afterwards turned to
such admirable account.   'Oh! if *we* had only clarinets,' he
writes from there in 1778. 'you cannot think what a splendid
effect a symphony makes with oboes, flutes, and clarinets.'
Nor was this a transient mark of admiration.   Mozart's new
enthusiasm bore immediate fruit in the Paris *Symphony*, and
steadily matured until the closing days of *Zauberflöte* and the
Requiem.

The development of the orchestra as a whole can most
readily be traced by the comparison of a few typical examples.
We may take the following, arranged in chronological
order :—

---

[1] Lacroix, *XVIIIme Siècle*, p. 415.   The date given is 1773.   Hiller mentions
clarinets at Mannheim in 1767.
[2] Yriarte (*La Musica*, canto iv) speaks of 'clarinetes marciales,' which seems to
bear this out.

1. Vienna Hofkapelle, 1740.   12 violins, 4 violas, 4 violoncelli, 4 contrabassi, 1 theorbo, 1 harpsichord, 1 cornetto, 3 oboes, 3 bassoons, 8 trumpets, 5 trombones, and 2 pairs of drums.

2. Berlin Hofkapelle, 1742.   12 violins, 4 violas, 4 violoncelli, 3 contrabassi, 1 theorbo, 2 claviers, 4 flutes, 4 oboes, 2 bassoons, 2 horns, and 1 harp.

3. Hasse's Orchestra at the Dresden Opera, 1754.   15 violins, 4 violas, 3 violoncelli, 3 contrabassi, 2 harpsichords, 2 flutes, 5 oboes, 5 bassoons, 2 horns, and a small force of trumpets and drums placed on platforms at either end.

4. The Mannheim Orchestra, 1777 [1].   'On each side' 10 or 11 violins, 4 violas, 4 violoncelli, 4 contrabassi, 2 flutes, 2 oboes, 2 clarinets, 4 bassoons, and 2 horns, with trumpets and drums placed, like those of Dresden, on separate platforms.

5. Vienna Opera, 1781.   12 violins, 4 violas, 3 violoncelli, 3 contrabassi, 2 flutes, 2 oboes, 2 clarinets, 2 bassoons, 4 horns, 2 trumpets, and 2 drums.

The first of these five preserved a traditional form which goes back to the time of our own Tudor sovereigns. In the court bands of Henry VIII and Queen Elizabeth we find the same preponderance of brass, the same want of balance and proportion, the same love of barbaric splendour and display. It is possible that the trumpets and trombones were in some measure kept apart, and reserved for royal entries and proclamations and other moments of pageantry; but there is nothing in current accounts to differentiate them from the rest, and we may note that from the Berlin Kapelle they are entirely absent. Thenceforward everything moves in the direction of progress: the gradual diminution of oboes, the inclusion of clarinets, the disappearance of the harpsichord as an essential part of

---

[1] See Mozart's letter to his father, Nov. 4, 1777.

the orchestral forces.   The strings are still somewhat ineffi-
cient, but with a slight increase in their number there would
be little difference between the Viennese opera band of 1781
and a typical 'small orchestra' of to-day.

It is probable that both at Mannheim and at Vienna there
was usually a harpsichord placed beside the stage for the purpose of accompanying recitatives, but the fact that it is not
mentioned in either list is strong evidence of its subordinate
position.   In this is implied another notable advance.   Traditional custom prevailed that the conductor should take his seat
at the keyboard, and hold his forces together by the simple
expedient of doubling their parts: a practice which tended to
make the orchestral colour thick and turbid, beside lowering the
responsibility and dignity of the players.   To France belongs
the credit of having first discarded this inartistic method.
Lully is said to have directed with the bâton, and from his
time onward it alternated at Paris with the bow of the first
violin[1].   At Mannheim Stamitz and Cannabich adopted the
French custom; from thence Mozart took it to Vienna; after
a few years of unequal contest the more rational policy prevailed[2].   It is no small thing that the conductor should give
a beat which the band can follow, and that instrumental tone
should be as pure as the skill of performers can make it.
Neither of these conditions was possible to Hasse; both were
secured to Beethoven.

Meanwhile, the keyboard itself was passing through a stage
of development which materially altered it both in structure
and in function.   The substitution of oil for tempera was not
more fertile in results than that of the pianoforte for the keyed-
instruments that preceded it: the change was slow to take

---

[1] See Mozart's letter to his father, Paris, July 3, 1778.   Wilhelm Cramer, the
pupil of Cannabich, is said to have claimed his right to conduct from the first
violin-desk when he came to England in 1772.

[2] The traditional custom of conducting from the keyboard survived in London
till Mendelssohn's first visit.   In Germany and Austria it seems to have been
practically discarded before 1800.

effect, but it ultimately revolutionized more than one province in the domain of musical art. Place the Diabelli variations beside those which Bach wrote for his pupil Goldberg; compare the *Hammerklavier* with a Bach sonata, or the *Emperor* with a Bach concerto. It is not only the thought that is new: there is an entire change of musical language.

The early history of the harpsichord and clavichord has already been traced [1], but it may be well, for the sake of clearness, briefly to recall their essential characteristics. The harpsichord was derived in principle from the psaltery; a key touched by the finger shot up a tiny quill, which plucked and released the string. Each movement thus produced a single vibrating note which no manipulation of the key could prolong or sustain, or alter in quality; and the instrument was therefore specially adapted to clean, cold polyphonic writing, in which the parts moved equally with an almost uniform tone. We must not conclude that harpsichord music was essentially inexpressive; we have ample proof to the contrary from the delicate fancies of Couperin to the capricious humours of Domenico Scarlatti. But it was expressive in the sense which that term bears as applied to line, not in the sense which is commonly applied to colour. Indeed, the instrument had less variety than that of a black-and-white drawing, for it was incapable of gradation. There were mechanical devices whereby the whole volume of tone could be suddenly increased or diminished; there were none for swelling it by insensible degrees or bringing into prominence some special note of the chord.

Two kinds were in current use. The larger, called Clavicembalo, or harpsichord proper, was enclosed in a ' wing-shaped ' case, and had sometimes as many as three or four strings to each key. The smaller, in which each note governed a single string, was still made after the oblong or trapezoid shape, and

---

[1] See vol. iv. pp. 110–19. Of course, when the harpsichord was enriched with stops it acquired contrasts of tone, but even so they were very different from those of the piano.

was beginning to exchange its pretty, old-world title of virginal for the more technical and commonplace spinet. It is probable that the former was generally employed for orchestral and concerted music [1], or on occasions of peculiar brilliance and display; the latter was quiet and home-keeping, dear to the hearth of many generations, but showing little taste or ambition for a public career.

Somewhat like the spinet in size, wholly distinct in principle, was the clavichord; a lineal descendant from the monochord of the early Church. In it the string was not plucked, but pressed by a small brazen wedge, technically known as a tangent; the sound continued as long as the note was held down, and the player could swell or vary its tone by exerting different degrees of pressure. At first it was made with strings of equal length, and obtained the several notes of the scale by an elaborate system of fretting; as time went on this cumbrous plan was gradually modified, until in 1720 a German named Daniel Faber constructed a 'bundfrei' or 'unfretted' clavichord, which gave two unison strings to each key, which was easy to tune, and which, as Bach found, was susceptible of equal temperament. But in spite of all discoveries there was one defect which it was found wholly impossible to eradicate. Though delightfully sweet and tender, the clavichord was so weak in volume of sound that it was useless for concerted music, and even alone could barely make itself audible in a large hall. Its exquisite poetry was like the voice of a dream, too thin and ethereal for the rough practical conditions of life. It was long the intimate confidant of the master; as his interpreter it could only endure until the rise of a more robust successor.

For the coming change preparation was already being made. While the century was still young a Paduan called Bartolommeo Cristofori exhibited in Florence an instrument which

---

[1] The power of vibrating sound to give the impression of a full harmony may be illustrated by the tambura, which one can hear to-day in any town of the Balkan provinces.

was constructed on the principle of the dulcimer, and produced its tone not by plucking or pressing the wires, but by striking them with a rebounding hammer. Shaped like a harpsichord, but able to control its volume of sound, the new invention was at once called 'cembalo col forte e piano,' a name easily corrupted after the Italian fashion into fortepiano or pianoforte. Besides the use of hammers, Cristofori made many alterations of internal structure; inverting the wrestplank, substituting a system of springs and levers for the simpler apparatus of quill or tangent, and attaching the strings, at their further end, not to the soundboard, as had been the former practice, but to a special 'stringblock' added to withstand the tension of stouter wires. It would fall beyond our present limits to describe in detail the various devices for directing impact and escapement, for damping strings, and regulating tone : enough that we have here the primitive model which, through successive adaptation and improvement, has been continuously followed up to our own day.

An account of Cristofori's invention was printed by Maffei in 1711 [1], and a German translation published at Hamburg in 1725. During the interval a somewhat similar plan was adopted by the Saxon musician Christoph Gottlieb Schröter. His pupils, he tells us, were in the habit of practising on the clavichord and performing in public on the harpsichord : a fact of considerable significance in the history of the two instruments. In order to remedy this evil he set about a means for rendering the harpsichord more expressive: a chance visit from Hebenstreit, the famous dulcimer player [2], determined his

---

[1] Sometimes misdated 1719, an error which gives priority to Marius' 'clavecins à maillets,' though these appear to have been harpsichords with small hammers, not pianofortes. Maffei's account was first published anonymously and was reprinted among his collected works in 1719. See Mr. Hipkins' article on the pianoforte (Grove, vol. ii. pp. 710-2, 1st edn. ; vol. iv. pp. 150-2, 3rd edn.), to which, as well as to his volume on the same subject, I am much indebted for facts and dates.

[2] Hebenstreit invented an improved dulcimer, to which he gave his own Christian name of Pantaleon; and one of Schröter's experiments was a keyed pantaleon in which the strings were struck from above. It was an instrument like this on which

direction: after a few preliminary experiments he hit upon the first German pianoforte, and had it made for him by his compatriot Gottfried Silbermann. But the evidence of independent origin is not so strong as would appear at first sight. It is unlikely that Schröter was a mechanician expert enough to have devised the scheme in all its details; it is highly probable that Silbermann, whose earliest known pianoforte is dated 1726, had already found opportunity of studying Maffei's article[1]. On the other hand, it is fair to add that the credit of carrying on and developing Cristofori's work belongs, in the first instance, not to Italy but to the Germans. It was he who discovered the new continent: it was Silbermann, Stein, and Streicher who colonized it.

For a long time, however, the value of the discovery was itself seriously questioned. J. S. Bach roundly condemned the first Silbermann pianofortes, both for heaviness of touch and for disproportionate weakness in the treble notes. His own favourite instrument was the clavichord—the 'well-tempered Clavier' of the famous Forty-eight—and though we are told that Silbermann ultimately converted him, it is certain that he never wrote a bar in his life with any special view of pianoforte technique. The same is true of his son, C. P. E. Bach, whose *Wahre Art das Clavier zu spielen* was written for the clavichord, and who is said to have declared that the pianoforte was 'only fit for rondos.' Mozart, in spite of his admiration for Stein's pianos, allowed both harpsichord and clavichord an equal share in his regard: even Beethoven printed his early sonatas with the superscription 'for pianoforte or harpsichord.' There was needed, in short, a whole genera-tion of mechanical progress before the new instrument could challenge the sweetness of the one rival or the brilliance and

Chopin played in 1824 to the Emperor Alexander. The dulcimer still survives in the Hungarian cymbalom, specimens of which are now made at Buda-Pest with a keyboard.
[1] Mr. Hipkins, from his examination of the Silbermann pianoforte at Potsdam, regards this as conclusively proved. See his volume on the pianoforte, pp. 99–100.

sonority of the other. At its first entry it found the field apparently occupied, and in its effort to accommodate two diverse ideals ran in some obvious peril of satisfying neither.

From this it was rescued partly by the energy of the great German makers, partly by an odd cosmopolitan alliance which, during the latter half of the century, was formed in our own land. The leaders were J. C. Bach and Muzio Clementi, the first two composers who showed a decided preference for the pianoforte, and under their direct stimulus and encouragement the London manufacturers came rapidly to the front. Zumpe's 'small square pianos' were soon in request through the length and breadth of England; Backers, a nationalized Dutchman, invented the so-called 'English action,' and with it the general structure of the grand piano; John Broadwood improved on both: every decade saw fresh devices, fresh modifications, further steps in advance, until, by 1800, the race was virtually won. Thenceforward the harpsichord and clavichord remained only as interesting survivals; in the course and development of composition they were no longer of practical account.

We have here a possible explanation of the fact that during the Austrian period the organ was almost entirely neglected. With Bach and Handel it had been essentially the vehicle for massive effects and rich harmonies, for large and stately utterance, for gravity and solemnity of tone; and as these became attainable by the pianoforte there seemed no longer any distinctive part for it to play. At any rate, whatever the reason, there can be no doubt that after 1750 the organ fell upon evil days. Mozart is said to have treated it brilliantly in improvisation, but as composer he never assigned it any position comparable to that of the clavier[1]: among his contemporaries, the Abbé Vogler was the only one who lifted it to a higher rank; among his successors it sank into even

---

[1] His seventeen 'sonatas' for organ, two violins and a bass are small and rather perfunctory works, in one movement apiece, mainly written for his own use at Salzburg.

further desuetude. The race of great organ-virtuosi died out of Germany with Bach's two sons Wilhelm Friedemann and Carl Philipp Emanuel; when Mozart visited Mannheim the only thing which could be said in favour of the second organist was that 'he did not play so wretchedly as the first'; Burney, who travelled through five European countries, includes almost every organ that he met under equal censure. The touch was bad, frequently requiring the weight of the whole hand, the pipes were harsh and strident, there was often no swell, there were sometimes no pedals, and the list of imperfections generally closes with the weary comment—'miserably out of tune as usual.' It is difficult to reconcile this with Silbermann's reputation as an organ-builder; it is yet more difficult to account for a degeneracy so sheer and rapid. Perhaps the rise of secular music, orchestral and chamber, tended to supersede an instrument which has always been primarily associated with the services of the Church[1]: but men do not voluntarily discard a medium until it has ceased to be valuable as a means of expression. In England alone did the old traditions remain, and in England, unfortunately, there was no one strong enough to make full use of them. In Austria the line was thinner and more frail; at the first touch of the new music it snapped asunder.

We are now able to form some estimate of the means which, during the latter half of the eighteenth century, the art of music had at disposal. Singers and violinists had attained a degree of proficiency which enabled composers to treat them without reserve; the pianoforte was beginning to make its way against harpsichord and clavichord; the orchestral voices were slowly gathering in strength and variety. At the same time there were special conditions by which the different masters were severally affected. Haydn's Eisenstadt symphonies were

---

[1] Yriarte, who awards to Spain the palm for Church music, speaks of the organ as the finest of all instruments (*La Musica*, canto iii). But among continental writers of the later eighteenth century he stands absolutely alone.

written for a private band of fourteen persons all told. The
early operas of Gluck and Mozart were modelled on a conventional scheme, which it required their mature genius to over-
throw. The Salzburg Masses were commissioned by an Archbishop who 'disliked fugues,' and prohibited some of the
orchestral instruments from appearing in his cathedral. But,
despite all difficulties and limitations, we cannot doubt that
the Austrian musicians had in their hand a fuller palette and
a richer gamut of colour than had been possible to any of
their predecessors. They were aided by mechanical invention,
by increase of executive skill, by a hundred gifts of industry
and experience ; they developed them by magnificent genius,
as well as by honesty and sincerity of purpose. And thus the
two artistic forces acted and reacted one upon the other,
gaining in power as the years advanced, working in har-
monious intercourse towards fuller freedom and more generous
opportunity.

NOTE.

There appears to be some confusion, both in nomenclature and in use, among the keyed instruments of the eighteenth century. They were different in mechanism, they were different in tone, they were different in capability of expression; yet we often find the names loosely applied, and the music written for one transferred without alteration to another.

In England the terms harpsichord and spinet were sometimes interchanged (as in the Tudor period the term virginal was used for both), but apart from this the names of the three families were clearly distinguished. Clavichord was used for instruments sounded by a tangent, Pianoforte for those sounded by a hammer, and any departure from this practice is not a matter of usage but merely the mistake of an individual author.

In Italy, France, and Spain the name of the harpsichord proper was fairly uniform :—clavicembalo or cembalo, clavecin, clavicimbalo. But between the names of spinet and clavichord there is often a serious confusion. The former, properly designated as spinetta or épinette, was frequently known in all these countries as clavicordo, clavicorde or clavicordio ; the old name manicordo, with its corresponding derivatives, was retained for the true clavichord, and Italy even completed the circle of error by occasionally calling the clavichord a spinetta, and using the term cembalo for all keyed instruments indiscriminately. Cristofori's invention, first known as cembalo col forte e piano, soon settled down into pianoforte in all three languages. In Germany clavier meant specifically the clavichord ; e. g. J. S. Bach's *Wohltemperirtes Clavier*, and C. P. E. Bach's *Wahre Art das Clavier zu spielen*. But it was also, like cembalo, broadly used for all kinds of keyboard, including that of the organ; and is at the present day the common German designation for the piano. The two sizes of harpsichord were at first distinguished as kielflügel or flügel and spinett; but the former name, which is merely pictorial, was afterwards assigned to any instrument enclosed in a wing-shaped case. For the pianoforte there was no distinctive German name—though Beethoven's *Hammerclavier* Sonata endeavoured to supply it with one—and it was usually called either by the general title of clavier, or by the specific Italian term fortepiano—the 'fortbien' of Frederick the Great's royal jest. The alternative 'pianoforte' was also current.

The following conspectus will exhibit the specific uses with such clearness as conditions allow :—

English.	Italian.	French.	Spanish.	German.
Harpsichord	(Arpicordo) Clavicembalo Cembalo	Clavecin	Clavicimbalo	Kielflügel Flügel Clavier
(Virginal) } Spinet }	Spinetta Clavicordo	Épinette Clavicorde	Clavicordio	Spinett
Clavichord	Manicordo Clavicordo Spinetta	Manicorde Clavicorde	Manicordio	Clavier
Pianoforte	Cembalo col forte e piano Fortepiano Pianoforte	Pianoforte	Pianoforte	Fortepiano Pianoforte Clavier Flügel

From this list two names are omitted—Gravicembalo and Claricordo—of which the former seems due to phonetic corruption, and the latter, in the first instance, to a misprint. Among rarer and more obscure members of the harpsichord family may be mentioned the clavicytherium or spinetta verticale, an upright spinet which was made in London as late as 1753. It may possibly have been the remote ancestor of our modern 'cottage piano,' though we can find no example of the latter until Robert Wornum constructed one in 1811. At any rate, in the history of the eighteenth century it is of very little account.

CHAPTER III

WITH the death of J. S. Bach there passed away the second
of the great contrapuntal schools. For nearly two hundred
years it had maintained an unbroken line, carrying its tradition
from the Gabrielis to Sweelinck, from Sweelinck to his pupil
Scheidt, from Scheidt to Buxtehude and Pachelbel, until it
culminated in the master who as a boy had travelled on foot
to Lübeck that he might hear Buxtehude play, and who in
his earliest compositions followed close upon the model of
Pachelbel's chorals and toccatas. Its principal characteristics
have already been fully described—the strength and dignity of
the northern temper and the Lutheran service, the uniformity
of tone natural to a recluse and cloistered art, the rich polyphonic texture that grew as it were spontaneously from the
organ keyboard ; each generation as it passed brought its own
accession of skill, or depth, or intricacy, each aided to develop
the gravity of religious feeling and the sturdy manhood that
disdained to palter with the world : at last the work was
crowned by supreme genius and raised by consummate
achievement into a monument for all time. Yet at no
period in its existence was the school a representative of its
age. Just as Milton joins the Elizabethan poets to those of
the Restoration, yet without belonging to either and without
exercising any serious influence on his contemporaries, so the
work of the great organ-contrapuntists, essentially Miltonic in
character, fills the space of years from Palestrina to Haydn
without ever really setting its mark upon the course and
current of events. From 1600 onwards the general tendency
of musical art was growing more and more monodic; it was
passing to the chamber and the theatre ; it was exchanging

polyphonic problems for those of the solo voice and the solo violin. The typical names in seventeenth-century music are not those of the organists, but those of Lully and Purcell and Alessandro Scarlatti; while the temper of the eighteenth may best be gauged by the famous dispute as to whether Graun or Hasse were the greatest of German musicians.

It is interesting to observe that Bach, who among all the members of the school came nearest into touch with the monodic movement, should also have perceived most clearly the discrepancy between its method and his own. It is, of course, notorious that he was rich enough to profit by more than one inheritance of his age. His violin-writing owes something to Vivaldi, his clavier-writing to Couperin; one of the most remarkable features in his choral work is the manner in which the polyphonic strands are, so to speak, shot with a sense of harmonic colour. But with him the polyphonic feeling was structural, the harmonic accessory; with his contemporaries the balance was steadily swinging to the other side, and the loss of firmness and solidity which the change involved was at least in part compensated by clearness, by transparency, and by new means of expression. For a time, no doubt, the abandonment of the contrapuntal ideal (in so far as it was abandoned) gave a certain licence to cheap effects and mechanical devices: but these were no worse in the decade which followed Bach's death than they had been, through Europe, in any decade of his lifetime; for the first half of the eighteenth century his method was exceptional, and the last half merely worked along the lines which were already habitual and familiar. To say this is not to undervalue the influence which he indirectly exercised through the greatest of his sons, but it must not be forgotten that the influence was indirect, that it was far more a matter of personal character and feeling than of actual style or technique. Emanuel Bach stemmed the tide of Italian frivolity because he was Sebastian Bach's son, but the dyke that he raised against it was very different from anything that his father had constructed. And it is a remarkable proof of the elder man's insight that he could see the signs of the times and realize that for all its apparent levity and prettiness the monodic movement held the key of the future. 'Die Kunst ist um sehr viel gestiegen,' he said towards the end of his life, 'der Gusto hat sich verwundernswürdig geändert. Die alte Art der Musik will unsern Ohren nicht mehr klingen.'

To trace the fulfilment of this prophecy is a difficult matter, not because there is any doubt of the ultimate facts, but because the lines of development are almost inextricably intertwined with one another. The three main issues may be stated clearly enough—growth of harmonic as distinct from contrapuntal treatment, change in the phrase and language of melody, extension of the possibilities of dramatic and emotional expression. But each of these reacted on the other two, and all contributed to the history of those cyclic or symphonic forms which are specially characteristic of the Viennese period. We shall endeavour, for the sake of clearness, to treat them separately, but in so doing we run the obvious risk of overemphasizing each several aspect as we come to it, and against this the reader may very well be cautioned at the outset.

Now, if we take an ordinary four-part song, a choral for instance, it is clear that we may consider its formal structure from two points of view. On the one hand we may regard it as consisting of four superimposed voices—treble, alto, tenor, bass, each of which maintains throughout a certain melody or 'part' of its own. On the other hand, we may regard it as a series of successive chords to each of which the four voices contribute, and which follow one another in orderly and logical sequence. To put the matter briefly and crudely, the former of these aspects is that of the contrapuntal method, the latter that of the harmonic. It will of course be seen that they are only warp and woof of the same texture : the fact that the voices are superimposed in simultaneous utterance means that they 'harmonize' with one another; the fact that the

chords are successive means that their constituent notes follow
each its own moving curve : but none the less the two aspects
are separable, and the general character of the composition will
vary according as one or other of them is brought into prominence.   To the contrapuntist the first care will be that his
parts should appear independent, suave, and melodious ; that
each should maintain its own character, without merely running
parallel to its neighbours, that each should exhibit the utmost
interest and variety which is compatible with the general
scheme.   To the harmonist it will be of chief importance
that this general scheme present the highest beauty attainable
by successions of simultaneous notes, that each chord stand
in some intelligible relation both to that which precedes and
to that which follows it, and that the whole be disposed in
some intelligible manner round certain tonal centres.   The
former is mainly concerned with a point of drawing, the
latter with a point of colour ; the former must needs treat all
its parts as melodies, the latter may if it choose treat one as
melody and the rest as accompaniment ; the former found its
purest expression in the days of the ecclesiastical modes, the
latter requires for its full development the tonality of the
modern scale and the consequent device of modulation.

Take for instance the following example from a madrigal of
Marenzio [1] :

[1] ' Dissi all' amata mia lucida stella.

Here it is obvious that the first consideration is the movement of each part as a separate singing voice. The fact that they harmonize is, in logical phrase, a property, not a difference of the composition; that is to say, while it is necessary to the beauty of the work it is a secondary, not a primary aspect of it. We may further observe that while the pattern of the texture is extremely varied the colour is virtually uniform, and that the passage may be described as a carefully drawn study in monochrome. Here, then, we have a simple and straightforward illustration of the contrapuntal method.

Contrast the opening phrase from the slow movement of Beethoven's *Appassionata* :

Here the first thing which strikes us is the succession of chords. We hardly notice as distinctive the movement of the inner voices ; and the movement of the bass, at the two cadences, is rather a parenthesis or an 'aside' than (as it was with Marenzio) an integral part of the conversation. Further, in the middle of the second strain Beethoven lightens the sombre gravity of the music with an extraordinarily beautiful point of colour, a device so far from being contrapuntal that the progression which it entails would, in strict counterpoint, have been condemned. But there is no need for any detailed analysis or explanation. It is impossible to hear, or even to see, the two passages without realizing that they represent entirely diverse aspects of the art of composition.

There is little doubt that the feeling for harmony, that is, for masses of tonal sound, may be traced back to some unconscious origin at least as early as the time of Orlando di Lasso. We may even hold that some of the contrapuntal rules imply it, and may observe it without anachronism in some of our own madrigalian writers, notably in Dowland and in Thomas Morley. But it is clear that this feeling was enormously fostered and developed by the monodic movement, and that though counterpoint still remained an essential part of musical education, the tendency of mature composition was growing more and more distinctively harmonic. With J. S. Bach the two methods were held in the most perfect balance attained by any musician of the eighteenth century. Handel no doubt could exhibit on occasion a remarkable sense of harmonic colour, but Handel valued colour rather for its dramatic possibilities than for its intrinsic beauty ; Bach evidently loved it for its own sake, and used it as no man has ever done before or since to enrich and adorn the pure outlines of contrapuntal style. A good example of this balance of ideals may be found in the choral, ' Thy bonds, O Son of God most high,' from the second part of the *St. John Passion* :—

This is saturated with harmonic colour, yet the drawing is as firm and clean and the progression of parts as characteristic and individual as the most rigorous contrapuntist could desire. And there are even places where the colour itself is affected

by contrapuntal considerations, notably the movement of the
tenor voice in the first strain and that of the bass in the
second.

But to maintain such a balance demands a firm hand, and
among men less able and less earnest than Bach the change of
method grew steadily more disastrous.   It is as hard to write
good counterpoint as to write good dialogue ; it requires something of the same concentration and effort, the same flexibility
of mind, the same power of adopting different standpoints and
working from them to a central issue.   So when musicians
began to see that their patrons and their public no longer
looked for characterization, and that the requirements of the
case could be satisfied by a little sentiment and a few patches
of colour, they allowed the natural indolence of mankind to
assert itself, and in place of the close-woven contrapuntal
texture turned out scores of facile melodies accompanied
either by simple chords or by conventional figures, which
gave the appearance of movement without the reality.   A
famous instance is the 'Alberti bass,' named from a composer
who founded upon it his one title to immortality :—

Here the bar has a factitious air of being busy ; it is full of
bustling semiquavers, and keeps the ear occupied with a continuous rhythm, but the real movement is disproportionately
small, and each figure contains not a melodic curve but a single
harmonic triad broken into its constituent notes.   Of a similar
nature and devised for a similar purpose were other arpeggio
figures of accompaniment, each the bare statement of a chord,
each confining its rhythmic effects within the simplest harmonic
limits.   One has only to contrast the running basses and the
intricacy of part-writing with which Sebastian Bach's melodies
were so frequently accompanied.

It was from Italy that the chief danger came. For one reason Italian music was essentially that of the singer and the violinist, and naturally devoted its chief attention to the simple melodic voice: for another, it had fallen into an easy-going *far niente* temper, which refused to take more trouble than the occasion demanded. To these we may add a certain childish simplicity, which has its good as well as its bad side, but which is not always compatible with high ideals or with sustained and strenuous attention. It would, of course, be wholly unjust to pass this judgement without qualification. The earlier period of Italian degeneracy saw Tartini writing for the violin, and Domenico Scarlatti for the harpsichord; during the later Sarti was experimenting in opera, and Cherubini was polishing his counterpoint. But when these exceptions have been granted, it remains true that during the eighteenth century the essential quality of most Italian music was a kind of facile prettiness, and such industry as was devoted to its elaboration tended more to glorify the virtuoso than to ennoble and elevate the composer.

The result was too often a style of music which recalls the lyrical prattlings of Ambrose Philips. The audience refused to listen to anything that demanded thought, the composer stood hat in hand ready to offer his patrons whatever they wanted, and the same fashion which filled the Venetian theatre with fairy extravaganza sent Music back to the nursery and set it once more at baby-language. Thus, for instance, in Galuppi's *Mondo alla Roversa*, produced with great success in 1758, there occurs a song for the heroine of which the opening words may be translated—

> When the birds sing,
> And when the birds sing,
> 'Tis Love that makes, that makes them sing.

while the music is as follows:—

In this perilous world an art so innocent may run some danger of demoralization, and we may perhaps see here the beginnings of that decadence which called down Wagner's tremendous epigram on the Italian music of the nineteenth century. At any rate, the melody is fairly typical of its time. There are scores and hundreds like it in the operas of the pre-Viennese period, not only among Italian composers, but even, in a lesser degree, among such foreigners as Hasse, who were most distinctively affected by Italian influence. Hasse was, no doubt, a man of greater ability than Galuppi, as well as of a more virile temperament, but yet of Hasse's composition there is a great deal that was writ in water. And the worst was that any one who possessed some measure of talent and had received some musical training could produce work of this kind without intermission: itinerant opera companies carried it through the length and breadth of Europe; it cost no trouble either to learn, or to sing, or to hear; it was not unpleasing, and it aimed at nothing more than pleasure. Serene Highness, wearied by a day in the council chamber or the hunting field, betook itself to the Court Theatre for an

evening's peace, and, provided that the tunes were pretty and
the accompaniments inconspicuous, was perfectly willing to be
satisfied with its entertainment.   Very soon the court band
adapted itself to the same taste, so did the court organist and
Kapellmeister: little by little the fashion percolated to the lower
strata of society; in a word, there was real danger that the
whole of European music would be swamped by a flood of
trivial commonplaces which should overspread it from coast to
coast, and should then stagnate.

For the first half of the century the chief bulwark against
inundation was the organ school, of which ·J. S. Bach was the
last and greatest representative.   But when J. S. Bach died, in
1750, Italian music was apparently going from bad to worse,
and its popularity through Europe was proportionately increasing.   The case appeared little short of desperate.   England
was too·remote; even Handel was almost entirely ignored on
the continent; Russia was still a frozen steppe; Austria lay
already submerged by Italian influence; France had no one
stronger than Rameau to withstand it ; and meantime the
tide was creeping through Germany and undermining the
national strongholds from Munich to Dresden, and from
Dresden to Berlin.   It is not too much to say that for a few
years the fate of European music depended on Emanuel Bach.
To describe him as 'the greatest composer of a dull period'
is to forget that before Handel died Haydn had written his
first symphony.   But if not the greatest, he was in many
ways the most influential, and it was largely his guidance
which trained the school of Vienna against those of Venice
and Milan.   'He is the father of us all,' said Mozart, and
before such an acknowledgement criticism must keep silence.

Of Sebastian Bach's twelve sons four survived him.   The
eldest, Wilhelm Friedemann (1710–84), was in common repute
the most gifted of them all: he was certainly the only one
who could have carried on the traditions of his school and
family.   A famous organist, a famous improviser, he possessed

at the same time great power of melodic invention and a complete mastery of counterpoint : his cantatas for the Church contain some magnificent passages; his fugues as examples of pure technique are sometimes not unworthy of the *Forty-eight*; even in his lighter pieces, the *Clavier Polonaises* for instance, he often recalls his father's firmness of touch and complexity of design. Unfortunately his whole career was marred by defects of character. The statement that he drank himself to death should, perhaps, be modified by the comment that he lived to the age of seventy-four : but there can be little doubt that he was a graceless ne'er-do-weel, idle, unbusinesslike, and self-indulgent; that in his first post, at Dresden, he performed his duties ill, and in his second, at Halle, left them almost entirely neglected; that his whole history is a miserable record of wasted genius and misused opportunities. Within his own immediate circle his works won instant and cordial admiration, but they never penetrated beyond, and they left the great movements of the time altogether untouched. There was no hope of leadership from a man so little able to command himself.

Nor, for different reasons, are the two youngest sons of any serious historical account. Johann Christoph (1732–95) lived a blameless and useful life as Hofkapellmeister at Bückeburg, wrote a large number of decent, colourless, ineffectual works, and left behind him a reputation of which all that can be said is that it reflected no discredit on the family name. Johann Christian (1735–82) migrated early to Milan, became thoroughly Italianized, and, in 1759, transferred his facile ability to London, where for three-and-twenty years he won fame and affluence as a purveyor of fashionable concerts. He possessed all the talents of the popular novelist, a style remarkably smooth and uniform, an almost prophetic insight into the wishes of his patrons, and just enough imaginative force to stimulate their interest without arousing their apprehension. In all his extant compositions there is not a page

which is really dull, nor a bar which the most conservative
hearer could have regarded as extravagant.   The result was
inevitable.   Our simple public, always on the look-out for false
idols, accorded him an enthusiastic welcome, and he accepted
the situation with good-humoured and genial cynicism.   We
are told that on one occasion some candid friends contrasted
his work in London with that of his elder brother in Berlin.
'It is easily explained,' said Johann Christian, 'he lives to
compose, I compose to live.'

This contrast brings the figure of Carl Philipp Emanuel Bach
into fullest relief.   Composition with him was not an episode
nor an industry, nor a means of popular appeal; it was the most
intimate expression of his nature.   He had less genius, he had
less opportunity than the great Viennese masters who followed,
but he set them a worthy standard of single-hearted earnestness and devotion.   By sympathy, by temperament, by predilection he belonged to the younger and more modern school;
from the older he had learned to treat his art with sincerity
and reverence;   on both sides he was entitled to represent the
period of transition, and in some measure to direct its course.
The very duration of his life is significant.   He was born in
1714, a few months after the death of Corelli; he died in 1788,
three years before that of Mozart.   Within his lifetime falls
every great work from *Ich hatte viel Bekümmerniss* to the
Jupiter symphony; he was a grown man when Handel wrote
the *Messiah*, he was still active when Haydn wrote the *Seven
Words*: so far as dates are concerned he might have heard the
production of Alessandro Scarlatti's later operas, and have seen
the young Beethoven conducting the Electoral orchestra at
Bonn.   It is indeed not infrequent that periods of widely
diverse mental activity should be connected by a single life.
Mantegna, the pupil of Squarcione, is said to have given lessons
to Correggio: Voltaire joins the age of Bossuet to that of
Chateaubriand; Schopenhauer was contemporary with Kant
and Nietzsche.   But not often has a single life witnessed the

shock of so many conflicting ideas, or rendered such material aid in their ultimate reconciliation.

Like many eminent musicians, he began his career as an amateur, took the law-course first at Leipsic and then at Frankfort-on-the-Oder, and only in 1737, at the age of three-and-twenty, decided to abandon Pandects and Institutes for the more congenial service of the arts. In 1746 he was appointed Kammermusicus to Frederick the Great, held the post until the outbreak of the Seven Years' War, and then retired to Hamburg where, in undisturbed quiet and comfort, he spent the rest of his days. He first made his mark as a composer with the six clavier-sonatas which he dedicated to the King of Prussia in 1742 ; two years later[1] followed the more famous ' Würtemberg' sonatas, and from thenceforward his position and reputation were assured. But neither ease nor security ever tempted him to relax his efforts or to lower his ideals. Throughout his long life he appears to have laboured incessantly, and his style, wonderfully mature and individual from the outset, grew steadily fuller and richer as the years advanced. It is true that of his choral compositions, which included twenty-two settings of the *Passion* and a large number of Church cantatas, there is only one, *The Israelites in the Desert,* which possesses any considerable importance at the present day. His orchestral works in like manner give one the impression that he is struggling with an uncongenial medium, and even the three symphonies, written in 1776, show little or no sympathy with the new methods of instrumental treatment. But from first to last his supreme command of the clavier was indisputable. As a virtuoso he was probably unsurpassed by any performer of his time : the treatise *Die wahre Art das Clavier zu spielen* placed him in the front rank of European critics, while among the noblest works of his later manhood stand the *Sonaten mit veränderten Reprisen,*

---

[1] Published in 1744. It is probable that all six were composed at Töplitz in 1743. See Bitter, p. 56.

of 1760, and the great collection *für Kenner und Liebhaber,* which occupied him from 1779 to within a few months of his death [1].

The two composers by whom he was most influenced were J. S. Bach and Hasse. From the former he learned the lesson of strength and solidity, a firm hand, and a sound design; from the latter a certain grace and suppleness of phrase, a certain clearness and transparency of texture, while to both he added a delicate taste and sensibility that were peculiarly his own. His relation to his teachers is well described by Baumgart: 'C. P. E. Bach vereinte in seinen Clavier-Compositionen die strenge Schule seines Vaters, dessen kunstvolle Architektonik und harmonischen Reichthum, mit dem Schmelz der italienischen Cantilene' [2]; but we must remember that the 'harmonic wealth' was very differently administered by father and son. J. S. Bach is here a contrapuntist experimenting in harmony, C. P. E. Bach a harmonist who has profited by the study of counterpoint. To illustrate the distinction we may take two passages in both of which the harmonic intention is evident: both in the same key, both containing the same general modulation, both exhibiting somewhat the same progression of the bass. The one opens the last chorus of the *St. Matthew Passion*:

---

[1] The dates of publication are 1779-87. But many of the sonatas were written earlier, one as early as 1758. See C. F. Bitter, *C. P. E. und W. F. Bach und deren Brüder,* vol. i. p. 212. The full title of the collection was *Sonaten nebst Rondos und freien Phantasien für Kenner und Liebhaber.* It has been reprinted in our own time by Baumgart.

[2] Preface to the new edition of *Sonaten für Kenner und Liebhaber,* quoted by C. F. Bitter, op. cit. i. 48. Contrast Burney's remarkable sentence (iv. 457) about 'Hasse's operas where Emanuel Bach acquired his fine vocal taste in composing lessons, so different from the dry and laboured style of his father.'

the other the first chorus of *The Israelites in the Desert*:

and despite their points of resemblance we can hardly deny that
by the time we reach the second our standpoint has shifted.
Or, again, take the following passage from the oddly named
Phantasie in tormentis [1]:

[1] See Bitter, op. cit. i. 223. It may be useful to contrast Bach's treatment of
colour in the Chromatic Fantasia. In C. P. E. Bach's setting of 'Leite mich nach
deinem Willen,' which is full of rich harmonic colour throughout, some of the
progressions are not justifiable on contrapuntal grounds.

It is impossible that J. S. Bach should have written these progressions, for he always uses colour as accessory to design; it is impossible that Hasse should have written them, for they lie altogether beyond his horizon. They belong distinctively to the harmonic method, they show a particular kind of interest in its problems which no other composer of the time was both able and willing to bestow on them. The curious, abrupt changes are determined not by the requirements of the drawing, but by the wish to set points of colour into strong contrast and relief; the modulation, if it were necessary, could have been effected in a couple of chords, the sequence, regarded merely as a sequence, would have been more telling if it had been less remote. In one word, the beauty of the passage depends upon the prominence of aspects which had hitherto been regarded as secondary. To find its nearest analogue we must look to the fantasies of Haydn and Mozart, and through them to the work of our own Romantic movement. It is no paradox to say that what Emanuel Bach was attempting in the eighteenth century Robert Schumann was achieving in the nineteenth. And behind them both there stands, silent yet approving, the figure of the great Leipsic Cantor.

It is not easy to overestimate the importance of this work. The divorce between contrapuntal and monodic methods had thrown each into an isolation, which was itself a source of weakness and peril.   Counterpoint apart from the harmonic sense was petrifying into the erudite dullness of Marpurg and Kirnberger; monody, unwilling to share the labours of the contrapuntist, was sinking into the sloth and indolence of the Italian opera. J. S. Bach showed that the most elaborate polyphonic writing could be vitalized by true feeling and warmed with rich colour; C. P. E. Bach extended the range of harmonic treatment, and showed that monody itself could be ennobled by the character bred in a contrapuntal school. We may add that the Viennese composers, who followed C. P. E. Bach, completed the reconciliation by absorbing the contrapuntal method into the harmonic. With Haydn and Mozart the fugue is subordinated to the sonata, with Beethoven it is, *qua* fugue, a laboured and uncongenial form of expression, with Schubert it has sunk to the level of a mere academic exercise.   Yet the harmony of Beethoven is richer than that of Mozart and Haydn, the harmony of Schubert is more varied than that of Beethoven : partly because in each generation it was learning to make more use of polyphonic resources, partly because the widening of the harmonic scope brought problems of colour, and even of emotional utterance, that pressed for a solution [1]. It is not, of course, to be forgotten that at the end of his career Beethoven set himself to develope a new polyphony. With that we shall deal in due time; enough for the present to point out that it was new, and to remind the reader that the Galitzin quartets belong to the same period as the *Et vitam venturi* of the Mass in D.

It has been said that the feeling for harmonic design was to some extent a consequence of the monodic movement.   But, in Italy at any rate, there soon came a close interaction between the two, and by the third quarter of the eighteenth century we

---

[1] A third important cause, the development of instruments and instrumental effects, is here for the sake of clearness omitted. It was accessory to the other two, and its discussion would be irrelevant to the present topic.

may almost say that the Italian composers were allowing their
harmonic sense to take the lead, and were treating melody itself
as auxiliary and subordinate. The reason of this fact is not
far to seek. A composition laid out, paragraph by paragraph
on harmonic lines, exhibits a certain logical fitness and propriety
which both satisfies expectation as it proceeds, and at the end
gives to the whole work a due impression of coherence. It is
in this respect, indeed, that the Italians helped to prepare the
way for the great cyclical forms, which are essentially harmonic
in basis, and so take their place among the forerunners of
Mozart and Beethoven. In two respects, however, Italian
influence stopped short at the point where progress was of
vital importance. It never really faced the problem of recon-
ciling harmonic design with melodic phrases independently
conceived : it took but little pains to extend or amplify the
range of its harmonic system. As a natural result its work
during this period was tending to become formal and mono-
tonous. The harmonies are usually restricted to the three
simplest chords, the modulations to the three most nearly
related keys, and the melodic phrase, with little or no rhythmic
variety, no longer dominates the general principles of the design,
but is itself determined by them. It is almost as though an
architect should allow the entire style and character of his
building to be settled by the shape of a conventional and
uniform ground-plan.

Take, for example, the following andante from a sonata by
P. Domenico Paradies (1710–92), a famous Neapolitan virtuoso
and teacher who spent most of his life in London:

There is no denying that it possesses a certain grace and charm, that it is pleasant and attractive so far as it goes; but it has remarkably little to say. The harmonic scheme consists of a few elementary cadences; the melody does no more than draw attention to them; the rhythm follows an almost uniform figure, in which there is nothing to arrest or stimulate the intelligence of the hearer. And it must be remembered that this is typical of a thousand compositions. Sometimes, as in Galuppi, the devices are treated with unusual dexterity of touch; sometimes, as in Sacchini, with more melodic sweetness and continuity; but through the greater part of contemporary Italian clavier music we find the same limitations, the same mental indolence, the same complacent want of enterprise, until in a natural impatience we are inclined, like Berlioz, to 'offer a hundred francs for an idea.' The lessons of Domenico Scarlatti were completely forgotten, if indeed they had ever been learned [1], and Italy once more settled herself comfortably down to follow her art along the line of least resistance.

In this matter, again, we may turn for contrast to C. P. E. Bach. It is true that he was too much the child of Hasse to escape altogether from formalism, but he uses the forms with a tact and a flexibility that neither Hasse nor his Italian masters could ever have displayed. His harmonic range was wider than theirs, his command of rhythmic figures was far more complete, and his unfailing taste enabled him to attain, within the limit of his resources, a most delicate variety of phrase and metre. Here, for instance, is the opening of an allegretto from the fourth of the 'Reprise' Sonatas :—

---

[1] Scarlatti wrote most of his clavier works in Madrid, and of the 329 pieces which he is known to have composed only 42 were published in his lifetime. Burney says that his music was very little appreciated in Italy. See vol. iv. pp. 160–8.

No doubt in 'materiality of thought' this may sound somewhat thin and unsubstantial, but in point of design it represents
a totally different ideal from the melody of Paradies quoted
above. The general scheme is perfectly logical and coherent,
yet the harmonies are sufficiently varied and interesting; in
no single phrase does it appear that the pattern of the music
has been suggested by its texture; the rhythms are abundant
and well contrasted; the whole work shows care, invention, and
a true sense of artistic effect. Indeed, the more we study the
sonatas of Emanuel Bach the more readily do we understand
the reverence in which he was held by his great successors.

They had more genius, they had deeper feeling, they had a wider experience to direct them; but in the pure technique of composition the debt that they owed to him was almost incalculable.

The new melody, however, could not stop here. It was still bound by a certain ceremonial politeness, and though it had acquired a meaning it had not yet learned to speak out. Even with C. P. E. Bach we are not quite free of the *salon* and the presence-chamber; the world of polished phrase and courtly epigram, of avowals which are often tender but never indiscreet, of a society in which ease of manner comes first, and it is considered ill-bred to give vent to the primitive emotions. It is all a hundred times better than the vapid commonplace which it superseded; it has wit and intelligence, and a true appreciation of style: but before it can become a real vital force it must discard its trappings, and strike with an unimpeded arm. He who begins with niceties of expression begins at the wrong end: the first requisite is that the thing said should represent some fundamental truth of human nature. And though Bach had far more humanity than the group of Italians with whom he is here contrasted, he had not enough to perceive the true direction of his art, or to solve the imminent problem that confronted it. In the conflict of styles he won a notable victory, but another hand had the credit of finishing the campaign.

Few events in Musical history are of more far-reaching importance than Joseph Haydn's appointment at Eisenstadt in 1761. He was then twenty-eight years of age, he had educated himself by a diligent study of Bach's early sonatas, he had already composed the early symphonies and quartets in which the influence of Bach is chiefly apparent. To any but the most inspired forecast it would have seemed certain that his course and career were definitely settled, and that he would continue to write in the style of his master, with more insight perhaps, and with a hint of deeper meaning, but with no considerable alteration of method or material.

Yet, even in the earlier works there are traces of an expression which does not belong to Bach, which draws from a different source, which breathes a new life, and acknowledges a new ancestry. Once established at Prince Esterhazy's court, with a patron, a competence, and a free hand, Haydn set himself to develope his own personality on his own lines. The son of a Croatian peasant, he retained through life the characteristics of his race and station, he was essentially a man of the people, and the turn of his fortune, instead of obscuring this fact, only served to bring it into greater prominence. Eisenstadt lay near his home, the whole country side was full of the folk-songs which he had loved from childhood—songs of the ploughman and the reaper, of rustic courtship and village merrymaking;—half unconsciously he began to weave them into the texture of his composition, borrowing here a phrase, there a strain, there an entire melody, and gradually fashioning his own tunes on these native models. His common employment of them dates from the Symphony in D (1762), to the Salomon Symphonies of 1795 : they find their way into everything,—quartets, concertos, divertimenti, even hymns and masses;—they renew with fresh and vigorous life an art that appeared to be growing old before its time [1]. There was no longer any need for precise and formal antithesis, for elaborate ornamentation, for all the rhetorical devices by which thought, however sincere, can be made to seem empty and artificial. In their place we have a living, breathing music with real blood in its veins and real passion in its heart; the free spontaneous utterance of the joys and sorrows of a nation.

In the history of melody this change is highly significant. The folk-song was to Haydn far more than the Chorals had been to the great German contrapuntists [2] : it was not only a means of direction and guidance, it was the natural perennial

---

[1] For a complete account of Haydn's debt to the Croatian folk-songs, see the pamphlet *Josip Haydn i Hravatske Narodne Popievke*, by Dr. Kuhač (Agram, 1880).

[2] See vol. iii. pp. 112–21.

source of inspiration. Hence the peculiar freshness and vitality of his music, especially of those works in which the popular influence is strongest. If we compare the Austrian National Anthem with any tune of Galuppi or Hasse, or even Emanuel Bach, we shall feel that we are in a different world. It is not only another language, it is another order of being; a stage of development which has crossed one of the great organic frontiers. And the Austrian hymn is simply a Croatian ballad which has been ennobled and dignified by the hand of a master.

The freedom which Haydn had won became the heritage of Mozart and Beethoven. He was on terms of personal friendship with both of them, he was considerably their elder, he exercised a decided influence on their style. It is not of course contended that their use of folk-songs is in any way comparable with his, but it is incontestable that the general shape and tone of their melodies is far more akin to the folk-song than to the artificial curves and traceries of polite music. And this is indeed the real point at issue. Melody, if it is to touch the heart must possess a spontaneous life, which, however indefinable, is totally distinct from all mechanical devices. Any one can make a tune; it requires no more than a pen and a piece of music-paper: a living tune cannot be made at all, it is born of a natural creative impulse with which its subsequent treatment is no more to be compared than the education of a child with its parentage. It is in folk-melody that this creative impulse is most readily to be observed; a true folk-tune may be beautiful or ugly, shapely or deformed, but in either case it is alive, it has a meaning, a personality which the most elaborate *Kapellmeistermusik* does not possess at all. And the melodies of true Genius have the same kind of life, they are of the same human family, the same blood, touched, it may be to a finer strain, aristocrat beside plebeian, but all in the last resort 'the sons of Adam and of Eve,' and derived from an ancestry which the peasant shares with Bourbon and Nassau. It is little wonder that the lords of music should so often have adopted their humble neighbours, still less that the children of their own family should grow up in the natural image of the race to which they belonged.

Indeed, given a like training and a like *entourage*, the two are often indistinguishable. The Air for Variations in Beethoven's septet is a folk-song of the Rhine Provinces: it is often quoted as a specially characteristic example of Beethoven's early manner. The two opening themes of the Pastoral Symphony are taken from a Servian ballad: a hundred critics might study the passage and find no trace of an external origin. And the reason is that Beethoven, like the other Viennese composers, was in close sympathy with these primitive expressions of natural feeling. At his hands they acquire a more artistic expression, a more subtle rhythm, a more complete and coherent stanza, but it is their fundamental thought which finds an echo in his own mind, and a nobler utterance in his own creations.

The influence of the folk-song brought into music a new emotional force,—so new, indeed, that some prudish critics censured Haydn for being 'fantastic and extravagant.' The censure reads oddly to us at the present day, but it is not more absurd than the hasty judgement which regards him as cold or self-contained. The quartets in which he found his most natural expression are vivid, nervous, sensitive, never of course approaching to the unplumbed depths of Beethoven, but in their varying moods wholly sincere and outspoken. His characteristics in short are those of his native melodies, primitive, simple, unsophisticated, lightly moved to tears or laughter, wearing his heart on his sleeve with the confiding frankness of a child. Then, at the appropriate moment, came those formative conditions that should train the art with a wider experience of life:—the great political upheaval which roused men's minds from apathy and indifference, the religious movements which stirred them to an unwonted enthusiasm, the growth of a national German literature with its twin stars of Romance and Philosophy, the return to nature in the poetry of England and France;—all affording to genius a fuller opportunity and a richer material, all bearing their part in that development of human character which it is the highest function of art to express. And so the new music passes to adolescence in Mozart and to maturity in Beethoven; the stream flowing further and further from its primary source, yet never losing its continuity or altering its essential character. The grown man feels more subtly and deeply, but not more truly than the child; experience brings more opportunities of joy and sorrow, but it can only develope, not create; and though the power of genius be incalculable, yet its wielder is the product of his age and country. No doubt when we think of Beethoven's later works—of the *Hammerclavier* Sonata or the Choral Symphony—we seem to be in the presence of forces, the origin of which it is impossible to trace. And in a sense this is true. There is no 'accounting' for that marvellous music: 'it is Beethoven' we say, and there is an end. But the greatest genius is the most indebted man; he who can best profit by the circumstances to which he is born. Not Dante, not Shakespeare, not Goethe could have come except to an age prepared to receive them: as little can we conceive Beethoven except as the inheritor of Haydn and Mozart.

To illustrate this development in detail would carry us beyond the limits of the present chapter. We are here concerned with points of departure, and these it may be convenient, at the close, briefly to recapitulate. The conditions which made the Viennese school possible were first, that the preponderating balance of musical style should swing from the contrapuntal to the harmonic side; second, that the harmonic method should be set forth by a composer of sufficient invention and sincerity to make it a vehicle for the highest musical treatment; third, that there should be found some type of melody which should at once dominate the entire scheme of harmonic colour, and express with a true and living utterance the emotions and passions of mankind. Of these the first was fulfilled by the general course of events. The feather-weights of the popular Italian music were piled high on the monodic scale, and pulled down the balance when the death of J. S. Bach removed the heavier counterpoise. Then came Emanuel Bach, turning to nobler purpose the accepted phraseology of the time, and saving it once for all from the reproach of triviality and platitude. Thirdly, Haydn took up the method of Emanuel Bach, breathed into it his own native inspiration, and taught it to speak a language that all men should hear and understand. Thenceforward a new page is turned in the history of musical art; a page on which are recorded many of its greatest and most enduring achievements.

CHAPTER IV

GLUCK AND THE REFORM OF THE OPERA

In the last chapter we followed the transition of musical style through C. P. E. Bach to Haydn. Before pursuing the further current of the stream we must here turn aside and trace from source to confluence the most important of its tributaries. Bach had left one field, that of opera, entirely untouched; his work was to prevent the popular operatic methods from overspreading other forms of composition. In order to complete the reform it was necessary that a more audacious master should invade the theatre itself, should attack false art in its very stronghold, and lead it captive from the fortress which it had deemed impregnable. It was of course impossible that any one man should have effected this conquest unaided. The influence of the general intellectual movement is more apparent here than in any other chapter of musical history. But the revolution required a musician for leader, and in the fullness of time it found one to its hand.

Christopher Willibald Gluck (1714–87) was born at Weidenwang, Upper Palatinate, in the same year as Emanuel Bach, with whose life, indeed, his own almost exactly coincided. His father, one of Prince Eugene's gamekeepers, observed the boy's talent, and squeezed a scanty purse to provide him with the means of education : an example of parental insight so rare in the history of music that it deserves more than a passing notice. We may add that it was immediately justified by the result. In 1736 Gluck left the Prague Music School and went off to seek his fortune in Vienna, where he met Count Melzi, an enthusiastic amateur, who at once engaged him for his private band, and carried him off to Milan for a more serious course of training under Sammartini. As might naturally be expected, he began his career by copying the style of his master, and his first seven operas[1] (produced between 1741 and 1745 at Milan, Venice, Cremona, and Turin) appear to have possessed no qualities which could militate against their ready and immediate success. Then came an auspicious failure, which at first checked and then diverted the current of his genius. In 1745 he was summoned to London, and there produced two operas and a pasticcio, which were all virtually hissed off the stage. For the cause of this defeat it is now useless to inquire. We cannot claim it as a proof of the superiority of English taste (though Gluck afterwards flattered Dr. Burney by assigning this as the reason), for the English taste of the time was little short of deplorable. Handel told Gluck that he had taken too much trouble, and in this cynical avowal we may perhaps be nearer the truth. But, however it be explained, there can be no doubt that ill-success is an admirable stimulus to reflection. Gluck realized that he was on the wrong line, gave the British public a derisive concert on the musical glasses, and, having thus vindicated his fame as an artist, went back to his study and reconsidered his position. For the next two years (1746–48) he set himself resolutely to the study of aesthetics and literature, and then, with a very different mental equipment, began his work of reformer in Vienna.

Arteaga[2] discusses the defects of Italian opera under three main heads, the unphilosophic character of the composers, the vanity of the great singers, and the total breakdown— 'abbandono'—of dramatic poetry. On no one of these counts can any adequate defence be set up. Philosophy, we are told, is 'musical as is Apollo's lute,' and the composers of the Italian

---

[1] *Artaserse* (Milan, 1741), *Demofonte* (Milan, 1742), *Demetrio ed Ipermnestra* (Venice, 1742), *Artamene* (Cremona, 1743), *Siface* (Milan, 1743), *Fedra* (Milan, 1744), and *Il Re Poro* (Turin, 1745).

[2] *Rivoluzioni del teatro musicale italiano*, chs. xiii, xiv, xv.

school derived their inspiration less from Apollo than from Marsyas. Their work was done without insight, without intelligence, without even the bare necessities of common sense and reason. The stage, loaded with useless pageantry, made the machinist master of the situation, except, indeed, where the young bloods of the audience insisted upon claiming their right to sit at the wings; the chorus stood in a double row 'like grenadiers on parade,' and sang tonic and dominant to the cadence of a few mechanical evolutions; there was no plot, there was no characterization, there was no touch of dramatic interest or propriety: and the spectators rattled their dice-boxes or called Basto and Punto, only suspending their game for a few moments when a Vestris was to dance or a Caffarelli to sing. The same libretti were set and reset, always after the same cut-and-dried conventional pattern, and the highest achievement was attained if another trill could be added to Dido's *Aria di bravura*, or if Artaserse could prolong for three more bars the holding-notes of his *Aria di portamento*. There is a passage in George Hogarth's memoirs[1] which, though well known, is worth reproducing as a summary. 'In the structure of an opera,' he says, 'the number of characters was generally limited to six, three of each sex; and if it were not a positive rule it was at least a practice hardly ever departed from to make them all lovers—a practice the too slavish adherence to which introduced feebleness and absurdity into some of the finest works of Metastasio. The principal male and female singers were each of them to have airs of all the different kinds[2]. The piece was to be divided into three acts, and not to exceed a certain number of verses. It was required that each scene should terminate with an air; that the same character should never have two airs in succession; that an air should

---

[1] *Memoirs of the Opera*, by George Hogarth.

[2] There were five kinds:—*Aria cantabile, Aria di portamento, Aria di mezzo carattere, Aria parlante* (called also *Aria di nota e parola*, or *Aria di strepito*, or *Aria infuriata*), and *Aria di bravura*, or *d'agilità*. For an example of each see the article on Opera in Grove's *Dictionary*, vol. ii. pp. 509, 510 (first edition); third edition, *v.* article ARIA, vol. i. p. 110.

not be followed by another of the same class; and that the principal airs of the piece should conclude the first and second acts.   In the second and third acts there should be a scene consisting of an accompanied recitative, an air of execution, and a grand duet sung by hero and heroine.   There were occasional choruses, but trios and other concerted pieces were unknown except in the Opera Buffa, where they were beginning to be introduced.'

The spirit of man has often allowed itself to be confined by narrow fetters, by the Unities falsely called Aristotelian, by the *Tabulatur* of the Meistersingers, by the formal logic of the schools, but never in all its history has it submitted to prescription so meaningless and so pedantic.   We may say of them, as Macaulay said of the Newdigate, that the only rule which possesses any common sense is that by which the length of the piece is restricted.   The rest are fatal not only to any freedom of movement, but to any intelligible vitality of idea.   They crush the very breath out of the body, and leave it, like a malefactor, hanging in chains.   Indeed, the only forms of music drama which still retained any semblance of life were the little comic operas and intermezzi, of which Pergolesi's *Serva Padrona* is at once the earliest and the most conspicuous example. These were at least human and personal; they presented not diagrams of classical heroes, but humorous portraits of contemporary manners; they were often, within their limits, pleasant and amusing.   But like their kinsmen the Zarzuela of Spain and the Singspiel of Germany they were too slight to maintain the conflict alone.   By common consent they were regarded as far below the level of Opera Seria, and even when they shared the stage with it, in alternate acts, were in no way allowed to challenge its pre-eminence.   It may have been that they afforded less leisure to the card-players; it may have been that they could be understood by common people who had never heard of Dido and Artaxerxes: at any rate, they were still of a rank comparatively humble, and fulfilled an office comparatively subordinate. It was to Opera Seria that the theatre belonged by right; it was to Opera Seria that Gluck's reform was directed.

He began tentatively enough with one of Metastasio's libretti —*La Semiramide riconosciuta*—which was produced at the Court Theatre on May 14, 1748, and given five times in rapid succession. Critics are divided as to the historical importance of this work. Pohl [1] declares that it gives little or no promise of the coming reform; Marx [2] draws attention to the power of musical scene-painting, and finds at least a presage of the future dramatist in the scene between Semiramis and Scytalco. As a matter of fact it suited Gluck's purpose to proceed by slow degrees. He was not yet quite sure of his ground, he could not afford to dispense with the collaboration of Metastasio, the conventions of the time were still too powerful to be successfully defied. Opera was a favourite form of entertainment in Vienna, and the traditional fashion had been set and stereotyped by a score of popular composers. Bonno, Wagenseil, and Reutter represented the native genius, and among their more august visitors came Hasse from Dresden, and Jommelli from Naples, and Adolfatti from Venice, all pledged to maintain the three acts and the six characters, and the five different kinds of aria, and the other dogmas of the Metastasian creed. Gluck had no desire to be burned as a heretic: at least he found it advisable to mature his own views before he proffered them as an open challenge to orthodoxy.

The success of *Semiramide* encouraged its composer to a further advance, and in 1749 and 1750 he paid two visits to Italy, where he brought out the two most important of his early operas—*Telemacco*, at Rome, *La Clemenza di Tito*, at Naples. The former of these may be taken as the turning-point of his career, his first definite attempt to break through customary

[1] *Joseph Haydn,* vol. i. p. 87.
[2] *Gluck und die Oper*, vol. i. pp. 158-75. See also Mr. Ernest Newman's volume on *Gluck and the Opera*, pp. 30-32.

trammels and to tell a dramatic story in a dramatic way. The scenes are so arranged as to emphasize the continuity of the plot, the characters are humanly conceived and contrasted, and Gluck thought so highly of the music that on no less than ten occasions he employs portions of it in his later works[1]. It says something for the catholicity of the Roman taste that the opera was received with unexpected favour, and that a few years later Gluck was rewarded by receiving from Benedict XIV the Order of the Golden Spur[2]. There is something almost of comedy in the spectacle of this arch-revolutionary at the Vatican. Not more incongruous is the story of Voltaire and the Papal dedication of Mahomet.

The succeeding events are difficult to explain without some hint of discredit. We can hardly suppose that Gluck was bribed either by his patent of nobility or by the Kapellmeister-ship which, in 1754, was conferred upon him at Vienna; but the fact remains that for over a decade he attached himself to the court, and with one exception produced nothing better than polite futilities for the theatres of Laxenburg and Schönbrunn. It is true that the exception was *Orfeo*, which startled the entire Viennese world in 1762, but its very brilliance only serves to accentuate the darkness. There must have been some spirit of time-serving in the man who, after writing the magnificent scene between Orpheus and the Furies, could go back to work which at its best reminds us of Jommelli, and at its worst of Reutter.

At the same time, *Orfeo*[3] is of such supreme importance that the history of operatic reform is commonly said to date from its production. In preparing it for the stage Gluck showed all the care and firmness which he could well display

---

[1] Notably the air ' Je t'implore et je tremble' of *Iphigénie en Tauride.*

[2] The same honour was conferred in 1770 on Mozart. But Mozart never used the title, Gluck never laid it aside: a characteristic example of the difference between the two men.

[3] For analyses of this and the subsequent operas of Gluck the reader may be referred to the volumes of Marx and Mr. Ernest Newman already cited.

when there was an artistic principle at stake. He discarded
Metastasio, and took Calzabigi as his librettist; rewrote the
words until the enraged poet threatened to withdraw his collaboration, domineered over the rehearsals until the Emperor
had to conciliate the singers in person, and met protests,
appeals, and remonstrances with the same fixed and stubborn
opposition. The play was to be acted, not sung through by
posturing soprani and clock-work choruses. *Che farò* was to be
given without embroideries—'add a roulade,' he said, 'and you
turn it into an air for marionettes.' No wonder that the cast
felt the very walls of the theatre insecure, and that the
audience listened to the first representation in pure bewilderment. It was not until the fifth performance that the work
received any intelligent appreciation, and then only at the hands
of a few connoisseurs. Count Durazzo, to whom Gluck owed
his appointment as Kapellmeister, made a bold bid for popularity by printing the score, but in the next three years only
nine copies were sold, and the whole undertaking appeared to
have fallen to the ground.

Gluck resigned himself to the inevitable, and returned contentedly to *Ezio* and *Il Parnasso confuso*, and other occasional
pieces, among which there stands out in relief a bright little
comic opera called *The Pilgrims of Mecca*. But *Orfeo* had
shown him his true strength, and with all his philosophy he
was not a man to be beaten. In 1767 he once more stepped
down into the arena, and flung to the world the most uncompromising challenge of his life. The opera of *Alceste* carried
the principles of *Orfeo* to their logical conclusion: it was
prefaced by a manifesto [1] which proclaimed the cause of reform
and condemned with judicial severity the errors of the accustomed method. The function of music, says Gluck, is to
support poetry, without either interrupting the action or dis-
figuring it by superfluous ornament. There is to be no concession to 'the misapplied vanity of singers'; the warmth of

[1] Quoted in Mr. Ernest Newman's *Gluck and the Opera*, pp. 238-40.

dialogue is not to cool off while the actor waits for a weari-
some ritornello or exhibits the agility of his voice on an
appropriate vowel; the old *da capo* form is to be given up as
undramatic, and even the sacred distinction of aria and recitative as far as possible obliterated.   The overture is 'to prepare
the spectators for the coming action, and give them an indication of its subject'; instruments are to be employed not
according to the dexterity of their players, but according to
the dramatic propriety of their tone; there is to be no parade
of difficulties at the expense of clearness, no virtuosity, no
violation of good sense; and as climax of audacity 'there is
no rule which may not be sacrificed in order to secure an effect.'

It was impossible to leave this unanswered.   The critics
fell upon Gluck as Scudéry had fallen upon Corneille, the
court consulted Reutter and looked askance; the public frankly
declared that it found *Alceste* tedious and unintelligible.   'For
nine days the theatre has been closed,' said one disaffected
voice, 'and on the tenth it opens with a Requiem.'   Gluck
in short had offended everybody at one stroke: his patrons
by seriousness, his rivals by denunciation, the singers by
a disregard of their privileges, the contrapuntists by an open
defiance.   No doubt there had been protests before:—the
delicate satire of Addison, the mordant wit of the *Teatro
alla moda*, the solid reasonings of Diderot and Algarotti;
they could be ignored or disregarded, or at most referred to
'the long-standing antagonism of poet and philosopher.'   But
here was a man in the very centre of the movement, a composer
of established position and repute, who not only asserted that
everybody else was wrong, but, worst of all, wrote operas to
prove it.   So the storm grew and gathered, and when, two
years later, Gluck produced *Paride ed Elena*, with another
rigorous dramatic scheme and another epistle dedicatory about
'pedantic harmonists' and 'ingenious negligences,' it broke
above his head in a full torrent.   Sonnenfels, Burney, and
a few other foreign visitors supported him with their applause

and sympathy: Vienna for the time being declared against him.

Discouraged but wholly unconvinced, he turned his thoughts toward Paris. Among his acquaintances was a certain Bailli de Roullet, then attached to the French Embassy in Vienna, at whose suggestion he set to work with Calzabigi on Racine's *Iphigénie en Aulide*. By the end of 1772 the score was completed, and meanwhile de Roullet sent home a long preparatory letter to the director of the Académie Royale de Musique, stating that the celebrated Chevalier Gluck was a great admirer of the French style of composition, that he preferred it indeed to the Italian, that he regarded the French language as eminently suited for musical treatment, that his opera of *Orfeo* had been a great financial success in Bologna, and that he had just finished a new work, in French, on a tragedy of the immortal Racine. In its creation he had exhausted the powers of art:—simple natural song, enchanting melody, recitative equal to the French, dance pieces 'of the most alluring freshness': everything that could please and nothing that could offend the most delicate susceptibilities. Surely he deserved some acknowledgement for so nobly defending the French tongue against the calumnious accusations of its own authors [1].

In order to understand the full diplomacy of this letter we must go back twenty years, and trace the course of French Opera during one of its most distracted periods. Up to 1752 Rameau was the unquestioned monarch of the Parisian stage. His opera of *Castor et Pollux* (1737) had placed him in the forefront of French composers, and the authority that he wielded was as absolute as that of Lully or Handel. But in 1752 an Italian troupe, popularly known as 'Les Bouffons,' obtained permission to occupy the hall of the Opera-house, and

---

[1] This letter, dated Aug. 1, 1772, may be found, together with the records of the newspaper-war which followed, in an anonymous volume entitled *Mémoires pour servir à l'histoire de la révolution opérée dans la musique par M. le Chevalier Gluck* (Naples, 1781).

there gave a season of those light intermezzi which showed the Italian vocal style at its best. Paris hesitated for a moment, and then split into two furious parties. The old Conservatives rallied round the banner of Rameau and native art, the revolutionary party upheld the foreigners; within a few months the 'Guerre des Bouffons' had all but assumed a political importance. Pamphlet rained after pamphlet and lampoon after lampoon : Grimm, in the *Petit prophète de Böhmischbrod*, threatened the French people with extinction if it were not at once converted to Italian music; the *Coin du Roi* answered with less wit but more acrimony; Diderot, who hated Rameau for his attacks on the Encyclopaedia, took abundant opportunity of avenging himself; Rousseau, who had just produced his *Devin du village*, turned his back on himself with sublime inconsistency, and proclaimed aloud that the French language was unsingable, and that French music was a contradiction in terms. An entire new school of Opéra Comique arose out of the controversy. Poets like Marmontel, Favart, and Sedaine set themselves to write after the Italian models : Duni brought over from Parma his *Ninette à la Cour*, and followed it, in 1757, with *Le Peintre amoureux* : Monsigny left his bureau and Philidor his chess-table to follow the footsteps of Pergolesi; lastly, in 1768, came Grétry from Rome and killed the old French operatic style with *Le Tableau parlant* and *Zémire et Azor*.

So far, the victory of the 'Guerre des Bouffons' lay definitely with the Italian party. In the contest of wits they had a clear advantage; the death of Rameau, in 1764, had removed the chief of their antagonists; the most distinguished composers of the time were almost without exception on their side. Hence the nationalists were looking out for a champion; for some one who should vindicate the majesty of the French style and silence once for all the audacious paradoxes of Grimm and Rousseau. At the nick of time came de Roullet's letter from Vienna with its astute points and its carefully calculated appeals. The Académie Royale sat in session to consider it, asked to see the first act of *Iphigénie*, read it with approval, and finally offered Gluck an engagement at Paris 'if he would pledge himself to write for them six. operas of the same kind.' If there were no one on the spot who could stem the tide of Italian partisanship, at least they would make themselves secure by a solid and lasting alliance.

To Gluck the condition appeared nothing short of prohibitive. He was nearly sixty years of age, his home and office were in Vienna, he had no mind to throw up a comfortable appointment and risk the chances of a precarious livelihood abroad. He therefore wrote to his old pupil Marie Antoinette, and asked her to use her influence with the Academy. The wife of the Dauphin was not lightly to be denied, the obnoxious condition was rescinded, and at the end of 1773 Gluck received a formal invitation to bring his work to Paris for rehearsal.

At first he found himself in a difficult position. He was a foreigner, and therefore an object of suspicion to the nationalist pamphleteers : he was a guest of the Académie de Musique, and therefore the natural enemy of the Bouffonists. But he left no stone unturned to secure his welcome. He wrote conciliatory letters, he called upon adverse critics, he obtained an introduction to Rousseau, and induced that potentate to believe that there were some secrets of dramatic expression which even the Italians had not mastered. Then came the usual trouble with the company. Vestris was obstinate, Legros was out of health, Larrivée, who had been cast for *Agamemnon*, showed no conception or understanding of his part, and Sophie Arnould, the greatest operatic actress of the day, marred her reading of *Iphigénie* by a faulty intonation. More than once the composer threatened to withdraw his work and return to Vienna, more than once Marie Antoinette had to intervene, and it was not until April 19, 1774, that the opera was declared ready for performance.

It was undoubtedly the finest work that Gluck had yet

written. Not less passionate than *Orfeo* and *Alceste,* it is
nobler and more majestic than either: the melody pure and
dignified, the dramatic interest unbroken, the characters firmly
drawn though presented with a due artistic reticence and
restraint. M. Gustave Chouquet [1] sums it up in one happy
phrase when he speaks of its 'Sophoclean' quality: its golden
transparency of style, its epic touch, its grandeur of proportion
are not incomparable with the *Antigone* and the *Oedipus.* In
a word it is a true classic, instinct with vitality and inspiration,
dominated throughout by reverence for a high ideal.

On the world of Paris the opera made a profound impression.
The Italian party essayed a few criticisms, but they found the
majority against them; they had lost their most powerful leader
by the defection of Rousseau; for the time they were obliged
to confess themselves defeated. New versions of *Orfeo* and
Alceste were at once prepared for the stage, and the former,
given on Aug. 2, 1774, consolidated the victory which *Iphigénie*
had already won. The war appeared to be over, when Gluck,
in a moment of incredible folly, offered the Court *La Cythère
assiégée,* one of the feeblest of his Viennese trivialities, and
in its swift and disastrous failure risked at a blow the loss
of his entire position.

Marmontel was not the man to let this error of strategy
pass undetected. The hero, it seemed, was not invulnerable;
the breath of popular opinion was veering round; opportunity
was ripe for meeting the Académie de Musique with its own
weapons. The Italian party had already vindicated its cause
in Opéra Comique, but it had no one at Paris who could
rival Gluck in serious opera. Let them then borrow from
their antagonists the policy of a foreign alliance, and invite
across the Alps a composer who should be their leader and
their champion.

The field of selection lay within narrow limits. Jommelli

---

[1] Article on Gluck in Grove's *Dictionary,* vol. i. p. 602 (first edition); vol. ii.
p. 400 (third edition). Mr. Ernest Newman (*Gluck and the Opera,* pp. 131–33)
takes a somewhat more disparaging view.

was dead; Traetta, 'the most tragic of the Italians,' had
just returned from St. Petersburg broken in health; Paisiello
was setting out to succeed him at the Imperial court; Sarti
left Copenhagen in this year to take up his appointment at
Venice. Sacchini might have been a possible choice: he was
then the idol of London, where he almost filled in public
estimation the place which the death of Handel had vacated.
But Sacchini's music, wholly typical of the Italian school,
was almost too suave and uniform for the purpose required,
and his idle and dissolute habits would have made him a very
precarious ally. There remained but one man of considerable
reputation, and to him accordingly the Bouffonists made appeal.

Niccola Piccinni, the countryman and contemporary of
Traetta, was born at Bari, near Naples, in 1728. At the age
of fourteen he entered Sant' Onofrio, studied there for twelve
years under Leo and Durante, and in 1754 made his début
at one of the smaller Neapolitan theatres. He found the
Comic stage in the possession of Logroscino (1700–63), a
witty and versatile writer of musical farces who had won
from an admiring public the title of Il Dio dell' Opera Buffa.
At almost a single stroke he ousted his rival from popular
favour, and established a reputation which soon spread beyond
the limits of his native province. It was at Rome, in 1760,
that he gained his greatest and most notable triumph. His
opera *La Cecchina, ossia La buona figliuola*, took the city
by storm: it was given at every theatre, it was sung in
every street, it stood godfather to villas, to taverns, to costumes,
it furnished the Roman populace with a store of catchwords
and an inexhaustible theme of conversation. Within a year
it was produced at every capital in Italy, within a decade
at nearly every capital in Europe. To its rapid and unqualified
success the whole history of eighteenth-century music can
supply no parallel.

The qualities of the work are easily enumerated: an amusing
plot, an abundance of bright and pleasing melody, some real

H

sense of colour, and an orchestral score of unaccustomed richness and elaboration [1]. It sounds but a light equipment when
we remember that during these same years Gluck was planning
Orfeo, but by some lucky accident it precisely hit the level
of the public taste, and so assumed an importance which
was, in part at any rate, factitious. There is genuine music
in *La Cecchina*; but its limitations, no less than its merits,
may help to explain the enthusiasm of its reception.

To Piccinni's modest and unpretentious temper these plaudits
meant opportunity rather than reward. He had no idea of
posing as a great master, his work lay before him, his popularity
was but a stimulus to further effort. Unluckily he allowed
industry to outrun discretion. In 1761 he wrote no less than
six operas, in the next twelve years he increased the number
by more than fifty; his quality degenerated, his patrons grew
weary, and in 1773 he was hissed at the very theatre which
had brought *La Cecchina* to its first performance. We are
told that he owed this disaster to the jealousy of his pupil
Anfossi: but that it could have been brought about at all
is highly significant.   He had lost the confidence of his public,
he had not the strength of character to fight for his laurels;
in bitter disappointment he withdrew from Rome, and retired
to seek his fortune anew in Naples. There, among his own
people, he recovered something of his former skill and invention: indeed, the operas of *Alessandro nelle Indie* and
I viaggiatori may challenge comparison with the best of his
early works. But they hardly penetrated beyond the city
for which they were written, and at a time when his old
masterpiece was being applauded from Lisbon to St. Petersburg
there were many parts of Italy in which his recent compositions
were unknown.

This was the man who, in 1776, was called forth *impar*

---

[1] Piccinni's operas were so fully scored that copyists demanded a sequin more
for transcribing one of his works than one of any other composer. Burney, *Present
State of Music in Italy*, p. 317.

congressus Achilli to contend with Gluck.   For such a struggle he possessed but a meagre armoury of qualifications.   His talent, unquestionable so far as it went, showed thin and slender beside the stalwart proportions of his adversary; his tragic writing touched the height of the conventional standard, but in no way rose above it; his comedies, from the very nature of the case, lay outside the point at issue.   He knew no word of the French language, he had no taste for intrigues and diplomacies, he was so little a fighter that he had fled from Rome at the first breath of antagonism.   Indeed, the wonder is that he ever consented to enter the field.   But the offer was tempting, the party enthusiastic, victory, he was assured, lay within his reach : in an evil moment he emerged once more from seclusion, and confronted the downfall which one fatal success had doomed him to incur.

At first, no doubt, the causes appeared equally balanced. Piccinni was received with acclamation, Marmontel wrote poems in his honour, Ginguené, d'Alembert, La Harpe, and a host of others assailed Gluck with invectives which strangely anticipate a more modern controversy.   The composer of *Iphigénie* was accused of ruining the Parisian voices, of sacrificing music to a drama which, as La Harpe said, ' would have sounded better without it,' of endeavouring to conceal his numerous errors under a noisy and strident orchestration. He had no melody, no refinement, no sense of beauty ; his recitative was uncouth, his harmony rugged, his modulation incoherent, his choruses were less appropriate than those of Rameau, his duets were stolen from Italy and marred in the stealing.   Suard and the Abbé Arnaud retaliated, the dispute waxed hotter and more intense, and when, a year later, Gluck produced *Armida*, and Piccinni *Roland*, it broke into a war beside which the ' Guerre des Bouffons ' was a mere display of the parade-ground.   No graver question had endangered national unity since Blue fought Green in the streets of Constantinople.

To bring the matter to an issue Berton, the director of the Grand Opera, proposed to the two rivals libretti on the same subject, that of Racine's *Iphigénie en Tauride*. Gluck accepted the offer as a challenge, put forth his full strength, secured the immense advantage of first representation, and on May 18, 1779, crushed opposition beneath the greatest and most enduring of his works. From the magnificent storm of the overture to the breathless drama of the sacrificial scene there is not a bar that is weak or superfluous, not a phrase that fails of its due effect. Pure musical beauty as sweet as that of *Orfeo*, tragic intensity deeper than that of *Alceste*, a firm touch, an undaunted courage, a new subtlety of psychological insight, all combine to form a masterpiece such as, through its entire history, the operatic stage had never seen. Envy itself could find no opening for attack : criticism was silenced by the tumult of approbation. The supremacy of a true dramatic ideal was completely vindicated, and not all the wit or malice of antagonism could gainsay it any more.

As an illustration of its boldness and unconventionality may be quoted the opening of the famous scene in which Orestes 'mistakes for repose of mind the prostration of physical fatigue.'

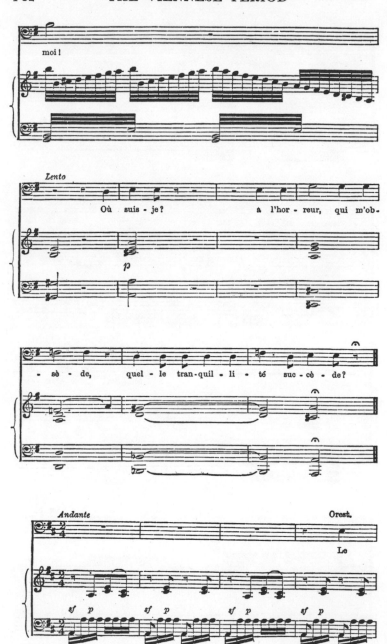

Six months later Gluck bade farewell to Paris. He had achieved his task, he had accomplished his purpose, he could well afford to leave the field to a beaten enemy. Yet, in idle and desultory fashion, the war lingered on : Piccinni gave his *Iphigénie* in 1781 and his *Didon* in 1783 ; Salieri, the pupil of Gluck, responded in 1784 with *Les Danaïdes* ; Sacchini introduced a diversion with his *Dardanus* and his *Œdipe à Colone*. But the question was really settled : these outbursts of guerrilla warfare merely prolonged a struggle that had become unmeaning, and in 1789 came the French Revolution and swallowed up the entire controversy.

So far, the history of operatic development has been virtually restricted to the career of a single man. Indeed, up to 1780, there is little else of any moment to record. The work of Italy during these years has already been considered. Spain had passed through her own 'Guerre des Bouffons' earlier in the century [1], and was now contentedly following the fashion of her successive courts—Neapolitan with Ferdinand VI, Castilian with Charles III—while her most notable composer, Perez, accepted a rival service at Lisbon. The darkness of England was barely illuminated by Arne's *Artaxerxes* (1762): the ballad-operas of Shield and Kelly had not yet appeared, and the British public was far too fully occupied in comparing J. C. Bach with Sacchini to have any mind for encouraging a native school. Germany was dominated by Graun and Hasse, both unflinching adherents of the conventional Italian style; the more distant countries of Europe had not yet awoken to the artistic life. It remains, then, to trace the further course of the movement, and in particular to note its influence upon the great masters of Vienna.

---

[1] See the account of the Compañia de Trufaldines in Carmena's *Crónica de la Ópera-italiana en Madrid* (Madrid, 1878).

CHAPTER V

THE OPERA FROM MOZART TO WEBER

In the history of operatic music the part played by Joseph Haydn may practically be disregarded. Of his fourteen operas all but two were occasional pieces written for the private theatres of Eisenstadt and Esterhàz, and of the exceptions *La vera Costanza* was driven from Vienna unheard, and *Orfeo*, intended for London, was never finished. He believed himself that he needed only opportunity and experience to become a master of the stage, spoke of *Armida* (1783) as his best work, and eloquently complained of the country exile which put all theatrical triumphs beyond his reach [1]. But it would seem that in this matter he miscalculated his own powers. His constructive genius was essentially symphonic in character; he had little power of breaking his design to suit the requirements of a stage situation, and the best of his dramatic work is to be found in such light comedies as *La Canterina* and *L'Infedeltà delusa*, in which the methods of the theatre most nearly approximate to those of the concert-room. Had Gluck never written a single note the work of Haydn would not have been appreciably altered.

With Mozart the case is different: indeed, the history of opera during the next ten years is little more than an account of the wealth which he inherited and bequeathed. In him converged all the streams of tendency which we have hitherto been separately considering: the sweetness of Italy, the mastery of C. P. E. Bach and Haydn, a dramatic insight which, though

[1] See Pohl's *Haydn*, vol. ii. pp. 344-58.

inferior to that of Gluck, was nevertheless its most worthy successor. He possessed a natural gift of melody, such as the world has never seen equalled, and a quickness of apprehension which learned by instinct all that the science of his day had acquired. Born in 1756, he was a composer at the age of four, a pianist of European reputation at the age of ten; at twelve he had written *La Finta Semplice*, at fifteen he took his place among the doctors of Bologna. Educated under the wise severity of his father, he attained a proficiency to which effort was needless and difficulty unknown; and he entered manhood a skilled performer on three instruments, a master in every known branch of composition, and a genius whose brilliance and fertility of resource were in their kind unsurpassable.

His early operas are cut after the customary Italian pattern, though they differ from the works of Galuppi or Hasse by their far greater melodic beauty and their far higher sense of musicianship. In the best of them, *La Finta Giardiniera*, for example, or *Mitridate*, or *Lucio Silla*, there is an abundance of fine melody and a style remarkably mature, but, except perhaps for the last, there are few indications of dramatic power, while in all alike there are a good many concessions to the tyranny of the singer. It would of course be unreasonable that we should expect otherwise. Mozart wrote these works at an age when most boys are studying the Latin grammar, and though the gift of music has often manifested itself early, some experience of life is needed for the understanding of the theatre. Again he had, as yet, been almost exclusively subjected to Italian influence, and though as a child he had witnessed the first performance of *Alceste* in Vienna, it was not until later that he realized its true artistic value. But, in 1778, after a prolonged study of the Mannheim orchestra, he paid a visit to Paris and arrived there in the very middle of the 'Gluckist and Piccinnist' controversy. In its actual movement he seems to have taken little or no part. Gluck was away, writing *Iphigénie en Tauride*; with Piccinni he was on terms of no more than formal courtesy, and though Grimm was his most cordial patron, yet Grimm was at this time beginning to waver in allegiance. Indirectly, however, this visit marked a crisis in his operatic career, and its effects were clearly shown when, in 1781, he produced at the Munich Carnival his opera of *Idomeneo*. Here the influence of Gluck is unmistakable. The story does not admit of such dramatic subtleties as those of *Alceste* or *Iphigénie*, but it is full of vivid and salient contrasts, and it affords abundant opportunity for stage-effect. And if we compare the score with any of Mozart's previous works for the theatre, we shall see at once the way in which he had profited by his new lesson. The formal overture is abandoned, and replaced, after Gluck's manner, by a short dramatic prelude. The chorus has become an integral part of the plot; indeed, at the most exciting moment it is virtually protagonist. The characters, though not yet free from conventionalism, are within their limits clearly defined; the rich and brilliant orchestration is evidently intended to give picturesque expression to the scenes. We know that about this time Mozart was making a careful study of *Alceste*: we may infer that the preface not less than the composition occupied his attention and directed his thoughts.

No doubt the differences are wide enough. 'When I sit down to write an opera,' said Gluck, 'I endeavour before all things to forget that I am a musician.' To Mozart, at any time in his career, such a confession would have seemed little short of artistic blasphemy. In his eyes the musical aspect was not an accessory but the supreme essential, and even dramatic expression must recognize the limitations imposed by pure beauty of design and colour. Again, *Idomeneo* is laid out on Italian lines, and to a large extent determined by the Italian style. The second tenor song, for example, is an *aria di bravura* of pure virtuosity, wonderfully ennobled by rich harmonies and recondite modulations, but belonging far more to what is called 'absolute-music' than to music with any definite poetic intention. In short, the main historical interest of the opera lies in its reconciliation of separate ideals. ᐧ A supreme work of individual genius, it is not less remarkable as the meeting point of many confluent streams.

It would be interesting to conjecture how much farther Mozart might have followed Gluck had he continued to throw his strength into tragedy. Circumstances, however, decided otherwise. A few weeks after his success at Munich he quarrelled with his patron the Archbishop of Salzburg, was turned penniless into the street, and there accepted a commission which affected the whole subsequent course of his operatic writing. It happened that at this time the Emperor Joseph II was endeavouring, as a part of his general policy, to establish a German opera-house in Vienna. The Burgtheater had been selected for the purpose, and reopened, in 1778, with *Die Burgknappen* by a composer named Umlauf : it was now, after three years of effort, languishing for want of genius to direct it. National German opera was as yet in its childhood. The only native form was the Singspiel, a sort of light comedy or vaudeville, which in the hands of Johann Adam Hiller (1728–1804) was beginning to attain an immense popularity at Leipsic. The titles of Hiller's best known works—*Der Dorfbarbier, Die Jagd, Liebe auf dem Lande*—will sufficiently indicate their character : pleasant little stories of village life, bright, innocent, and amusing, which introduced the folk-song to the stage as Haydn was introducing it to the concert-room. Their example was followed by a host of other composers, by Wolf and Schweitzer, by André of Berlin, by Neefe, who was Beethoven's first instructor, by Georg Benda, who brought the style to Austria and showed Dittersdorf how to use it[1]. Naturally, therefore, the Burgtheater looked to comedy as its means of expression, and finding Mozart at the door called him in forthwith to collaborate.

[1] Dittersdorf's *Der Apotheker und der Doktor* (Vienna, 1786) is perhaps the best extant specimen of a Singspiel pure and simple.

There can be no doubt that he was a fitting ally. The natural bent of his genius was, on the whole, for comedy; his brilliance, his wit, his playfulness moved more easily in the sock than in the buskin; despite many preoccupations he had always been interested in the Singspiel, and had testified his interest both in his early operetta of *Bastien et Bastienne,* and in the comic opera of *Zaïde* which was still unfinished. When, therefore, the management offered him Bretzner's *Entführung aus dem Serail* he accepted it gladly, worked through the winter with something more than his customary enthusiasm, and, in 1782, effected with it the same minor revolution on the stage of Germany which Philidor and Grétry had effected on that of France. The book was an ordinary Singspiel, and had recently been set in that form by André of Berlin. Mozart deliberately readjusted its balance, cut down the spoken dialogue, added new lyrics, revised the plot, polished the characters, and produced what was no longer a mere comedietta with incidental songs, but a true comic opera in which, as he said himself, 'the music should be everything.' Indeed, so far did he carry his principle, that in one or two numbers, notably in Osmin's immortal aria, the music was written before the words.

The success of *Die Entführung* led Mozart to believe that German opera would take permanent root in Vienna. His letters are full of it:—advocacy of the German language as 'not less fitted for singing than French or English and more so than Russian,' projects of a new comedy, 'the text by Baron Binder, the first act already finished,' predictions that the Italian company would soon give way to a worthier rival. But as time went on his tone grew less hopeful and more denunciatory. The whole scheme, indeed, was ruined by sheer mismanagement. True the directors offered him a libretto of their own, *Welche ist die beste Nation,* but it was so bad that he refused to set it, and in a moment of absurd pique they quarrelled with him, turned him out of the theatre which he had helped to create, and went back to Gassmann and Umlauf and the rest of their docile mediocrities. The sole result of all his endeavours was a little farce called *Der Schauspieldirector,* which he wrote in 1786 for the Emperor's private opera-house at Schönbrunn. And by that time the German theatre had died of inanition, and Italy, led by Gluck's pupil Salieri, was once more in possession of the field.

Mozart adapted himself to circumstances. Vienna wanted its operas in Italian, in Italian it should have them: and with *Figaro* (1786), *Don Giovanni* (1788), and *Così fan tutte* (1790), he permitted himself to concede to popular fashion. The change, however, was of less moment than at first sight would appear. In these three opera-books there is nothing distinctively Italian except the versification and the phraseology: two of them are adapted from French originals, the third, forced upon Mozart by the Emperor's command, is an ill-wrought tissue of impossible intrigue which belongs to no country in the reasonable world. It is, in short, a mere historical accident that the three great operas were set to Italian texts. Had they been written for the German, in which they are so often played, we cannot suppose that the quality of the music would have been sensibly affected. For Mozart's dramatic method was always singularly independent of the poet's collaboration. It was focused mainly on two points: first, the presentation of each scene as a separate unit, second, and dependent on the first, the portrayal of such dramatis personae as successively take part in the action and movement. For the general development of the plot he cared little or nothing; for the actual words uttered far less than for the type of emotion which they suggest. The situations, one by one, are vivid and picturesque; the characters, point by point, are discriminated by a hundred subtle and delicate touches; but in no one of the great operas is there a coherent story or even any serious attempt at dramatic illusion. They take us from the issues of human life into a fantastic fairyland of their own, a land in which we feel that anything may happen, and that to sympathize or censure is to emulate Don Quixote at the puppet-show.

At the same time it is no paradox to urge that they are, in their way, highly dramatic. Given the scene, and admitting for the sake of argument that it could possibly have occurred, we feel that the whole colour and movement of it are set before us with extraordinary skill and invention. The ball-scene in *Don Giovanni* strains credulity beyond the breaking-point, yet how well-marked is the contrast, how vigorous the denunciatory close. The imbroglio in *Così fan tutte* is, dramatically speaking, little short of an outrage: yet at the time it so holds our imagination that we almost forget to disbelieve it. On each successive event is concentrated everything that music can do, every appropriate device of rhythm and figure and orchestration; there is not a motion, not a gesture that is not illustrated by voice or instrument, there is not a shade of feeling which lacks its natural expression. The scene is always laid in Cloud-cuckoo-town, but it maintains the laws of its kingdom.

Even more striking is Mozart's treatment of his characters. They are no more like real life than the Mirabells and Witwouds of Congreve: allowing the utmost for necessary operatic convention we see that they are drawn to a different scale, that they occupy a different canvas from ours. But though artificial they are wholly consistent; they stand upon their own feet, they breathe freely in their own atmosphere. To have created Figaro and Leporello, Donna Anna and the Countess, Despina and Susanna, is no small feat of characterization; and, in every single case, we may say that the limitations belong mainly to the librettist, the merits entirely to the composer[1].

Yet, when all is said and done, it is the music and not the play that remains with us: the intricacy of thematic treatment, the novelty and vigour of rhythm, the volume of sound, rich,

---

[1] On this point the reader should consult the analyses of the operas in Jahn's *Mozart*, vol. iii.

pure, and transparent, and above all the 'little dew-drops of celestial melody' which hang sparkling upon every scene. To think of *Figaro* is to think of 'Voi che sapete' and 'Dove sono' and 'Deh vieni'; to think of *Don Giovanni* is to recall 'La ci darem' and 'Batti batti' and the great sestet in the second act. All the rest is there, everything is there if we have only the wit to see it; but to the most experienced critic as to the most unsophisticated auditor, it is the music that comes first.   Plot and character, pathos and wit, all are idealized in the light of a serene and absolute beauty, which, even if it shines more abundantly to those who can dissect its rays, yet illuminates to the full measure of capacity every eye that beholds it.   When we are told that in these operas Mozart shows himself a great dramatist, we accept the proposition as one which is beyond denial: when we are told that he shows himself a great musician it is our heart that assents.

The same is true in even further degree of his last work for the stage. *La Clemenza di Tito* (1791) may, for critical purposes, be disregarded: it was a mere court-pageant put together in eighteen days for the Emperor Leopold's coronation at Prague, and though it contains some fine numbers, it is not unjustly described as 'a weak copy of *Idomeneo*.' But in *Die Zauberflöte* (1791), produced but two months before his death, we have Mozart's method in quintessence. A plot so hopeless that after the first few scenes we give it up in despair: an atmosphere of magic which is merely an excuse for absurdities: a set of characters who are as ineffectual in action as they are unaccountable in motive: a bird-catcher dressed in feathers with a padlock upon his lips: a goddess from the machine who cuts every knot that stupidity could tie:— such was the harlequinade which Schikaneder handed over and which Mozart has turned into a living breathing masterpiece.   As we listen to the music the ridiculous incidents pass out of our field of vision, the doggerel verse ceases to annoy us, and, most wonderful of all, the characters grow into distinct being and personality. The magic of Tamino's flute has passed into the hands of the composer himself, and before it all criticism lies powerless and spellbound. Indeed, if we want a ready measure of Mozart's genius we have but to read this libretto and remember that, after witnessing a performance of the opera, Goethe seriously proposed to supplement it with a second part.

With *Figaro*, *Don Giovanni*, and *Die Zauberflöte*, the opera of the eighteenth century attains its climax. Before carrying on the story to its next great halting-place, in *Fidelio*, we must diverge for a moment to gather and group the lesser records of contemporary events, and may begin by noting an innovation which, though it had no immediate result, yet possesses in the history of the time a certain value and significance. Hitherto it had been an accepted convention that tragic opera should be based on a 'Classical' subject, that it should follow Virgil or the Greek dramatists, or the poets of the Trojan cycle. Men had not yet come to conceive the idea, on which in our own time Wagner so strongly insisted, that each country should draw its material from its own national history or legend: as yet, the dignity of the buskin demanded that the hero should be Aeneas or Achilles or Dardanus, or some such other remote and alien figure. But, in 1786, Gustavus III wrote for his new theatre at Stockholm a patriotic libretto on the subject of 'Vasa,' and two years later Catharine II followed this royal precedent, and herself set upon the Russian stage the story of Prince Oleg, the mythical founder of the Muscovite empire. In the former case the composer was Naumann, a respectable and mediocre musician, who stood for the time in high favour both at Stockholm and at Berlin: in the latter, the music was divided between Canobbio, Pachkievich, and Giuseppe Sarti, who had recently taken up his residence in St. Petersburg, and had there made his reputation with his romantic opera of *Armida*. Sarti (1729–1802) is a man on whom history has been unduly severe. He fell foul of Mozart on a famous occasion [1], and the story is always remembered against him: but it is forgotten that he was at the same time a composer of real invention, an extremely skilful contrapuntist, and a brilliant and audacious master of the orchestra. The score of *Armida*, for instance, contains many of the devices which have been carelessly attributed to Berlioz and Wagner: the use of muted trumpets and clarinets, experiments in combination of instrumental colour, and a remarkable freedom in the treatment of the strings. The ballet music and the cavatina 'Vieni a me,' should alone be sufficient to rescue this work from neglect. It is true that his other operas, *Le Gelosie villane*, *Giulio Sabino*, *Dorina*, and *Il Rè Medonte*, in no way approach to this level; yet a man's capacity can fairly be estimated by his best achievement, and history may well pay some honour to the versatile artist who extended the range of orchestral expression, who taught Cherubini to write fugues, and who founded the conservatorium of St. Petersburg.

Meanwhile there was arising a new generation of Italian opera composers, nearly all of whom show in some measure the influence of their time. Jommelli had died in 1774, Galuppi in 1784, Sacchini in 1786, and with them the old conventional school passed away, though it still haunted the stage in the shadowy productions of Guglielmi and Zingarelli. Of the younger eighteenth-century composers, two may be dismissed in a few words; Cimarosa, whose *Matrimonio segreto* (Vienna, 1792) is still a landmark in the history of comic opera, and Paer, whose *Camilla* (Vienna, 1799) gained him his post of Kapellmeister at Dresden; but there are three who deserve a more detailed mention, both for the space which they occupy in contemporary events, and for the historical interest of their work.

---

[1] See later, ch. ix, p. 264.

Giovanni Paisiello (1741–1815), born at Tarento, and educated at Sant' Onofrio, was only prevented from being a great composer by the uniformity of his success. His whole life was one long triumphal procession from Naples to St. Petersburg, from St. Petersburg to Vienna, from Vienna to Paris. He was the favourite of Ferdinand IV, of the Empress Catharine, of Joseph II, of Napoleon: his early operas *Il Marchese di Tulipano* and *L'Idolo cinese*, ran the round of Europe, his *Barbiere di Siviglia* became so established an institution that Rossini was hissed, thirty years later, for venturing to set the same libretto. But to us who have outgrown Paisiello's music, the main interest of his career is that it marks more clearly than that of any other Italian the transition between the eighteenth and the nineteenth centuries. His greatest opera *Il Re Teodoro* (Vienna, 1784), actually shows us the change of style in process; recalling in Lisetta's rondo the influence of Mozart :—

and in *Se voi bramate* almost anticipating Verdi's earlier manner :—

An artist, who knows that whatever he produces will be equally sure of approbation, will need a more sturdy fibre than Paisiello's if he is to resist the temptations of indolence. Even in *Il Re Teodoro* the writing is curiously unequal; now a phrase of real melodic invention will be answered by some careless platitude, now a bit of sound scoring or a touch of dramatic effect will be neutralized by whole pages of perfunctory irrelevance. And in this matter, as might be expected, his later compositions display no improvement. From 1785 to 1797 he was court composer to Ferdinand IV, and during that time poured out upon the Neapolitan stage a flood of hasty, ill-considered, and superficial eloquence. His fertility was no doubt remarkable, and it may well be considered a paradox to ascribe indolence to a musician who, in three quarters of a century, produced 94 operas and 103 works for the Church; but the highest labour of the artist is that which rises from self-criticism, and to this level it would seem that Paisiello never attained. Of his Neapolitan operas, *I Zingari in fiera, Nina o la pazza d'Amore*, and *La Molinara* had perhaps the greatest vogue, but all alike were acclaimed with facile enthusiasm when they appeared, and all alike are deservedly forgotten now.

Of more serious consequence to the historian is Antonio Salieri (1750–1825): the master of whom Beethoven did not disdain to profess himself a disciple[1]. Born at Legnano in the Veneto, he went early to Vienna where Gassmann took him under protection, and where, in 1770, he won his first success with a comic opera *Le Donne letterate*. Austria was still ringing with the controversies of *Alceste*, and the young musician, actuated we are told by diplomatic motives, betook himself as pupil to the composer whose rivalry he had most reason to fear. His assiduity was rewarded: Gluck soon raised him from the position of pupil to that of assistant, and, in 1781, on returning from the French campaign, entrusted him with the libretto of *Les Danaïdes*, which had been sent as a commission from the directors of the Académie de Musique. With this work, produced in 1784, the reputation of Salieri was definitely established. There is no need here

---

[1] 'Der Schüler Beethoven war da.' But the instruction which Beethoven received from Salieri does not seem to have extended beyond the declamation of his Italian arias.

to discuss the unworthy strategy by which he allowed his master's name to appear on the bills: in any case, the opera brought him fame and fortune, both of which he augmented next year in his brilliant comedy *La Grotta di Trofonio*. But the climax of his popularity was yet to come. In 1787 Paris witnessed the first performance of his *Tarare*, which, despite a poor libretto, was received with such a transport of applause that, for the first time in operatic history, the composer was called before the curtain and publicly crowned. It says much for Salieri's modesty and earnestness of purpose that after this triumph he withdrew the work, rewrote it to his greater satisfaction, and, in 1788, produced it afresh at Vienna, under its better-known title of *Axur, Rè d'Ormus*. There have been many instances in which an artist has been taught by failure that second thoughts are best: there are not many in which he has learned this lesson from popular approbation.

The rest of Salieri's dramatic work is of less importance, though he continued to write for the stage until 1804. But his three principal operas give him an honourable position among the composers of his time, and should at least be sufficient to save his name from oblivion. That his music no longer holds our attention is incontestable. It falls between the methods of his two great contemporaries; it is less dramatic than that of Gluck, it has less melodic genius than that of Mozart, and it has gone the way to which evolution unerringly directs all compromises and intermediaries. Yet in its kind it possesses a certain strength and dignity; it is the work of a man of talent who wrote his best and who never degraded his art into an appeal for popularity. An odd historical accident has linked his name with the two most famous of the early nineteenth century. He gave lessons to Beethoven, he was director of the school in which Franz Schubert was educated; and amid this constellation of genius he holds a minor, but not an ignoble place; a star self-luminous indeed though not of the first magnitude.

Third, and most remarkable of the three, was Luigi Cherubini (1760–1842), the autocrat whose despotism was for so many years tempered by the epigrams of Berlioz.   He was born at Florence, where his father held the post of Accompanist to the Pergola, exhibited the usual precocity of musical genius, and, in 1777, received an endowment from Leopold, duke of Tuscany, in order to prosecute his studies under Sarti, at Bologna.   His education was a curious mixture of the practical and the theoretic.   On the one hand, Sarti employed him as a collaborator in minor parts, and even allowed him to produce one or two operas of his own—*Quinto Fabio* in 1780, *Armida* and *Adriano* in 1782; on the other, he was kept to a course of counterpoint exercises more rigorous and more uncompromising than had been set since the days of Palestrina.   Both alike were of considerable service : from the one he gained an early acquaintance with stage effect and a working knowledge of the theatre and its methods ; to the other he owed that transparent style and that mastery of polyphonic resource which have kept his work alive to the present day.   In an age when operatic writing was too often slovenly and careless, when it moved from act to act with slipshod feet and uncertain aim, we can hardly over-estimate the value of such steady discipline.   It brought its attendant dangers in the narrowness and pedantry for which Cherubini became notorious in his later life ; but at least it made possible such unquestioned masterpieces as *Les deux Journées*, and the overture to *Anacréon*.

Up to 1786 he remained in Italy, writing some half-a-score of operas, and producing them with success at every great theatre from Rome to Venice.   Then followed two years of wandering, at the end of which, in 1788, he transferred his allegiance to the French Académie, and from thenceforward made Paris his home.   He arrived at a moment singularly opportune.   The old war of Gluckists and Piccinnists was virtually over, indeed controversy found itself more fully occupied with the prospect of the States General, and amid the shock of graver issues art was enjoying a period of comparative peace. That the great Revolution should have stimulated the taste for popular amusements will appear strange to those alone who are unacquainted with the buoyant courage of the French nation. The same spirit which, in 1870, filled the comic papers with caricatures of the siege, and invented the 'Danse des Obus' for impromptu festivity, is equally apparent as we turn back to the record of those ominous years which witnessed, in earthquake and hurricane, the birth of the Third Estate. In 1791, the year of the king's flight, no less than seventeen new theatres were opened in Paris; between that date and 1800 the number had increased to thirty-five. In 1794, the year of Robespierre's execution, Sarrette brought forward his project for a Conservatoire de Musique, and carried it into operation the next autumn. And with all this increase of opportunity came a comparative freedom from artistic discussion. Patriotism had a more serious cause to maintain than the singing qualities of the French language. It was of more moment whether a man were Jacobin or Girondist than whether he preferred the Austrian or the Italian versions of *Iphigénie*. There were threats of foreign invasion more formidable than the 'Bouffons': there were weapons of conflict more deadly than the sarcasms of Grimm and Vaugirard. The fighting instincts of the people had found their issue in the political field, and art, for the time, was common ground where men could meet and shake hands.

When Cherubini arrived in Paris the first place among French composers was held by Grétry, whose early success in Opéra Comique has already been recorded. Since the days of *Zémire et Azor*, Grétry had been prosecuting his career with varying fortune; and though he had gained no very certain hold on the fickle affections of the Parisian populace, had more than once roused them to a pitch of enthusiastic and well-merited approbation. *L'Épreuve villageoise* (1783) by a few judicious amendments turned its first defeat into a signal victory; *Richard Cœur de Lion* (1784) became the watchword of the Royalists, and on one memorable occasion fanned to a fervour of excitement the smouldering indignation of Versailles[1]; *La Caravane de Caire* (1784) hit the national taste for the picturesque, and attained a vogue which lasted over five hundred representations. Against these, no doubt, may be set many failures: they were forgotten on the morrow of their birth, and we have little need to recall their memory. But they may serve to remind us that Grétry, more than any other composer of eminence, was curiously compact of strength and weakness. Gifted with real melodic ability, he frankly avows that he regarded Haydn as 'a dictionary which any one might consult who would.' Often graceful and delicate in style he is sometimes so unsubstantial that, as was epigrammatically said, 'one could drive a coach and four between the bass and the first violin.' His sense of stage effect is frequently deficient; his sense of colour is usually keen and pure; and the overweening vanity, so amusingly illustrated in his *Essais sur la musique*, exaggerated his merits and left his faults uncorrected. It is precisely the same with his criticism. He lays down the principles of dramatic writing with a luminous good sense which recalls the prefaces of Gluck, and supports them by a psychology which shows no advance on the paradoxes of Helvetius. Of Sacchini, of Jommelli, of Galuppi, he speaks with truth and insight: yet it was he who said that Mozart 'put his statue in the orchestra and his pedestal on the stage.' And the climax is reached in a memorable sentence which links his own name with that of his favourite librettist: 'C'est avec franchise que je dis n'avoir jamais cherché à imiter Pergolèze : j'étois sa suite comme Sedaine est celle de Shakespeare[2].'

Beside Grétry there were two other notable composers in

---

[1] See the chapter 'O Richard, O my king,' in Carlyle's *French Revolution*, bk vii, ch. ii.

[2] *Essais sur la musique*, iii. 431.

the field. The first, François Joseph Gossec, the Belgian (1733–1829), was already a man of position and repute, the reorganizer of the Concerts Spirituels, the founder (in 1784) of the Parisian École de Chant. He had made his début in Paris as early as 1751, he had written symphonies and quartets before 1760 [1], he had won his fame as a brilliant colourist, and a bold and skilful master of orchestral effect. In 1764 he began to write for the theatre, and during the next twenty years produced about the same number of dramatic works, mainly on the scale of grand opera; all successful in their day, all at present unknown or unheeded. He was essentially a clever artist; lacking in force and inspiration, but quick and ingenious, ready and fertile in resource, almost boundless in audacity. The result is that while his work is forgotten he has in many ways influenced the training of better men. Like the Worship of Reason, with which, in Revolutionary times, he was officially connected, he plays but a transitory part in the great drama: yet the scene in which he appears is full of significance, and it bears its due share in the development of the plot.

Of a different stamp was Étienne Henri Méhul (1763–1817), who, in 1788, had exchanged his native Ardennes for Paris, and had begun to write opera under the direct encouragement of Gluck himself. Gentle, modest, and reserved, he had little taste for the conflicts and intrigues of the theatre; his first three dramatic works were written solely for practice, with no thought of publication or performance, and the fourth, *Cora et Alonzo*, was still waiting its turn in the ante-rooms of the Académie. It is something to the credit of the age that in a few years' time he became Cherubini's most serious rival, and that a talent so little enhanced by arts of diplomacy was recognized and estimated at its true value. But as yet he had brought nothing to the test, his name was barely

[1] See later, ch. viii, p. 225.

known, his career still open before him, and even his equipment partial and incomplete.

Such was the state of affairs in Paris when, at the end ,of
1788, Cherubini brought out his new tragedy *Demophon*. The
work as a whole is not of his best : it is a compromise between
the methods of Gluck and those of Sarti, and like all compromises it failed to satisfy. Next year, however, brought
aid from an unexpected quarter. Léonard, the barber of
Marie Antoinette, obtained leave to collect a company for
the performance of Italian opera, sent Viotti to Rome for
singers, and offered the conductorship to Cherubini. The
new venture opened in a hall of the Tuileries, then, dislodged
by the fall of the Bastille, removed to what Fétis calls 'une
espèce de bouge' at the Foire St.-Germain, where, in 1792, it
built and occupied the famous Théâtre Feydeau. Here Cherubini
found his opportunity. The accommodation, no doubt, was
somewhat meagre, but he had an excellent cast with a first-
rate orchestra, and after practising his hand by adding songs
to the works of Cimarosa and Paisiello—a deplorable practice
from which, for half a century, French music was never entirely
free—he set his reputation beyond cavil with the brilliant
masterful rhetoric of *Lodoïska*. It is interesting to compare
the score with those of Mozart's later operas. There is something of the same breadth, there is much of the same lucidity,
the texture is almost equally rich, the instrumentation almost
equally sonorous ; but in the one we have the work of a poet, in
the other that of an orator, vigorous, clear, persuasive, yet lacking
the divine inevitableness of *Don Giovanni* and *Die Zauberflöte*.
In a word, the Parisian critics who accorded to *Lodoïska* the
welcome which, a few months later, they refused to *Figaro*,
unconsciously anticipated the epigrammatic judgement which
spoke of a lyric poem as 'beau comme la prose.'

In the meantime Méhul had been set in charge of the Théâtre
Favart, whither, in 1791, he transferred from the Académie his
neglected score of *Cora et Alonzo*, and for the next ten years

the two theatres maintained a friendly rivalry, until, in 1801, they amalgamated into the Opéra Comique.   During this period, indeed, they shared the dramatic field between them.   Grétry was now coming to the decadence of his power, and though he still continued to write operas, failed to maintain the level of his old reputation : Gossec deserted the stage for hymns to the Republic and services to the Goddess of Reason : occasion favoured the two younger men, and they both had ability to make use of it.   It is to this opportunity that we owe Méhul's *Euphrosine et Coradin* (1790), *Horatius Coclès* (1794), *Doria* (1797), and *Adrien* (1799), beside a host of lesser works which led up, in due course, to the two masterpieces, *Uthal* (1806), *Joseph* (1807), by which his name is best remembered in history.   To their challenge Cherubini responded with *Elisa* (1794), *Médée* (1797) and, greater than either, *Les deux Journées* (1800), which shows a conciseness of expression and a warmth of feeling unusual in his compositions.   These were succeeded, in 1803 and 1804, by the two ballet-operas of *Anacréon* and *Achille à Scyros* : both admirable of their kind, and both received with unmistakable favour.

Corneille was 'condemned by the Duumvirs, acquitted by the people' : Cherubini in like manner was paid for his popularity by the alienation of the court.   The directorship, which he had almost a right to claim, was given in 1801 to Paisiello, and in 1803 to Lesueur; his name was omitted from the first list of the Legion of Honour (1802), which included those of Gossec, Méhul, and Grétry : and Napoleon, whose enmities were seldom generous, appears to have taken delight in subjecting him to the pettiest forms of public humiliation.   It was, therefore, an odd irony that when, in 1805, he accepted a commission from Vienna, and there produced *Faniska*, the last and greatest of his operas, he should have seen his prospects entirely destroyed by the invasion of the French army with his Imperial enemy at its head.   The work was so far successful that it attained a few representations, and won the cordial eulogy of Beethoven: then it was silenced by the echoes of Austerlitz, and the composer returned to France, broken in health, overwhelmed with disappointment, and fully determined to abandon the theatre [1].

A far more important opera was imperilled by the French invasion of 1805. On November 20, a week after Napoleon's occupation of Schönbrunn, *Fidelio* was produced at the Theater an der Wien, given for three nights to scanty and preoccupied audiences, and then withdrawn in a fit of disgust. A few months later it again essayed its fortunes, but it was *vox clamantis in deserto*, and there were none to hear : after April, 1806, it disappeared from the boards, and returned for no less than eight years to the dusty shelves of its composer's bookcase. We have no means of knowing whether Napoleon had heard about Beethoven's relations with Bernadotte: at any rate retribution speedily followed the offence, and Florestan was sentenced by the discarded patron of the *Eroica*.

The history of *Fidelio* is too well known to need more than a brief recapitulation. Ever since his arrival in Vienna, Beethoven had kept in view the prospects of a successful opera: indeed, Haydn invited him from Bonn, in 1792, with the express purpose of training him to write for the stage. But as the years went on the prospect grew fainter, partly from the set of his genius towards other forms of composition, partly from his extreme difficulty in finding a suitable libretto. His sturdy puritanism revolted from the frivolous morals of the Austrian theatre; to the stories of *Figaro* and of *Don Giovanni* he expressed the most open dislike, and so long as these represented the prevailing fashion he had little hope that his scruples would be satisfied. At last, in 1804, his friends brought him, from Dresden, the text of Paer's *Eleonora*

---

[1] He so far repented as to compose, in 1809 and 1810, the two small operas of *Pimmalione* and *Le Crescendo*, and to follow them with *Les Abencérages* in 1813 and *Ali Baba* in 1833. But despite these generous exceptions, it remains true that after the return from Vienna he devoted himself mainly to sacred music.

ossia l'amore conjugale, a book of which the subject at least
was unexceptionable: during the winter a German translation
was prepared, and, in 1805, Beethoven retired to Hetzendorf
and wrote the music. Then followed a rigorous period of
alteration and recension[1]. The opera was first presented in
three acts, with the overture commonly known as 'Leonora
No. 2.' In 1806, at the urgent entreaty of Breuning, Beethoven
sacrificed three numbers, reduced the whole work to two acts,
and rewrote the overture from beginning to end (Leonora
No. 3). In 1807, he composed an entirely new overture in
C major (Op. 138), erroneously called Leonora No. 1, for
a performance at Prague, which was projected but did not
take place. In 1814 the work was again revised, the title
altered to *Fidelio,* the action quickened, and yet another
overture composed, that in E major, commonly called 'Fidelio'
or 'Leonora No. 4.' To make the story complete it may be
added that the first performance in 1814 was introduced by
the overture to the *Ruins of Athens,* as the *Fidelio* was not
finished in time. Such a method is of ill-augury for a dramatic
career. We know, from a note in one of the sketch books,
that in spite of all this labour and disappointment, Beethoven
still continued to feel the attractions of the stage, but we need
have little wonder that he returned to it no more. The incidental pieces which he wrote for the plays of Collin, Goethe,
and Kotzebue are not more dramatic in quality than the ballet-
music to *Prometheus*: in opera he concentrated his entire
genius on one superb example,—*unum sed leonem.*

As to the beauty of the music there cannot be two reasonable
opinions. It belongs to the time of the fifth symphony, of
the Rasoumoffsky quartets, of the violin concerto, the period
in which Beethoven attained his most perfect balance of expression and design, nor is it in any way unworthy of its
compeers. The richness of its melody, the brilliance of its

---

[1] See the critical edition of *Leonora* by Dr. Otto Jahn (Breitkopf & Härtel,
1851).

orchestration, the splendid strength and vigour of its greatest overture combine to give it rank among the first masterpieces of composition. Yet in the history of operatic literature it stands alone. It follows no precedent, it has created no school, with the possible exception of *Les Troyens* it has not seriously influenced any theatrical work of the nineteenth century. Till the time of Wagner it remained the one supreme instance of an epic drama; and Wagner's whole conception of the stage was so different from Beethoven's that, in this matter, no fruitful comparison can be drawn between them. We may remember that when Beethoven took *Fidelio* in hand he had for fifteen years been training almost exclusively on the cyclic forms. Sonata, concerto, symphony, quartet, these had been his work, in these he had matured his thought and developed his style. Add that the bent of his mind was essentially symphonic, just as that of Bach's was essentially contrapuntal, and we may possibly explain both the strength of *Fidelio* and its isolation. To call it a dramatic symphony would overstate the case: but it is a drama conceived and executed on symphonic lines.

To illustrate this position we may lay the score side by side with that of *Don Giovanni*. It has already been noted that Mozart goes far to hold the balance between 'absolute music' and the requirements of the stage: but whereas in his work the dramatic ideal is made compatible with the melodic, in that of Beethoven it is commonly subordinated. Take for instance the two famous quartets—*Non ti fidar, o misera*, from the one, *Mir ist so wunderbar* from the other. In both alike we have an imbroglio of cross-purposes: different issues to maintain, different emotions to express; tangled threads of feeling, to be woven somehow into a texture of musical beauty. This is Mozart's solution of the problem [1]:

---

[1] For reasons of space only the opening stanza of Mozart's is quoted. But fully to appreciate the contrast it is necessary to compare the two quartets throughout.

Here it is easy to trace the formal design, yet Mozart has not only employed it as the vehicle of three distinct emotional moods, but, at the end of Don Giovanni's phrase, has pressed it into the dramatic service as a note of irony. And the case is even stronger at the entry of the second theme, where, as suspicion ripens, Donna Elvira grows more urgent, Donna Anna and Don Ottavio more concerned, and Don Giovanni more insistent in his reiterated protests of innocence. Beethoven, on the other hand, like many great poets, is too autocratic for the theatre: he makes his characters say not what they want, but what he wants, and, in this example, even subdues their will to the strictest and most exact of musical forms:—

glück - lich, ich wer - de glück - - lich, glück - lich sein. Er
- lo - se, o na - men - lo - - - se Pein! . . . . Wie
fällt kein Mit - - - tel ein, mir fällt kein Mit - tel
Paar, sie wer - den glück - - lich, glück - lich sein; sie

liebt mich, es . . ist klar . . . ich
gross ist die . . Ge - fahr . . . . wie
ein, mir wird so wun - der - bar, mir fällt kein Mit - tel
liebt ihn, es ist klar . . . ja,

wer - de glück - - - lich sein.
schwach der Hoff - - - nung Schein!
ein, mir fällt kein Mit - tel ein.
Mäd - chen, er wird dein.

Here there is no attempt at characterization: Marzellina expresses her hopes, Leonore her fears, Jaquino his perplexity, and Rocco his comfortable paternal blessing to precisely the same phrase with precisely the same treatment. Beethoven's quartet, in short, is for pure delight, for the pleasure of dainty melody, and flexible part-writing: it thrusts all emotion into the background, and gives us 'simple beauty and naught else.'

But, it will be urged, *Fidelio* contains some dramatic numbers: Pizarro's 'Ha! welch' ein Augenblick,' Leonore's 'Abscheulicher, wo eilst du hin,' and above all, the great prison-scene in the second act. True: they are as dramatic as the first movement of the D minor sonata, as the scherzo of the Fifth symphony, as the slow movement of the concerto in G. One of Beethoven's highest endowments was his power of writing intense and passionate melody, and it was not likely that this power should be paralyzed by the opportunities of the stage. But he never stands clear of his characters, or lets them tell their story in their own way; he projects his personality into them, he makes them speak with his voice and utter his thoughts: it is not Florestan that we see, but Beethoven himself, sitting in darkness and solitude and thinking of the 'ferne Geliebte.' There is hardly a song which may not find a parallel among his lyrics; there is hardly a figure or a phrase which does not recall the method of his instrumental compositions. And this is the reason why even so academic a device as a quartet in canon does not strike the hearer as incongruous or out of place. It is like the canon in the Fourth symphony, it is like the double counterpoint in the 'Pastoral' sonata; merely a point of musical design set with unfailing tact in a scheme, the essential purpose of which is musical.

With *Fidelio* the great period of Viennese opera came to an end. Schubert, like Heine, so far mistook his genius as to attempt the stage, but his first opera, *Die Bürgschaft* (1816), was left unfinished, his second, *Die Zwillingsbrüder* (written 1818, produced 1820), entirely failed, and the others cannot

be said to have obtained a hearing[1]. Even the exquisite
incidental music which he wrote for Helmine von Chezy's
Rosamunde (1823) shared, after two nights, the disaster of
that unfortunate play. No doubt this may partly be referred
to the astonishing apathy with which Schubert's work was
received by his contemporaries: but a more positive cause
was the fact that, in 1822, Rossini arrived at the Kärnthnerthor,
and that in the flood of his facile genius all native growth
was overwhelmed.

Meantime Paris had been passing through another period
of turmoil, which divided court, professoriate, and populace,
and which at one time bade fair to rival, in violence if not
in wit, the hostilities of the 'Guerre des Bouffons.' Two
French composers had arisen to follow in the footsteps of
Grétry and Méhul. The elder, Jean François Lesueur (1765-
1837), began as a Church musician, and indeed was admitted
by the Archbishop of Paris into minor orders. But, in 1792,
he deserted Notre Dame for the stage, and next year established his reputation by producing *La Caverne* at the Théâtre
Feydeau. Two or three unimportant successes followed, then
a period of inaction, and then, in 1804, he won, with *Ossian*,
the greatest triumph of his life. Napoleon, who had recently
appointed him Maître de Chapelle, sent for him, loaded him
with favours, and treated him thereafter as the accredited
representative of the National party in French music. Lesueur,
a gentle, amiable scholar with a taste for Greek modes, accepted
his honours modestly, and after one more opera (*La Mort
a'Adam*, 1809), retired into the professorial chair, where he is
best remembered as the teacher of Berlioz, Ambroise Thomas,
and Gounod.

[1] *Sakontala* (1821), left unfinished: *Die Verschworenen* (1823), printed by
Spina, but not performed in Schubert's lifetime: *Alfonso und Estrella* (1822)
and *Fierabras* (1823), both rejected: *Rosamunde* (1823), given at the Theater
an der Wien, Dec. 20, 1823, and withdrawn after two representations. There
was also a boyish extravaganza, *Des Teufels Lustschloss*, and one or two small
operettas, none of which were ever performed.

The younger, François Adrien Boieldieu (1775–1834), may be called the Béranger of the French stage. He was a tender and graceful composer of lyric melody, whose operatic style is well described by Hiller as the artistic continuation of the *chanson*. His first important work was the *Calife de Bagdad*, given at the Théâtre Favart in 1800; the two masterpieces on which his fame principally rests are *Jean de Paris* (1812) and *La Dame blanche* (1825), the last of which is still justly regarded as one of the two or three finest examples of French light opera. It is noticeable that an artist who so readily gained the ear of his public should have addressed it so seldom : but Boieldieu was of a timid and retiring disposition, and always hesitated long before confronting Fortune. A professor at the Conservatoire, he used to submit his manuscripts to his pupils; an acknowledged master, he took lessons from Cherubini; and at the time when the strains of his *Dame blanche* were echoing from one end of Paris to the other, he could find no better reason for his success than 'a reaction from Italian influence.' Seldom in the wars of art has a campaign been headed by leaders so diffident and so unassuming.

Against these two there came up from Italy a figure so strange that it can hardly be portrayed without the suspicion of caricature. A compound of punctilio and intrigue, of lavish generosity and sordid meanness, of pompous vanity and sound common sense, Gasparo Spontini fills the measure of his contradictions by standing, in the field of opera, as an intermediary between Mozart and Meyerbeer. He was born, near Jesi, in 1774, made his début in 1796 at the Argentina, and in 1803, having already written more than a dozen operatic works, set out, like his master Piccinni, to conquer Paris. For a time he met with a discouraging reception. His first appearance was courteously welcomed, his second wearied the patience of his auditors, at the third he was hissed off the stage. But, in 1804, his little opera of *Milton*, which is saturated with Mozart, gained him more serious attention, and in 1807, after three years' hand-to-hand contest with the authorities, he made his mark once for all in *La Vestale*. The success of this work is not difficult to understand. The libretto, by Étienne Jouy, is of considerable merit; the music, though extremely pretentious, is full of display and colour; the whole arouses much the same interest as we should take in a great public pageant. It was, in short, a distinctively spectacular opera, and, as such, appealed to the most spectacular of capitals. With its production Spontini stood upon firm ground. There was to be no more hissing his dramas at the theatre or shouting down his oratorios at the Concerts Spirituels: for once he had said his say, and Paris owned itself convinced.

As *Milton* follows the method of Mozart, so, with a wider latitude *La Vestale* follows that of Gluck. It has something of the same grandeur of conception, coarsened in the transfer, like Roman sculpture in comparison with Greek, but strong and massive in construction, and not unfrequently dignified in tone. Its worst fault, apart from a certain roughness of harmony, is its fondness for sheer noise, a vice which grew upon Spontini to the end of his life, and which he transmitted to the most characteristic of his successors. In conducting, as in composition, he exaggerated every *nuance*: ' his *forte*,' says Dorn, ' was a hurricane, his *piano* a breath, his *sforzando* enough to wake the dead.' It was he who made his prima donna shout so loud in an impassioned scene that she lost her voice for the rest of the evening. It was he who rated the straining 'cellists for insufficient tone until they restored themselves to favour by singing while they played. And it was he who, when Mendelssohn came to see him and the occasion demanded an aphorism, pointed to the dome of a church across the way, and summed up his artistic experience in the solemn warning, ' Mon ami, il vous faut des idées grandes comme cette coupole.'

However, at the time, ' des idées grandes comme cette

coupole' were in fashion, and Spontini took full advantage
of the popular taste. His next opera, *Fernand Cortez* (1809),
fully carried on the promise of *La Vestale*: the next, *Olympie*,
which he took nearly ten years to write, set the final seal upon
his reputation [1]. But France had now become too narrow for
his ambitions: Alexander needed a new world, and, in 1819,
he accepted an invitation from Frederick William III, and
carried his bâton to Berlin.

The condition of German opera had much improved since
the days of Graun and Hasse. It is true that among the
numerous courts there were still some which regarded formal
roulades as the highest achievement in music, and French
comedies 'mit obligatem Hanswurst' as the highest achievement in drama, but at Berlin, Dresden, and Hamburg, to
name no others, the répertoires were well chosen and the
pieces well executed. Berlin in particular, under such directors
as Döbberlin, Iffland, and Count Brühl, had risen to a high
state of efficiency. It had given a hearing to Gluck in 1782;
it had presented all Mozart's operas from *Die Entführung*
to *Die Zauberflöte*; it was the first house outside Austria to
venture on *Fidelio*; in recent years its performances of *Cortez*
and *La Vestale* had come near to rival Paris. It possessed an
excellent company of German singers; its orchestra, trained
by Bernhard Weber, was one of the best in Europe. As yet,
however, it had no native school of composition. Reichardt
(1752–1814), and Himmel (1765–1814), who held successively
the post of Hofkapellmeister, were but feeble luminaries to
guide the steps of a national movement, and though both
wrote for the stage it was to little purpose and with little
result. One man alone had attained sufficient prominence
to take the lead, and he disregarded his opportunity.

Louis Spohr (1784–1859) has often been ranked by his-

---

[1] It was coldly received on the first night, apparently from faults in the libretto.
But in its revised form it obtained an immediate success. See Dr. Spitta's article
on Spontini, Grove's *Dictionary*, iii. 670, first edition; v. 106, third edition.

torians among the composers of the Romantic period, with
which indeed the latter half of his long life almost exactly
synchronized. But he is far more justly estimated as the
outcome of Mozart, to whom he stands, in Hullah's fine
phrase, 'as flamboyant architecture to the purer Gothic which
preceded it.' The design is weakened, the ornament exaggerated, the style often passes into mannerism, but the
tradition is unmistakably present, and is maintained with
a real feeling for absolute beauty. It is like the tracery of
Orleans beside that of Chartres; it is like the colour of
Correggio beside that of Raphael : the work of a lesser genius
which fears to be simple lest it should fail to charm.

Part at least of his deficiency was due to want of concentration. He was one of the most versatile of artists : a violin-
player of European repute, an able and amusing writer, a painter
who could support himself by his miniatures when composition
proved unremunerative. His facility was astonishing, his gift
of melody considerable; all that he needed was a wider knowledge and a sterner power of self-criticism. He himself tells us
that feeling his counterpoint to be imperfect, he read Marpurg's
treatise and 'wrote six fugues'; after which he returned to
work fully satisfied with this light equipment. And there
is a well-known story that, on hearing one of his pupils
play Beethoven's E minor sonata, he asked in a tone of
budding interest, 'Have you composed anything more in that
style ? '

The greater part of his voluminous work will be considered
later : at present we are concerned only with his position in
the history of opera. Like most of his contemporaries he
began with failure : his first attempt, *Die Prüfung* (1806),
went no further than the concert-room, his second, *Alruna*
(1809), though accepted at Weimar and approved by Goethe,
was laid aside after a single rehearsal. It is true that at
the end of the same year a little comedy, *Der Zweikampf
mit der Geliebten*, was performed with success at Hamburg,

but it hardly compensated for the disaster of the larger works, and Spohr allowed almost a decade to elapse before he endeavoured to retrieve his fortunes. In 1818, after a tour in Austria, he accepted the post of conductor to the opera-house at Frankfort, and then, secure in his own domain, produced his first two great operas, *Faust* and *Zemire und Azor*. The latter won at the time the more ready welcome, the former is undoubtedly the finer work, and ill deserves the neglect into which it has been allowed to fall. It shows a real power of delineation, it is full of characteristic melody, and in several numbers, notably the Witches' scene, it turns to admirable effect Spohr's gift of rich and changing colour. We may grant that Gounod has won his right to hold the stage : but it is a pity that musical partisanship will not allow two compositions on the same theme.

Such was the position of affairs when Spontini arrived in Berlin and at once set himself to produce, in full magnificence, his revised version of *Olympie*. He opened his campaign badly : began by quarrelling with Count Brühl, kept his copyists waiting, bullied his singers until they nearly revolted, and behaved towards the entire theatre with a ludicrous assumption of imperious arrogance. The populace grumbled in the newspapers, the court-party hesitated, even the Emperor protested at the long delay and the lavish expenditure; Spontini paid no attention to any one, but insisted on change after change and rehearsal after rehearsal, wholly indifferent to black looks or murmured comments. It was to a very tense and critical audience that, on May 14, 1821, the curtain rose upon the first scene of Voltaire's tragedy.

The performance is said to have been one of the finest ever known in the history of Opera, and the triumph was brilliant and complete. Count Brühl offered his most generous congratulations; friends and foes vied in applause; the voice of Berlin proclaimed that *Olympie* stood without a rival, and that *Don Giovanni* and *Fidelio* were as nothing in comparison. We can imagine Spontini holding his stick 'like a field-marshal,' and turning with imperturbable face toward that surging sea of acclamation. The truly great-souled man recognizes that there can be no honour equal to his merit, yet he will accept the worship of his inferiors because he knows that they have nothing better to give.

Another five weeks and Spontini's reign was at an end. On June 18 a new theatre opened in Berlin, and chose for its first performance a peasant comedy called *Der Freischütz*, by Carl Maria von Weber, who had endeared himself to every German student by the folk-songs of 'Leier und Schwert.' At once the fickle populace transferred its allegiance: *Olympie* was deserted, and in an incredibly short time not only Berlin but the whole of Germany was ringing with the Bridal chorus, and Caspar's drinking song, and the tunes of Agathe's scena. Spontini was not less astounded than Goliath at the challenge of David. It was impossible to believe that he, the Emperor's protégé, the monarch of the opera-house, the wielder of the most gigantic forces in Europe, could be cast down by the onset of a mere ballad-writer; and in great anger and disdain he set about a means of reasserting his supremacy. But at present he had nothing ready, and his dilatory methods exposed him to another blow. Early in 1823 Spohr conducted a performance of *Jessonda*[1] at the Berlin opera-house, and the mortified potentate felt his own stronghold trembling beneath his feet. He made two pathetic attempts to adapt himself to the new conditions. In 1824 he divided public opinion with *Alcidor, eine Zauberoper*: five years later he struck his last blow, and failed, with *Agnes von Hohenstaufen*. Spohr, indeed, he might have met upon equal terms; but neither by use of the supernatural nor by appeal to German sentiment could he rival the creator of Max and Zamiel.

[1] Produced with great success at Cassel, shortly after Spohr's appointment there, in 1822. The rest of Spohr's operas, which fall outside this period, were *Pietro von Albano*, *Der Berggeist*, *Der Alchemist* (all 1829–30), and *Die Kreuzfahrer* (1844). None of them gained any reputation comparable with that of *Jessonda*.

The downfall of Spontini closes the history of opera so far
as it is covered by the present volume. It remains to add
a word on the humble, but not insignificant, part played by
England during this later period. The ballad-opera is a form
which we may justly claim as our own: it was in full growth
before Hiller wrote *Der Dorfbarbier*, or Rousseau *Le Devin du
Village*; and though it be of tiny scale and slender material
it affords ample opportunity for the lighter gifts of composition.
In the last three decades of the eighteenth-century music of
real merit was produced by Dibdin (*The Waterman* and *The
Quaker*); Storace (*The Haunted Tower*, *No Song no Supper*,
and *The Iron Chest*); Attwood (*The Prisoner*, *The Smugglers*,
and *The Magic Oak*); and above all by Shield, whose *Castle of
Andalusia* is charming, and whose *Rosina* is a work of genius.
After Shield the tradition began to degenerate: with Kelly and
Horn it sank to a lower level of ability, with Bishop it became
professorial and academic; but at the worst it always shows
some character, some native sweetness of phrase, which may
trace back its ancestry through the songs of Arne to those
of Purcell. It was a meagre harvest that we gathered through
these barren years, but the best of the grain was sound and
wholesome; and no other nation in Europe would so lightly
have cast it away to the common dust-heap of oblivion.

CHAPTER VI

ORATORIO AND CHURCH MUSIC

WE have already observed that during the eighteenth century
the line between sacred and secular music was often slender
and ill-defined. Opera was allowed to take subjects from
Holy Writ[1]; divine service admitted 'jigs and balletti' without
scandalizing either priest or congregation; in reading the
compositions of this period the student may frequently doubt
whether a given score was originally intended for worship or
for entertainment. It is not, therefore, surprising that oratorio
should have been accepted as an intermediate form, occupying
a march-land in which there were no settled boundaries. Almost
all Handel's oratorios were produced either at Covent Garden
or at Lincoln's Inn Fields; indeed the *Israel* was made palat-
able to its audience by the insertion of operatic songs; and
this practice was still further extended on the continent, when
oratorio fell into line with grand opera, and alternated its most
impressive scenes with the humours of *Ninette*, or the sprightly
dialogue of *La Serva Padrona*. It must be remembered that
until the opening of the Gewandhaus at Leipsic (1781) there
was practically no such thing as a public concert-hall in
Europe. Concerts were given either in private houses, or in
the rooms of musical clubs[2]: for the populace at large the
alternative was between the Church and the theatre, and despite
S. Philip Neri, the Roman Catholic tradition still preferred
to restrict its music to its own ritual. Even in Protestant

---

[1] Three of Kozeluch's most famous works were *Judith*, *Deborah*, and *Moses in
Egypt*: the first two operas, the third an oratorio.

[2] A conspicuous example was the Viennese Tonkünstler-Societät, which opened
in 1772. See Hanslick's *Concertwesen in Wien*, p. 18.

England the tradition was hard to break. Our three-choir festivals began in 1724, but no oratorio was admitted into a cathedral until, in 1759, the *Messiah* was given at Hereford, and in 1787, the *Israel* at Gloucester. The whole form, in short, was treated as a kind of sacred drama; distinguished throughout by the absence of action, but only very gradually detached from scenic effects and the surroundings of the stage.

In point of style it maintained a compromise between the two methods which it united. Recitative, aria, and duet remained, for the most part, operatic in character; they were counterbalanced by large massive choruses, sometimes contrapuntal, and almost always determined by an ideal of ecclesiastical dignity. Yet even on this side there were occasional lapses, particularly among the more theatrical of the Italian writers who took their ideals lightly, and were reluctant to forego the glitter and display of vocalization. Porpora's first oratorio is a significant example. It was written for Charles VI who disliked florid ornament, and the young composer, guided by a friendly warning, forced himself along a path of simple melody until he came to his final chorus. Then he could endure it no longer, outraged nature reasserted herself, and he concluded his work with a fugue on four trills, which, we are told, had the result of throwing the Emperor and the court into convulsions of laughter. And though there are no other instances so gross and naked as this, yet throughout the entire period Italian oratorio seems to fail of its purpose. The polyphony, noticeable in *à capella* compositions, is here replaced by a lighter and more superficial style, the workmanship is often hasty, and we miss that solid strength which may be found in the contemporary music of Germany and Austria. The most notable exceptions are Jommelli's *Passione* and Piccinni's *Jonathan*, neither of which exercised any real influence on the development of the art; the oratorios of Sacchini, Paer, Salieri, Paisiello, and Cimarosa in no way enhanced their composers' operatic reputation; those of Guglielmi and Zingarelli were merely trivial and vulgar.   In other forms of sacred music there were Italian composers who did good service: in the field of oratorio their record is, at this time, singularly empty and undistinguished.

For different reasons the same fact holds good of England and. France, in both of which, especially the latter, sacred music was assiduously written, but in both of which the chief strength lay outside oratorio.   Arne's *Judith*, produced in 1764, has a touch of historic interest as being the first work of the kind in which female voices were admitted to the chorus[1], but both it and Arnold's *Prodigal Son* (Oxford, 1773), have long passed beyond the reach of discussion or criticism.   Indeed, the Handel Commemoration of 1784 may well have shown our musicians that there was no suitor who could bend the bow of Ulysses.   Gossec made some mark with *Saul* and Lesueur with his *Christmas Oratorio*; but to the French mind this form of composition has never been very attractive, and in the eighteenth century it stood no chance amid the conflict of theatrical parties.   Spain and Russia stood apart; the one preoccupied with her Passion-plays, the other, under Bortniansky[2], concentrated on the reform of her ritual music.   Thus, for all historical purposes, the course of oratorio during this period is virtually restricted to two countries: Germany at the beginning and the end, Austria in the intervening time.

As will naturally have been anticipated, it begins with C. P. E. Bach.   In 1749 he had made his first offering to the Church, a fine manly setting of the *Magnificat*, in which, among all his compositions, the influence of his father is most apparent: twenty years later, now long established as Kapell-

---

[1] This was at a famous performance in Covent Garden, Feb. 26, 1773.

[2] Born 1752, educated mainly in Italy, made, in 1779, director of the Imperial Choir at St. Petersburg.   He entirely reorganized Russian Church music, and set it upon the basis which, with slight modifications, it has adopted to the present day. _ Even on festivals it is extremely simple, but it is made very effective by the absence of accompaniment and by the great richness and compass of the voices.

meister at Hamburg, he produced in close succession his two oratorios *Die Israeliten in der Wüste* (1769), and *Die Passions-Cantate* (1769), and followed them in 1777 with a third, *Die Auferstehung und Himmelfahrt Jesu*[1]. In these three important works we find a definite revolt against the old traditions, and, on some sides, a definite anticipation of later methods. Though two of them contain some good fugues, the choruses are not as a rule contrapuntal: indeed, there are cases in which the laws of counterpoint are actually violated. It is difficult, for instance, to realize that a son of J. S. Bach wrote the following passage, which occurs in the first number of the *Passions-Cantate* :—

[1] A complete analysis of all these may be found in Bitter's *C. P. E. und W. F. Bach und deren Brüder*, vol. ii. pp. 1–60. For an equally full account of the *Magnificat* see the same book, vol. i. pp. 117–31.

On the other hand the melody is always pure, the feeling often, in the best sense of the term, dramatic, and the harmonic choral-writing unusually rich and effective. And, as these characteristics appear most clearly in the first and greatest of the three, it may be well to present it to the reader in a brief descriptive analysis.

There is no overture: a few bars of orchestral prelude (scored for two flutes and strings *con sordini*) lead at once into the first chorus, 'Die Zunge klebt am dürren Gaum.' Its extremely beautiful opening phrase has already been quoted on p. 72; not less characteristic is the second theme, in which despair turns to reproach:—

There follows a duet, in which two Israelitish women lament their present dearth, and regret the land flowing with milk and honey from which they have been brought to die in the wilderness. Aaron (whose part is written for a tenor voice) counsels patience and trust, but to little purpose, and he can only check the revolt by announcing that his brother is at hand. A short majestic symphony, and Moses enters with

words of rebuke. He is met by a fine denunciatory chorus,
'Du bist der Ursprung unsrer Noth'; full of passionate
declamation, and swift agitated accompaniment. ` At its close
he reasons with his people, is answered by another pathetic
cry, 'Umsonst sind unsere Zähren,' given in duet to the two
Israelitish women: then, after a superb aria, he stands by the
rock with rod uplifted and bids his rebels prepare for the
miracle. The scene which follows has turned a new page
in the history of oratorio: there is a rapid alternation of
recitative and choral outburst, a moment of breathless expectation, the rock is stricken, and the people break forth
into a shout of jubilant wonder as the water streams and
eddies between their ranks :—

hört.　　　　Gott hat uns er - - hört.

The second part opens with a great hymn of thanksgiving, followed by a very elaborate, and very beautiful, soprano song, 'Vor des Mittags heissen Strahlen,' florid in style and exacting in compass, but far purer and sweeter than any formal aria of the time. Well might an enthusiastic hearer declare, in the highest words of approbation that he could find, 'Graun und Hasse haben nie schöner gesungen.' At this point the interest of the work declines; the libretto ceases to depict and begins to moralize, the music passes into a contemplative mood for which the genius of C. P. E. Bach was not altogether suited. But up to the first two numbers of the second part this oratorio deserves our most careful consideration; not only for its intrinsic merit—and it is eminently worth reviving at the present day—but for its remarkable resemblance to Mendelssohn's *Elijah*. We can hardly doubt that it served in some degree as a model for that noble though unequal composition.

The other German oratorios of the time need no more than a passing mention. Graun's *Der Tod Jesu* (1755) belongs to the preceding epoch, and has already been discussed in vol. iv.[1] Hasse's oratorios were almost all burned in the bombardment of Dresden, and the single survivor, *I Pellegrini al Sepolcro,* is of no great moment or account: Naumann (1741-1801)

---

[1] See vol. iv. pp. 45, 46.

produced in this form a dozen works, the character of which may best be gauged by his unqualified condemnation of Handel's *Messiah*. Twice in the eighteenth century were attempts made to introduce that masterpiece to a German audience. Stamitz put it on at Mannheim, and the first part aroused such a storm that the second had to be omitted. Hiller put it on at Leipsic, and Naumann led an overwhelming chorus of disapproval. It was not until Mozart rescued it, in 1789, for a Viennese musical society that any one outside England grew alive to its beauties.

Apart from his revision of Handel, Mozart showed but little interest in oratorio. His *Betulia liberata* (1771) belongs to the time of his early Italian operas, and precisely resembles them in style and treatment: his *Davidde Penitente* (1785) is little more than a pasticcio from the Mass in C minor. Among his lesser contemporaries, Kozeluch, as we have seen, hovered between oratorio and sacred opera; Dittersdorf wrote a few works of the former class—*Isacco* at Grosswardein, *Davidde* on his first arrival in Vienna, *Ester* and *Giobbe* for the Tonkünstler-Societät; but in this connexion the one great name of the early Viennese period is that of Haydn, who before the close of the century produced two masterpieces [1], the one now entirely neglected, the other, in English estimation, ranking almost next to the *Messiah*.

For the disfavour into which it has fallen, *Il Ritorno di Tobia*, like many other works of the time, may thank its libretto. The verse is poor and turgid, the scheme mechanical, the sentiment often trivial and undignified. Raffaelo is a very mundane angel, Tobias a somewhat histrionic hero; there is at least one song of an extremely undevout character; and when Tobit recovers his sight his first exclamation is 'Consorte Anna, la tua bellezza non soffra in otto anni oltraggio alcuno.' But the music, though by no means of a uniform level, contains some of Haydn's finest and most brilliant writing. It

---

[1] The interludes to the *Seven Words* are more properly classed among Haydn's instrumental compositions.

was composed in 1774 for the newly organized Tonkünstler-Societät, and was evidently designed to tax to their utmost the resources of Viennese executance. The orchestra is, for the time, gigantic [1], the scoring extremely rich and elaborate, especially in the two soprano arias of the second part, the songs are gorgeous with colouring and ornament, and the choruses, whether harmonic or fugal, laid out on a large and broad design. The great difficulty of the work renders it unlikely that a performance could be undertaken at the present day, but some acquaintance with it is almost necessary to an understanding of Haydn. We may add that ten years after the first production he inserted a new chorus, 'Svanisce in un momento dei malfattor lo speme,' which, refitted to the words 'Insanae et vanae curae,' is often giver. separately as a motet [2].

When, in 1795, Haydn left London for the last time he took with him a libretto which had been compiled by Lidley from *Paradise Lost*, and intended, in the first instance, for Handel. On his arrival in Vienna he submitted it to his friend Van Swieten who translated it 'with considerable alterations'; for two years he worked at it almost incessantly, and on April 29, 1798, aged 66, he produced at the Schwarzenberg palace this most famous of all his compositions. The beauties of the *Creation* are too well known to require any further discussion. We have but to recall the choral recitative which narrates the birth of light, the fall of the dark angels and the rise of the 'new-created world,' the descriptive songs of Raphael and Gabriel, the great choruses which stand like monuments four-square; all are endeared to us by long familiarity and countless associations. Sometimes we may smile for a moment

---

[1] It includes two flutes, two oboes, two corni inglesi, used with great effect, two bassoons, two trumpets, two horns, two trombones (alto and tenor), drums, and strings.

[2] Its popular name of 'Sturmchor' has led to its confusion with a chorus which Haydn wrote in England to Peter Pindar's 'Hark the wild uproar of the waves'; an entirely different composition.

at the *naïf* realism; it no more affects our love of the music
than does the detestable English into which the libretto has
been retranslated.   The score is full of learning and invention;
it carries them both lightly; and its freshness and vitality,
remarkable in any case, come with double force from a musician
who was nearing his seventieth year.

It may be convenient to add here a mention of *The Seasons*,
which appeared in 1801, although this work is not properly
speaking an oratorio.   The words are taken from Thomson's
poem, translated and modified by Van Swieten, and the music
was for a long time almost as popular as that of the *Creation*.
Our modern criticism, which allows no half-lights, has decided
that because it is inferior it is therefore not worth performing—
much as though one should refuse to play the *Two Gentlemen
of Verona* because it is not so great as *Hamlet*—an error of
judgement which it is to be hoped that a more discriminating
generation will repair.   As a matter of truth it is far too
beautiful to neglect: the songs are nearly all charming, the
choruses are written with Haydn's accustomed skill, and the
storm-scene (to name no others) is a notable instance of vivid
pictorial effect.

If we doubt about the classification of *The Seasons*, what
are we to say of Beethoven's *Christus am Oelberge*, which
followed it, in 1803, at a distance of two years?   It is commonly
called an oratorio; it more nearly resembles a musical Passion-
play, if we could imagine one written by an un-Christian hand.
The figure of our Lord is treated without reticence or restraint,
the style is 'not only secular but in certain places actually
sparkling'[1]: the great 'Alleluia' at the close is purely pantheist,
as different from Handel's as Goethe is from Milton.   Yet, if
we are indifferent to the title and unmoved by the impropriety
of treatment, we must acknowledge that the music is of high
interest and value.   It is first-period work, written before the

[1] See Rockstro's article on Oratorio, Grove, ii. 553.   In England the libretto
has been re-written, and the story transferred to *David at Engedi*.

Eroica Symphony, and marked therefore by that tentative manner in which Beethoven as yet handled all forms outside those of chamber-music: but it is an exceedingly fascinating experiment, and well repays our most careful and accurate study. The recitatives in particular are wonderfully flexible and dramatic, and the melodies, whether appropriate or not to their situation, have all that limpidity which is so notable a characteristic of Beethoven's early writing. Again, this is the first composition in which he shows his own special mastery of the orchestra, and on this ground it lays a foundation upon which so many magnificent superstructures were afterwards reared.

Schubert's only attempts at oratorio were the fragment *Lazarus*, which contains a fine bass aria, and the short *Song of Miriam*, which, though beautiful, does not fairly represent his genius. From Beethoven, therefore, the course of historical development returns to Germany, and there closes, for the present volume, upon the figure of Louis Spohr. His four achievements in this field cover a period of thirty years: *Das jüngste Gericht*, written in 1812, laid aside after three performances, and never published; *Die letzten Dinge*[1], produced at Düsseldorf in 1826; *Des Heilands letzte Stunden*[2], written in 1833, and brought out a couple of years later at Cassel; and *The Fall of Babylon*, commissioned for the Norwich Festival of 1842. It was on this last occasion that the Elector of Hesse-Cassel refused him leave of absence to conduct his work, and remained obdurate in spite of a voluminous petition from England and a special request from its Foreign Secretary, Lord Aberdeen. There must have been something exceptionally attractive in an artist who could thus imperil diplomatic relations.

To estimate these compositions is a matter of some difficulty. Their faults are obvious: the monotony of sliding-semitones, the cloying harmonies which recall Lamb's epigram of 'sugar

---

[1] Known in England as *The Last Judgement*.
[2] Known in England as *Calvary*.

piled upon honey,' the academic fugues which always give the
impression that they were begun with reluctance and finished
with relief, the rhythms which, in moments of the highest
solemnity, sometimes descend to the triviality of the dance.
One brief illustration, from the Chorus of Saints in *The Last
Judgement*, will exhibit a characteristic point of style :—

Lord God of Heav'n, and Earth, we a - dore   Thee.

The general tenour of the phrase is like a large and simple
utterance of Mozart; but on such an occasion Mozart would
never have weakened his primary colour with a half-tone at
the cadence. Spohr does so as a matter of course, here and
everywhere; indeed, he touches his extreme of asceticism if
once in thirty times he refrains from harmonizing it on
a diminished seventh. His whole conception of the art is
soft and voluptuous, his Heaven is a Garden of Atlantis and
even his Judgement-day is iridescent.

Yet we cannot deny that it is real music, and music which
Spohr alone could have written. Grant everything that can
be said against it, grant the overcharged sentiment and the
overloaded palette, there still remains a sense of beauty which
the world would be the poorer for having lost. The attenuated
outlines are wonderfully clear and precise, the colour is exquisitely refined, the hedonism of his prevailing mood 'loses
half its evil by losing all its grossness.' One feels instinctively
that he was incapable of a coarse or violent phrase. Add that
he had genuine emotion and a true gift of pictorial effect; it
will not be hard to explain the enthusiasm with which, during
his lifetime, he was everywhere received. And after all, among
German composers of oratorio, he is the most conspicuous
figure between C. P. E. Bach and Mendelssohn.

Such, in brief, is the century's record of its compromise
between dramatic and devotional expression. Of more historic

account is the music which was directly intended for the Church. And since the best part of this was claimed by the Roman Catholic ritual, we may begin by recapitulating the order of service, and so proceed to the compositions which were designed for it.

According to old tradition Low Mass was celebrated without music: but before the eighteenth century there had arisen, among the village churches of France, Germany, and Austria, the practice of introducing Hymns, Litanies, and the like for congregational singing. The art appears to have been rude and primitive, the accompaniment restricted to a serpent or violoncello (rarely an organ), which doubled the melody and kept the voices up to pitch; there was little guidance or supervision, and the most famous example that we know— Haydn's *Hier liegt vor deiner Majestät*—consists merely in the successive verses of a sacred poem set to a string of Croatian folk-tunes. High Mass, on the contrary, was always choral, and on state or ceremonial occasions might be reinforced by an orchestral accompaniment. It was to this, therefore, that Church composers turned for their inspiration and their opportunity.

The first choral number is the Introit, sung while the Celebrant repeats the *Iudica me Deus*, and the *Confiteor*. It consists of three parts, an antiphon[1], the words of which are usually though not invariably taken from the Bible, a psalm, of which one verse is chanted, with the *Gloria Patri*, and thirdly, the repetition of the antiphon in full. Throughout the history of the Roman ritual the Introit has always occupied an important position. A special antiphon is appointed for each service, and the Sunday has often been familiarly called after its opening words, just as the Mass for the Dead is known throughout Europe as the Requiem. At the same time the music of the Introit has usually been regarded as

---

[1] It is from this word, taken from the French *antienne*, that our term 'anthem' is derived.

a separate form of composition, since, like the anthems which follow it later in the office, it varies from day to day, while the liturgical portions of the Mass remain unchanged.

Next come successively the Kyrie and the Gloria, the latter of which is commonly divided into separate movements— Laudamus, Gratias agimus, Domine Iesu, Qui tollis, Quoniam, and Cum Sancto Spiritu. At its close there follow the Collects for the day; then the Epistle and Gospel, between which the choir sings an anthem called the 'Gradual,' and after it, according to the day, either a short versicle (Tractus) or the Sequentia, a hymn written in stanzas of accentual rhythm. Five Sequentiae were authorized by the Council of Trent, and they are among the noblest in Christian hymnology:—*Stabat Mater* for the Friday before Holy Week, *Victimae Paschali* for Easter, *Veni Sancte Spiritus* for Whitsuntide, *Lauda Sion* for Corpus Christi, and *Dies Irae* for the Requiem Mass.

After the sermon comes the Credo, divided like the Gloria into separate numbers; then, while the Celebrant is censing the Oblations, the Offertorium, followed either by a Motet or by an organ voluntary [1]. The remaining numbers continue in the course of the service; the Sanctus before the moment of Consecration, the Benedictus after the Elevation of the Host, the Agnus Dei while the Celebrant is communicating; and the rite closes with the plain-chaunt 'Communio,' and the post-Communion prayers.

Thus the office of High Mass invites the service of music, not only for its six chief choral numbers—Kyrie, Gloria, Credo, Sanctus, Benedictus, and Agnus Dei—but for the smaller forms of Introit and Gradual, of Offertorium and Motet. Besides these there are many other orders, recurrent or special; the

---

[1] These names have fallen into much confusion. Strictly the *Offertorium* was a portion of Scripture recited to a plain-chaunt; and the *Motet* an anthem, often on the same words. But by the eighteenth century the *Offertorium* had itself become an anthem; its name is now practically interchangeable with *Motet*, and the organ voluntary is often entitled, by French composers, an *Offertoire*.

Psalms at Matins, at Vespers the Psalms, Antiphons[1] and
Magnificat, the Miserere for the Tenebrae in Holy Week, the
Te Deum for occasions of national rejoicing. We cannot
wonder that in all ages the Roman Church should have had
the highest genius at its command, and that even a light
and frivolous generation should have recognized its splendour
and acknowledged its control.

Indeed, the historian is here confronted with a problem of
sheer multitude. A bare catalogue of the Church compositions between 1750 and 1830 would fill a substantial volume :
Paisiello wrote 103, Michael Haydn 360, Zingarelli over
500 ; almost every composer, except Beethoven and Schubert,
held an official position as Kapellmeister, and was stimulated
to ceaseless activity by his Chapter or his Patron. It is obviously impossible to review these thousands of compositions ;
we may add that it is needless, for most of them were mere pieces
of occasion, written with perfunctory haste, and intended for
no more than an ephemeral existence. But as, for this purpose,
the period falls roughly into three principal divisions, it may
be well to trace them in outline, and briefly to indicate their
most salient features.

The first, from 1750 to about 1770, is on the whole the
least interesting and important. It begins well with Haydn's
first Mass[2] (F major, 1751), a very remarkable composition
for a self-educated boy of nineteen ; it continues with the fine
Te Deum which, in 1756, Graun wrote for the victory at
Prague : but, after these, compositions of any real merit are
few and far between. Galuppi produced at Venice a good

---

[1] In particular the four 'Antiphons of our Lady' :—*Alma Redemptoris, Salve
Regina, Regina Caeli,* and *Ave Regina.*

[2] No. 11 in Novello's edition. It may here be stated that the current English
editions of the Masses of both Haydn and Mozart are extremely misleading.
They are not in chronological order, they do not correspond either with Haydn's
catalogue or with that of Köchel, and they persistently include among Mozart's
works an ill-compiled pasticcio, popularly called the 'Twelfth Mass,' the greater
part of which is undoubtedly spurious.

deal of Church music, some of which is still performed at St. Mark's: Gossec, in 1760, astonished Paris with a *Messe des Morts* which partly anticipates the extravagances of Berlioz: the only other considerable name is that of Jommelli, who, during his residence at Stuttgart (1754–69), developed his style under German influence, and wrote with a force and dignity that were beyond the reach of his Italian contemporaries. His setting of the *Passion*, his Mass in D major, above all his famous *Requiem* for the Duchess of Wurtemberg are marked by sound science and by genuine religious feeling, and this growth of experience bore yet nobler fruit when, shortly before his death, in 1774, he composed the very beautiful *Miserere*, which still ranks as the greatest of his works.

During the last thirty years of the century four Church composers are conspicuously prominent:—Sarti, Michael Haydn, Joseph Haydn, and Mozart. The first of these held successive appointments, as court-composer to the King of Denmark (1753–75), Director of the Ospedaletto at Venice (1775–79), Maestro di Cappella at Milan (1779–84), and Master of the Music to Catharine II (1784–1802). At Venice and Milan he wrote a great deal of Church music, full of fresh melody and amazing contrapuntal skill: at St. Petersburg he materially assisted Bortniansky in the reorganization of the Russian services, and produced, among many important works, his famous *Te Deum* for Potemkin's capture of Ortchakov. It is unfortunate that so little of his sacred work has been published. Some of it is still performed in Milan Cathedral, many of the scores are preserved in manuscript at the library of the Paris Conservatoire, but there is nothing currently accessible beyond the Russian *Te Deum*, two choruses, printed by Breitkopf & Härtel, and the numbers *Kyrie* and *Cum Sancto Spiritu* (the latter, one of the finest eight-part fugues in existence), which are quoted respectively in the text-books of Fétis and Cherubini.

Much, too, of Michael Haydn's work has been submerged

by the river of time. Appointed, in 1762, to the office of
Kapellmeister at Salzburg, he continued for the next forty-three
years to write at requisition whatever was wanted for his two
churches or his Episcopal chapel; he was crushed and brow-
beaten by a tyrannous patron; as a natural result his compositions were often wholly unworthy of his undoubted genius.
Still there are some considerable exceptions. The *Missa
Hispanica* which, in 1786, he exchanged for his diploma at
the Stockholm Academy, is said to be noble and impressive,
his Mass in D minor, his *Lauda Sion*, and his *Tenebrae* in E♭
are still highly esteemed, and the forty-two Graduals, printed
in Diabelli's *Ecclesiasticon*, take level rank with the work of
his brother, to whom, by the way, many of his compositions
have been falsely assigned. Particularly noticeable are those
of the 'Missa Rorate prima,' the 'Missa Rorate secunda,' the
'In conceptione Beatae Mariae Virginis,' and, best of all, the
Benedictus from the second Christmas office, which begins :—

Be - ne - dic - tus,   Qui ve - nit   in   no - mi - ne Do - mi - ni.

History cannot afford to disregard an artist whom Joseph
Haydn considered as his equal, and Mozart for many years
as his master.

Mozart wrote nineteen Masses of the ordinary office : the
first, in 1768, for the opening of a new church in Vienna, the
last and greatest[1], performed at Salzburg in 1783, to com-
memorate his marriage with Constanze Weber. The others
were produced, like those of Michael Haydn, to the order of
Archbishop Hieronymus, and, though written with all Mozart's
pellucid style and abundant melody, they are merely the
episodes of a genius working without interest and under
stress of stupid prohibition. Three stand out from among
their number : the *Missa Brevis* in F (No. 9, K. 192) written

[1] This was the Mass in C minor (K. 427) which he afterwards used for his
oratorio *Davidde Penitente*.

in 1774; the 'Coronation' Mass (No. 17, K. 317) in 1779, and the *Missa Solemnis* (No. 18, K. 337) in 1780: yet even these fall far below his highest level. To see his Church music at its best we must turn first to the smaller compositions:—the three Vesperae, the Litanies 'De venerabili,' the Offertories and Antiphons, the Motets which culminated in the immortal beauty of his *Ave Verum*; and lastly to that very crown and climax of his artistic life, the unfinished Requiem.

It is not here proposed to repeat the conflicting testimony as to the part played in this work by Mozart's most unscrupulous pupil. There are three numbers—the *Sanctus, Benedictus,* and *Agnus Dei*—for which no originals have been found, and we may perhaps believe, without extravagant credulity, that in editing them Süssmayer was dependent only on the memory of his instructions. Again, the orchestration of Nos. 3–9 is left incomplete in the autograph score, though so much is indicated that there is no room for anything but the work of a secretary. To admit Süssmayer's claim as composer is to violate every canon of probability, and to resign every attempt at a critical standard. On this point the internal evidence is conclusive, and there is no escape from the dilemma that either the Requiem, from its opening to the end of the *Hostias*, is the composition of Mozart, or that he divided it with a collaborator of equal genius [1].

For it is only in the doubtful numbers that the inspiration ever seems to falter or the workmanship to decline. The *Introit*, the *Kyrie*, the *Sequence*, the *Offertory* attain to a summit of achievement such as the art of music had not scaled since the death of J. S. Bach. We have but to recall the opening phrases—Requiem aeternam, Recordare, Lacrymosa,— and we are reminded of music which in beauty, in pathos, in unerring mastery of its medium, touches 'the outside verge that rounds our faculty.' The work is as far beyond

---

[1] For a complete account of the controversy, see Pole's *Story of Mozart's Requiem.* See also Jahn's *Mozart,* iii. 363, 387, and the note in Köchel's catalogue.

praise as it is beyond criticism; we might as readily pronounce upon the Parthenon or the Vatican Hermes. It is of that kind of genius about which we wonder, not how it accomplishes its aim, but how it has ever come to exist at all: there is no analogy with the characters and abilities of ordinary men, no common measure, no common standpoint. From its serene and unapproachable majesty commendation recoils, and to advocate its excellence is to pass sentence on our own opinion.

Mozart's Requiem stands alone, but between it and his other Masses the work of Joseph Haydn may find an honourable place. It is not what we at the present day should call religious music: it often lacks that gravity and seriousness which we justly associate with worship; yet this is due not to indifference—for Haydn was the most devout of musicians—but to a natural gaiety of temper which even the sacred precincts could not repress. 'I do not think,' he said, 'that God will be angry with me for praising Him with a cheerful heart'; and it was in all the frank simplicity of a child that he offered at the altar blossoms from his garden, and even wild-flowers from his native hedgerows [1]. If then we consent to waive this objection and to meet him in his own spirit, we shall admit that in the sixteen masses there is much of the best and purest of his composition: fresh, spontaneous melody often penetrated with true feeling, great technical skill of design and treatment, above all that artistic power of concealing art which gives to the lightest phrase its own value and significance. It is wholly free from self-consciousness or affectation; it speaks out of the abundance of a heart that never grew old.

Haydn's music for the Church may be divided into two groups, which centre respectively round Eisenstadt and Vienna. The former ranges from 1771 to 1783 (the period of 'Tobias')

---

[1] The Mass *Hier liegt vor deiner Majestät* has already been mentioned. Besides this there are Croatian folk-tunes in some of the settings for the office of High Mass: e. g. the *Christe Eleison*, of that in C major, No. 16 (Novello, 2).

and includes a Stabat Mater, a few motets and antiphons, and the five Masses which stand as Nos. 4–8 in his autograph catalogue[1]. The latter, covering the period of the *Creation*, ranges from 1796 to 1802, and includes the last eight Masses, and some smaller forms among which may specially be noted the Austrian National Anthem of 1797. It will be observed that in 1783 both Haydn and Mozart ceased, for a time, to write Masses. The reason is that in this year Joseph II issued an order forbidding the use of orchestral instruments in church, and the prohibition lasted until in 1791 (the year of Mozart's *Requiem*) it was cancelled by the Emperor Leopold. Between 1791 and 1795 Haydn was mainly occupied with his two English visits, and it was not, therefore, until 1796 that he was able to take full advantage of the Imperial rescript.

The five Masses of the earlier period are, in order of composition, the *Grosse Orgelmesse* in E♭ (No. 4, Novello 12), the *Missa S. Nicolai* in G (No. 5, Novello 7), the *Missa Brevis S. Iohannis de Deo* in B♭ (No. 6, Novello 8), the *Missa S. Caeciliae* in C (No. 7, Novello 5), and the *Mariazeller-Messe* in C (No. 8, Novello 15). Of these the two finest are the *S. Nicolai*[2] and the *Mariazeller*: the former more sweet and melodious, the latter vigorous and manly with a good deal of sound scholarship. The *Sanctus* is usually the least impressive number: before its sublimity Haydn seems to quail, his accustomed resources of tunefulness and ingenuity stand him no longer in stead, and he writes a few bars of choral recitation and passes on. But the settings of the *Kyrie*, the *Credo*, and the *Agnus Dei* are always admirable, and surpass in all but external qualities any work of the kind which, during these years, was written by Mozart.

On the other hand, the later Masses owe much of their

---

[1] His first Mass, as we have seen, was written in 1751. The second and third (*Sunt bona mixta malis* and *Rorate coeli*) are lost, and the date of their composition is unknown.

[2] Simrock's edition of this work supplements the *Kyrie* by a portion of that from Jommelli's *Requiem* : a remarkable instance of editorial methods.

richness and colour to Mozart's influence. In more than
one form of composition it is clear that Haydn carefully
studied the work of his great contemporary: in none is the
result more apparent than in this. The orchestra is larger,
the style more mature, the melody not more beautiful than
before, but beautiful in a different way. Take for instance the
Christe of the fifteenth Mass, which begins as follows :—

Everything. in this, the chromatic motion, the accompaniment figure, the treatment of the appoggiatura, bears more
resemblance to Mozart than to Haydn's earlier manner, and

there would be no difficulty in finding a score of similar examples.

It may be convenient to add a catalogue of the last eight Masses, since, although they are the best known, their order has not always been very clearly determined. The first two of them (Nos. 9 and 10, Novello 2 and 1) were written in 1796, the former (C major) called *In Tempore Belli*, from the fact that the French were then occupying Styria, the latter (in B♭) once made notorious in England by a pasticcio, entitled the *Oratorio of Judah*, which was mainly compiled from it. In 1797 Haydn celebrated the coronation of Francis II with the great Mass in D minor, sometimes known as the 'Imperial' from the occasion for which it was composed, sometimes as the 'Nelson-Mass,' because Nelson, on a visit to Eisenstadt, exchanged his watch for the pen with which Haydn wrote it. Then follow three more in B♭ (Nos. 12, 13, 14, Novello 16, 4, and 6), the last of which is unusually grave and meditative in character: then the fifteenth, in C major (Novello 9), and finally, in 1802, the Mass in C minor[1] (Novello 10), a noble and pathetic composition, in which Haydn has approached more nearly than usual to the dignity of his subject.

The Mass-music of this period closes, in the nineteenth century, with the work of Beethoven, Schubert, and Cherubini. In discussing the parts which they respectively sustain, it is useless to follow the chronological sequence of composition: they all wrote during the same thirty years, they exercised, on this side of their art, no appreciable effect on one another; we may therefore take them separately in the ascending order of their historical importance. Cherubini's first Mass was composed in 1809: his best work dates from 1816, when he

---

[1] There are two more in Novello's edition: No. 13, in C major, a poor composition, which, if genuine, represents Haydn at his weakest, and No. 14, in D major, very operatic, and consisting of *Kyrie* and *Gloria* alone. Possibly these may belong to the two lost Masses of the earlier period.

was appointed Master of the Chapelle Royale, and comprises, amid a host of smaller compositions, the Mass in D minor, the Coronation Mass in A, written for Charles X, and the two Requiems (C minor and D minor), one written in 1817, the other in 1836. As a rule his Church music is somewhat dry and formal, inclined to be prolix, and deficient in that happy inspiration which can sum up a train of thought in one telling phrase. But, as we should expect from Sarti's pupil, it is extremely solid and dignified, and it shows a command of contrapuntal resource which no musician of the time could rival. We may find an instance in the *Credo* edited by Dr. Ulrich: a vast *à Capella* composition in eight parts which exhausts almost every device within the range of learning. He has melody, too, a little cold and unsympathetic, but drawn with the firm hand of a master; such for example as the *Et in Spiritum* of the D minor Mass—

which would move us more if the curve were not quite so conscious of its perfection. Apart from all the others, both in date and in character, stands the *Requiem* in D minor for male voices. It is far the most dramatic and emotional of all his Church compositions, earnest and serious in tone, but at the same time poignantly expressive. No one who has ever heard it can forget the harmonic colour of the *Gradual,* or the pathos of the *Offertorium,* or the hurricane of sound which introduces the *Dies Irae.* There was more than scholarship in a man who, at seventy-seven years of age, could turn aside from his accustomed method, and produce a work so eloquent and so poetic.

Yet even here we miss that sense of profound conviction without which, on such a theme, neither poetry nor eloquence can satisfy.   And the contrast between what is given and what is withheld grows even more salient when we turn from his Masses to those of his younger Viennese contemporary.   It is said that on one occasion, attracted by the quiet of a village Rectory, Shelley debated the prospect of taking orders; his appearance in the pulpit would not have been more incongruous than is that of Franz Schubert directing the music of the office. So far as can be gathered from his biographers, Schubert appears to have possessed little or no religious belief: he wrote for the Church because his friend Holzer happened to be choir-master at Lichtenthal[1], and he treated the words of the ritual with far more appreciation of their value as poetry than understanding of their deeper and more intimate meaning as expressions of worship.   For the special methods of ecclesiastical composition he showed but little interest: his counterpoint was instrumental rather than vocal; his fugues are often the perfunctory accomplishment of an unwelcome task.   On the other hand, the solo numbers are of an inherent beauty which even his greatest songs can hardly surpass: the *Gratias* of the Mass in A♭, the second *Benedictus* of the Mass in C, are gifts of pure loveliness which we may well accept without cavil.   They have received the consecration of Art, though they revolt from the severer discipline of Religion.

It is interesting, in this matter, to contrast Schubert with Spohr.   Both derived some of their inspiration from Mozart, both were indifferent contrapuntists, both alike were lacking in sternness and self-restraint.   Yet in all essential attributes they are poles asunder.   Spohr's melody is often a mere echo, Schubert's is entirely his own: Spohr is full of mannerisms,

---

[1] He composed six Masses for the Lichtenthal Church: No. 1 in F major (1814), well described, by Professor Prout, as the most remarkable first Mass by any composer except Beethoven, Nos. 2 and 3 in G and B♭ (1815); No. 4 in C (1818, with the second *Benedictus* added in 1828), No. 5 in A♭ (1819-1822), and No. 6 in E♭ (1828), the longest and most elaborate of them all.

Schubert almost wholly devoid of them : Spohr aims at conciseness, yet wearies by monotony, Schubert is the most diffuse
of writers, yet we follow him with unflagging interest and
delight. The reason is that Spohr's range of expression was
comparatively narrow, and that it included little beyond those
direct appeals to sense or feeling which cease to be impressive
when they become familiar. Schubert's range was unlimited,
his invention was inexhaustible, and his command of emotional
colour, far greater than that of Spohr, was yet among the least
of his endowments.

Beethoven composed two Masses : one (C major) written in
1809 and published in 1812, the other (D major) occupying
the greater part of the four years from 1818 to 1822. Of
these the former is a standing puzzle both to critic and to
historian. It appeared in the very climax of Beethoven's
second period, midway between *Fidelio* and the Seventh
symphony, yet, despite some fine moments, it is on the
whole singularly dry and uninspired. The prevailing style
is antiquated, it goes back to the preceding century, it seems
to forget all that has been learned in the violin concerto
and the Rasoumoffsky quartets : even when it breaks new
ground, as in the remarkable opening of the *Sanctus* :—

the effect is more that of a somewhat uncertain experiment than of a genuine discovery. A possible reason may be that Beethoven was always curiously cautious in approaching a new medium, and that his mastery of resource came to him not by intuition but by long and painful industry. It would be difficult to believe on internal evidence that the sonata in D minor (Op. 31, No. 2) belongs to the same year as the Second symphony : the former was at the time a new revelation, the latter, notwithstanding the beauty of its slow movement, reads, in comparison, almost like a formal exercise. Such also may be the case here. With the forms of the sonata, the quartet, the symphony, the concerto, Beethoven was now absolutely familiar, he could mould them to his purpose, he could make them the unerring interpreters of his thought : with the great vocal forms he was still somewhat in conflict, and he sometimes purchased their obedience by concession.

The same conflict, though with a different issue, appears in the history of his second Mass, the *Missa Solennis* in D major, intended (though not finished in time) for the installation of the Archduke Rudolph as Archbishop of Olmütz. It is probable that no artistic achievement ever cost more incessant and determined labour. Begun in the autumn of 1818, shortly after the completion of the *Hammerclavier* sonata, it took Beethoven's entire time, except for a few days, until the end of 1821, and again for the first two months of 1822. We have a vivid picture of him, wild, haggard, dishevelled, oblivious of sleep and food, tearing the music from the very depths of his being, and bending it by sheer force into the appointed shape. Think for a moment of Mozart :—the tunes 'coming to him as he rode in his carriage'; the fugue 'composed while he was copying out the prelude'; the overture written impromptu in a single night. It is a far cry to these months of concentrated effort, and the prize wrested from fate by such titanic energy and such masterful self-will.

The whole character of Beethoven's Mass is in keeping with

the circumstances of its production.   It is gigantic, elemental, Mount Athos hewn into a monument, scored at the base with fissure and landslip, rising through cloud and tempest beyond the reach of human gaze.   It has been called dramatic, but the word is ludicrously inadequate: if this be drama it is of the wars of gods and giants with the lightning for sword and the clamorous wind for battle-cry.   It does not, like Mozart's *Requiem*, defy criticism, but simply ignores it.   'The fugal writing,' says one, 'is defective,' and we feel that the judgement is wholly true and wholly irrelevant.   Never before had the voice of music spoken with such depth, such earnestness, such prophetic intensity: there is more beauty in Mozart, in Bach, or in the white radiance of Palestrina, but not even they have uttered truths of such tremendous import.

There is little need to cite examples:—the solemn *Kyrie*, the *Credo* which upholds belief like a challenge, the descending flight of music which heralds the *Benedictus*: yet for illustration we may recall one passage, typical of the whole work, from the opening of the *Agnus Dei*.   It is the more noticeable because, in the Mass-music of the eighteenth century, this number is commonly treated with little sincerity or reverence: its first part often formal or perfunctory, its second often serving as a light and even trivial finale to the rest.   But with Beethoven there is an entire change of standpoint.   The music is so far removed from formality that we can hardly force ourselves to consider its technique at all: the bounds of art seem to be transcended and we are carried into regions where our accustomed standards are no longer applicable. Here is no charm, no gracefulness of melody, no device of cunning workmanship: we almost forget that we are listening to music, we set aside all questions of taste and pleasure: we are brought face to face with that ultimate Reality, of which beauty itself is but a mode and an adumbration.

Here, then, we may fitly conclude our survey of Church music during the period of Viennese influence. We have seen it making its way through lightness and frivolity, maintaining on the whole a sincere purpose, and gaining, not only in technical skill, but in earnestness and in power of expression. To expect that its course should be continuous is unreasonable; there are always alternations of ebb and flow in the current of human life: but we cannot doubt that from C. P. E. Bach to Haydn, and from Haydn to Beethoven, there was a real and sensible advance, and that in it the great artists of each generation materially aided. On the religious side of the question we have touched as lightly as possible; it belongs to a different order of investigation, and is mentioned here only because Art must be in some measure gauged by its relation to its object. But it is not without reason that the two aspects culminated together, and that the climax of the form was at the same time the fullest expression of its devotional spirit.

NOTE.

Two countries lie outside the course of historical development: England, from its adherence in the main to the Protestant Liturgy, Spain for no better ascertainable reason than that it was situated beyond the Pyrenees. Both, at this time, accomplished work of substantial value, and no account of the period can be complete without some record of their respective schools.

In 1755 Dr. Greene died, leaving his unfinished collection of Church music to his friend and successor Dr. Boyce (1710–1779). Boyce completed the work with great diligence and judgement, and published it, under the title of 'Cathedral Music,' in three volumes, the first in 1760, the last in 1778. Twelve years later appeared a continuation by Arnold (1740–1802), also in three volumes[1], which, though it be only the gleaning of Boyce's harvest, contains a good many notable anthems and one or two fine services. It should be added that the best of these date from an earlier period. Our Church composition in the eighteenth century was artificial and rococo, and though Boyce, W. Hayes (1707–1777), and Battishill (1738–1801) save themselves by a certain manliness and vigour, they seldom succeeded in breaking through the conventionality of their time. But the turn of the century brought forward two musicians on whose names an English historian may be excused for dwelling. Thomas Attwood (1767–1838) began life as a chorister of the Chapel Royal, was sent abroad by the Prince of Wales, and studied successively at Naples under Latilla and at Vienna under Mozart. Shortly after his return to London he was made organist of St. Paul's and composer to the Chapel Royal; in 1813 he helped to found the Philharmonic Society, and was one of

---

[1] With a supplementary volume containing the organ part.

its first conductors. His early compositions were mostly operatic: in later life he turned his attention to Church music and wrote anthems and services, of which the two Coronation anthems (for George IV and William IV) are remarkably fine works; and the hymn 'Come Holy Ghost,' it may be said advisedly, is not unworthy of the hand that wrote 'Ave Verum.' Indeed, his name has come down to us linked with one imperishable commendation. 'Attwood,' said Mozart, 'has more of my style than any scholar I ever had,' and in such a judgement we may well be content to acquiesce.

Of equal merit, though different in character, was the work of Samuel Wesley (1766–1837), nephew of John Wesley, and younger son of his brother Charles. He was a remarkably precocious musician; at eight years of age he wrote his first oratorio, at eleven he published a set of lessons for the harpsichord, on which, as also on the violin and the organ, he was already an accomplished performer. England had every reason to hope that a genius was arising who would once more raise its art to the level of Humphrey and Purcell. But in 1787 he met with a severe accident which clouded his life for the next twenty years, and left its mark afterwards in long periods of nervous irritability and depression. To this is due not only the fewness of his important compositions, but the gloomy and hypochondriacal temper which hindered his advancement, and the curious uncertainty of purpose which kept him vacillating between the Church of England and that of Rome. His ability was incontestible. He is said to have been the greatest organist and improviser of his day: he was the first musician in Europe to promote the study of John Sebastian Bach: and his compositions, many of which remain unpublished, include four Masses, over thirty antiphons—among them three noble settings of the Psalms 'In exitu Israel,' 'Exultate,' and 'Dixit Dominus'—about a dozen anthems and services, and a considerable number of instrumental works. His fame even in England has been somewhat dimmed by the more genial lustre of his son; but

we owe more than a passing attention to the man who opened
for us the pages of Bach, and in whose own style we may
sometimes catch an echo of their majestic harmonies.

It is not of course claimed that either of these men stands
beside the great masters. The art of both was in some measure
derivative, the amount of their production, tried by the lavish
standard of the time, was slight and parsimonious. But it is
claimed that they take honourable rank among the composers
of secondary importance: that they were pupils in a great
school: and that they are infinitely better worth studying than
nine-tenths of those careless and facile artists who have flooded
this period of history by sheer volume. Their work is not
Kapellmeister-musik: it has a genuine truth and beauty of its
own, and it maintained, through our darkest age, a tradition
of sincerity to which English music of the present day is
deeply indebted. Our poetry has often been kept alive by
achievements which fall short of the highest genius,—there
cannot always be a Milton or a Wordsworth,—and though in
our musical history the interval is wider between the summits,
this is a poor reason for confusing the humbler ridges with
the dead level of the plain.

Spanish Church music, during this period, was working along
two separate lines of development, distinguished by Eslava as
those of the Valencian and Catalan schools respectively. The
former was conservative, maintaining the old traditions of
dignified severity and purity which had been handed down
since the great days of Morales: the latter allowed itself to
be influenced by operatic methods, by ideals of sensuous colour
and melody, by the more obvious and popular forms of emotional
expression. The contrast may be seen at its widest point of
divergence if we compare two consecutive works quoted in
the *Lira Sacro-Hispana* [1], the hymn 'Oh Madre' by Pons,
and the psalm 'Memento Domine' by Cabo. The one is

---

[1] Siglo XIX, Tom. i. pp. 179 and 190 respectively.

wholly theatrical in tone and treatment, sometimes vivid and expressive, sometimes merely sentimental, but no more religious in character than the *Stabat Mater* of Rossini. The other, written in seven-part counterpoint, is grave and restrained almost to the verge of asceticism: there is no intrusion of colour, no appeal to sense or passion; the music flows on with that large unconscious beauty which we have come to associate with the character of Mediaeval art. It is true that these two examples fall at the extreme end of the period under consideration: they are for this reason none the less salient: and it follows therefore to consider, through the eighteenth century, the determining lines from which they respectively issued.

For the first three-quarters of the century the pure style held undoubted supremacy, and it was still possible to say, with Eslava, that the distinguishing feature of Spanish Ecclesiastical Music was its severity and its close adherence to plain-song [1]. The earliest composer whom it falls within our province to consider was Rabassa (d. 1760), who held office successively at Valencia and Seville, and, beside a famous treatise on counterpoint, wrote a vast amount of Church music in four, eight, and twelve parts. A motet of his *Audite universi populi* for twelve voices and organ is quoted by Eslava, and affords an interesting example of his method. The parts are treated not in imitation but in large choral masses, note against note, alternating very effectively with passages for a single part or for two or three together. The whole work is as solid as a row of Norman pillars, connected one with the other, by the lines of arches, and all the more impressive from their disdain of ornament. Among Rabassa's younger contemporaries may be mentioned Líteres, second organist at the Chapel Royal in 1756; Julià (d. 1787), monk of Montserrat and organist to the monastery; Fuentes (d. 1768), an excellent composer, who for the last eleven years of his life was chapel-master at

---

[1] Eslava, *Lira Sacro-Hispana*, Siglo XVII, pp. 28 and 32.

Valencia; and Soler (1729–1783), organist of the Escurial, whose work was held in high estimation by no less stern a critic than Padre Martini. In the next generation the tradition of the pure style was continued by Ripa (1720–1795), chapel-master at Seville, which in 1789 gave a great festival in his honour; Lidon (d. 1826), master of the Chapel Royal for over forty years, a voluminous writer of Church music and a distinguished composer for the organ; Montesinos (1748–1822), organist of the Collegio del Patriarca in Valencia; and Cabo (d. 1832), who entered the cathedral of Valencia as an alto singer, and rose successively to be first organist and chapel-master. It is worth noting that the last of these is selected by Eslava for special praise as a typical representative of the school. In no other country of Europe could we find a man who was contemporary with Schubert, and who still wrote after the pattern of the Middle Ages.

Meanwhile the dramatic or melodic ideal was, from the middle of the century, beginning to make its way; and its first point of divergence may be traced to a composer who in the main bulk of his work is usually ranged under the opposite banner. In 1740 Don Josef Nebra made his début in Madrid as a composer of light operas and zarzuelas. His talent attracted the attention of the Court, where the influence of Farinelli was paramount, and he received the somewhat incongruous reward of an appointment as organist of the Chapel Royal, with a commission to rewrite its music, most of which had been destroyed some ten years before by a fire in the library. Nebra seems to have adapted himself with remarkable skill to the new conditions. His list of works includes twenty-two Masses, a considerable number of smaller Church compositions—Hymns, Lamentations, Misereres, Litanies, and the like—beside the famous Requiem which he wrote for the death of Queen Barbara; and they are for the most part written in that strict contrapuntal style which was still regarded as the proper vehicle for devotional art. But his

early experiences in the theatre could not be altogether repressed. The Requiem, for instance, begins with two numbers
set to a *Canto fermo* from the plain-song, and then, with the
introduction of the *Dies Irae*, breaks into a definite attempt
at dramatic treatment. The devices are very simple and
primitive—not much more than rapid repeated notes and
a gradual sweep upward to a climax—but they are the same
in kind as those used later by Cherubini, with whose genius
that of Nebra may be said to bear some affinity. In any
case there is here an unmistakeable instance of the intrusion
of dramatic elements into worship: and it is interesting that
the frontier should have been crossed by a composer who,
like Cherubini, made his first public appearance upon the
stage.

Of a very different character was Garcia, called Españoleto
(1731–1809), whose quiet and saintly life was spent almost entirely in his cathedral of Saragossa. But in Garcia's work also
may be found traces of the Nuova Musica, not so much in
dramatic expression—though of this there are some hints—as
in a tendency towards melodic phrases and variegated harmonies.
It is more like the colouring of a Missal than that of a picture,
but the colour is there, and is laid on with an evident love of
it for its own sake. After Garcia the area widened still
further, through Secanilla[1] (1775–1832), who was chapel-
master at Calahorra, and who, next to Yriarte, was the greatest
of Spanish critics; through Prieto[2] (1765–1844), and Altarriba
(1777–1833), who were fellow pupils at Saragossa, the one
a famous tenor, the other a famous organist, until the dramatic
style reached its climax in Pons (1768–1818), who carried the
war into the enemy's country, and, as Valencia had an outpost
at Montserrat, retaliated by taking his oratorios and his operatic
hymns into the very citadel of strict counterpoint, the cathedral
of Valencia itself. It is an odd example of the irony of events

[1] See his Hymn to Sant' Iago, quoted by Eslava.
[2] See his *Salve Regina*, quoted by Eslava.

that Cabo, to whom his work must have been unspeakable heresy, should have sung in his choir and, after an interval, succeeded to his office: and that Valencia which, at the beginning of the period, imposed its style on the whole of Church composition, should, at the end, have seen its services directed, in near succession, by the leaders of such widely antagonistic parties.

CHAPTER VII

THE INSTRUMENTAL FORMS

C. P. E. BACH AND THE GROWTH OF THE SONATA

THE development of the great instrumental forms may, without undue emphasis, be regarded as the chief contribution made to musical art during the latter half of the eighteenth century. Before the time of C. P. E. Bach instrumental music had been on the whole subordinated to vocal, and had held a place honourable indeed but of secondary importance and promise. In the absence of public concert-rooms the Church and the theatre gave principal opportunity for display and reputation : the dignified ritual of the one, the ready popularity of the other, offered attractions to which there was then no counterpoise : skill of vocalization far outran that of any other medium ; and melody itself moved with the greater confidence if it went hand in hand with verse. No doubt J. S. Bach wrote in every contemporary form and excelled in all : yet even with J. S. Bach the balance inclines to the side of the Christmas Oratorio and the Passions and the Mass in B minor : for the rest it was but rarely that a solitary virtuoso like Couperin or Corelli could dedicate the best part of his life to the service of violin or harpsichord. But with C. P. E. Bach there begins a new era. It was especially his work in the development of the Sonata form which won him the unstinted admiration of Haydn and Mozart, and which, through them affected the subsequent course of events. In this his main historical interest lies : and it is therefore worth while to consider in brief outline the character of the forms as he found them and the kinds of modification which he adopted and employed.

The principles on which Sonata-writing depends are those of balance and contrast, of key-distribution and recurrent phrase, in short of such organization of musical theme as may be roughly compared with the plot of a drama or a story. And just as, in a story, plot of some kind is the most primitive requirement, so these principles, in one form or another, lie at the root of all the earliest folk-tunes and dances, more or less coherent according to the degrees of civilization which these imply. It would of course be here superfluous to trace the history back to its first origin: the nature of Bach's material will be sufficiently indicated if we start from his great predecessor Archangelo Corelli. Now in the Sonatas of Corelli we find two principal types of structure, each with two subdivisions[1]. The one, which is commonly known by the name of Binary, consists of a couple of musical ' paragraphs ' equal, or approximately equal in length, and set against each other in exact balance and antithesis. With one of its species the first paragraph ends in the key of the piece, and its modulations are wholly internal and incidental, e. g. the following Corrente from the Sonata da Camera in F, Op. 2, No. 7 :—

---

[1] This, of course, refers chiefly to the dance-movements in the Sonate da Camera, not to those less organic forms which seem to have been mainly determined by contrapuntal methods.

With the other species the first paragraph modulates out of the key, and the second works its way back, as in the Sarabande of the Sonata in A, Op. 4, No. 2 :—

The second type, which, on all logical grounds, should be called by the analogous name of Ternary [1], consists of three similar paragraphs, the third of which more or less exactly reproduces the first. This again is subdivided in the same way. If the first paragraph ends in the key of the piece, there is nothing, except the fancy of the composer, to prevent the third from restating it precisely, as it does in the Tempo di Gavotta of the Violin Sonata in A, Op. 5, No. 9:—

[1] In most English text-books on Form it is called Ternary if the first paragraph ends in the key of the piece, Binary if it does not.

3rd Part = restatement of 1st.

If however the first paragraph modulated away its restatement could not be precise, for there was an accepted law that the movement as a whole must end in the key in which it began. Thus the phraseology of the third paragraph needed such alteration as might bring it ultimately to a full close in the tonic, e. g. the following Corrente from the Sonata da Camera in A minor, Op. 4, No. 5 :—

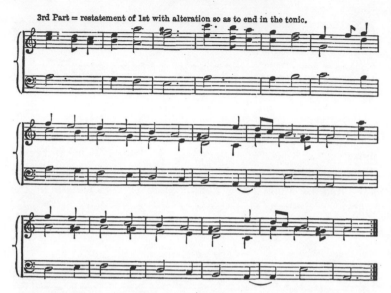

3rd Part = restatement of 1st with alteration so as to end in the tonic.

Of these four alternative types of structure the first is the
least organic and the least satisfactory.   It suggests indeed not
one movement but two: the opening half is complete in itself,
and the rest appears to be a mere appanage or after-thought.
There is little wonder, therefore, that in Corelli examples of it
are rare and that after his time it practically dropped out of use.
On similar grounds the third fell into disfavour : it represented
a low level of constructive skill, it seemed too obvious, too
easy, to give scope to ingenuity or invention.   At the same
time it was not ill-adapted to simple uses, and, as it survived
in the Folk-song and the ' da capo ' Aria, so after a period of
neglect [1] it was resumed in the Sonata for those lyric or elegiac
movements which from the nature of their subject required
little complexity of organization.

The second . type, that of the Binary structure in which the
first part modulates away from the key and the second returns
to it, was the form of predilection during the first half of the
eighteenth century.   Corelli employs it far more frequently

[1] Even during this period some examples may be found in Rameau.

than any other: it is almost invariable with his Italian successors, it is almost invariable with J. S. Bach. Its neatness and exactitude were admirably suited to the logical temper of the time; it afforded a ready solution to the problem of variety in unity; it kept a check on all tendency to divagation or extravagance; it soon became a convention as unquestioningly accepted as the Alexandrine in France or the heroic couplet in England. But even a convention cannot remain stationary through forty years of artistic progress. Racine's Alexandrine is not like that of Corneille, Pope's couplet is not like that of Dryden, and in the same way the history of this Binary form shows a continuous development, until at last it breaks its own bounds and passes into a higher stage of evolution.

It will be noticed that in the instances quoted from Corelli the thought is somewhat indeterminate. The outlines are clear enough, but they are filled with details and incidents which, as they stand, look more like impromptus than parts of a predetermined design. The first advance, then, was towards greater precision, towards a clearer articulation of members, and their disposition so as to exhibit in fullest light the organic unity of the composition. This was most readily effected by a direct, epigrammatic antithesis of clauses, so placed across the modulation that each, as the movement proceeded, should transfer its key to the other: a device which may be represented by the mechanical scheme :—

$$a_1 - b_2 \parallel a_2 - b_1$$

(when a and b represent the clauses, 1 and 2 the keys): and illustrated by the following example from Marcello :—

Of this sharp-cut and polished antithesis there are, in the music
of the early eighteenth century, many hundreds of instances.
Its strength and its weakness are both equally apparent. On
the one hand it is supremely lucid, it reaches its point without
parade or circumlocution, it is absolutely perfect in rhyme and
rhythm. On the other hand it stands in imminent danger of
formalism, it lacks altogether the element of expectation or
surprise: after a few instances the hearer knows what is coming
and can foretell the entire issue at the double-bar. Hence it
was of great service in rendering the form familiar to audiences
of little musical experience: but as composers advanced in skill
and hearers in understanding there grew almost unconsciously
the need of a more developed and elaborate method. This is
particularly noticeable in the work of J. S. Bach, whose Suites
and Partitas bring the old Binary form to its highest degree of
variety and flexibility. Sometimes he takes a passage or figure
from the first part and plays with it contrapuntally, sometimes
he intertwines it with a new theme, sometimes he alters its
curve or enriches its harmony, often he carries it easily and
continuously through a chain of modulations: in every case he
arouses attention, stimulates curiosity, and challenges intelligence by confronting it with some new problem of design.

One more point. This elaboration of thematic treatment
naturally required a somewhat larger field, especially when it
extended itself through a series of modulating passages, and
thus the Binary movement came to consist not of two equal
parts, but of two parts, the second of which was longer and
more diverse than the first. In short the mechanical scheme
had grown from

$$a_1 - b_2 \, \| \, a_2 - b_1$$

to $\quad\quad a_1 - b_2 \, \| \, a_2 - c_3 - b_1$

where c_3 represents the prolongation of the second part by the further development of its themes or the introduction of new episodes. But here occurs a difficulty. The tonic key is only touched for a few bars at the beginning and end of the movement; all the rest is gathered round different tonal centres, and the whole scheme of balance and proportion will therefore be dislodged unless the tonic can be asserted at the end of the piece with some special emphasis or insistence. One means of securing this would be to introduce, immediately after the episodic passages, an allusion to the opening theme in the tonic key (thus reinforcing it by actual recurrence of phrase) and to maintain that key with the briefest and most incidental modulation till the final cadence. A remarkable instance may be found in the *Polonaise* of J. S. Bach's Sixth French Suite :—

The double-bar breaks this movement into two unequal parts of eight and sixteen bars respectively. The first eight bars begin in E major and modulate away to the dominant: the second eight bars begin with a reminiscence of the opening phrase and then modulate continuously till they reach a cadence in C♯ minor: the third eight bars reintroduce the tonic key, again with a reminiscence of the opening phrase, and centre round it until the end. The reader cannot fail to be struck with the resemblance between this form and the fourth of the structural types quoted from Corelli [1]. In both alike there is a first part which starts in the tonic and modulates to a related key: in both alike there follows a passage of further modulation: in both alike the conclusion of the movement consists of a sentence which begins and ends in the key of the piece. But whereas in Corelli the last part maintains the tonic throughout and uses it as a vehicle for restating

[1] See p. 189. Compare also with Bach's *Polonaise* Corelli's *Giga* from the Violin Sonata in A major, Op. 5, No. 9.

the first, in Bach the last part allows incidental modulation and, after a brief allusion to the opening theme, passes away to other topics. Bach's movement, in short, is still an example of the old Binary form, though so extended and developed that it stands at the extreme verge and frontier. One further step and the modern sonata-form was inevitable. Its ground-plan had already been sketched, and the sketch laid aside until men had worked out the utmost possibilities of the narrower design. But the narrower design had so widened its boundaries that by very force of momentum it was bound to transcend them: the form which Corelli had regarded as too hazardous and experimental for common use[1] was now approached once more after a generation of skill and experience; to C. P. E. Bach fell the opportunity of seeing in the fullness of time that the threefold form was possible, and that no other could any longer satisfy the requirements of the sonata.

The particular type of movement which was established by C. P. E. Bach thus marks the converging-point of two preceding lines, the one arrested since the time of Corelli, the other working round to join it by a longer and more devious circuit. In his hands it assumes the familiar 'three-canto' form, though not yet fully organized; an Exposition divided between two contrasting keys, a Development section modulating more widely afield, and a Recapitulation, the office of which is to restate the first part in the tonic key, and then to give a sense of unity and completeness to the whole. For the sake of clearness it may be represented by the following mechanical scheme:—

Exposition.	Development Section.	Recapitulation.
Begins in the tonic and modulates away to the dominant or relative major.	Begins with an allusion to the opening theme, in dominant or relative major, and then breaks away into free modulation.	Restates the themes of the exposition (with some omissions or changes) entirely in the tonic.
$a_1 - b_2$	$a_2 - c_3$	$a_1 - b_1$

So far as concerns the general ground-plan this is, of course, the form commonly employed in the first movement of the

[1] He employed it not more than a dozen times in the whole of his compositions.

'Classical' sonata: but its opening canto is not yet differentiated into determinate 'subjects'; the organs are still in
some degree embryonic.   In other words the Exposition fulfils
its function of contrasting two tonal centres, but its different
parts are not yet duly related and proportioned; if we try to
analyse it into 'first subject,' 'transition,' and 'second subject'
we shall see at once that the analysis is arbitrary and that the
names are misleading: the style is too uniform and the process
of modulation too gradual to admit of any such method of
division.   Take, for example, the Exposition of the opening
Allegro from the first Würtemberg Sonata, composed in
1743:—

This absence of distinctive themes is not a mark of deficient melodic invention, for C. P. E. Bach had a very remarkable gift of melody, nor of inexperience, for he had been engaged in sonata-writing since 1732. It was simply an inherited tradition, which, preoccupied with clearing the outlines of his form, he did not think it worth while to discard. His main business was to mark out the ground and lay the foundations:

it is unreasonable to expect that he should foresee the full
capabilities of the superstructure.   As he neared the end of his
ninety clavier-sonatas [1] he began more firmly to differentiate
his themes; but by that time Haydn was already famous.

Three results follow from this comparative want of organization.   First, that in a large majority of these movements it is
the opening theme which most readily attracts the attention and
which remains longest in the memory.   Indeed the music often
enters with a striking and vivid phrase and then settles down
to scale passages or assertions of some elementary harmonic
progression : as, for instance, the Sonata in G minor (comp.
1746) which, after a few rhapsodical bars of introduction, breaks
into the fine stormy opening :—

and then seems to lose itself in the sand.   Not less remarkable
is the Allegro of the third Würtemberg Sonata (E minor),
which starts with an almost Handelian breadth and dignity, and
after four bars sets about considering how it may most easily
arrive at the contrasted key.   Indeed, until the Reprise Sonatas
there is not one of Bach's Expositions which maintains a uniform level of interest throughout.   The melody rises with a bold

---

[1] The total number of C. P. E. Bach's compositions for Clavier Solo was 210,
of which rather more than 90 were sonatas.

enough flight, but the wings begin to flag before it reaches the double-bar.

Secondly, Bach's treatment of the 'Development section' is always rather simple and rudimentary, setting out with the opening theme in the contrasted key, and continuing a sober and even tenour with very little in the way of adventure or episode. This is, of course, an inevitable consequence of his Exposition: the characters are not yet distinct enough to admit of dramatic incidents and situations, the phrases, with one exception, are not sufficiently salient to be readily recognized in a new context. As the son of his father he was naturally acquainted with some of the possibilities of thematic variation, but they were not with him a matter of chief interest, and he did not and could not realize the immense range which would be opened out by a sharper discrimination of subjects. Hence, compared with Haydn and Mozart and still more with Beethoven, his work in this respect is usually somewhat uniform and colourless: it is the drama of Thespis not yet humanized by the introduction of the second actor.

Thirdly, he cuts rather than solves the problem of the Re-capitulation; the problem how, with least appearance of effort, to restate in one key the music which the exposition had divided between two. Our experience of the consummate skill with which Beethoven effected this may tend to make us forget that, at the inception of the sonata, it was a matter of real difficulty: the shifting of the tonal centre required some alter-ation and readjustment, and it was by no means clear how this could be neatly and deftly brought about. At any rate, in the early sonatas, Bach never seems to be entirely master of his form. Sometimes he secures the necessary transposition by entirely rewriting the passage that leads up to it, or even by substituting a new episode altogether: sometimes he shortens his dénouement by a considerable omission and joins the edges together with a somewhat obvious seam: in both events he leaves us with the unsatisfactory impression that the last act of the play has caused some perplexity to the dramatist. It is necessary to add that in this respect his later work shows a very noticeable advance: the fine Sonata in E major [1] (composed 1766) is a model of constructive skill, as are many others in the series 'für Kenner und Liebhaber': but we are here less concerned with a criticism of Bach's ability than with a statement of his place in the history of musical forms. This place he owes almost wholly to his first two volumes (the 'Frederick' and 'Würtemberg' Sonatas), for it was from these that Haydn derived his education, and it is therefore on these that the attention of the reader should mainly be concentrated. Bach, in short, is less important to us in the full maturity of his genius than in the earlier days of trial and experiment. In the eyes of Burney he was the kindly old virtuoso, in whose writings the instrumental music of the eighteenth century attained its consummation: in ours he is the inspired pioneer who cleared the paths for the feet of his Viennese successors.

So far we have considered Bach's treatment of the particular structural type which is most closely associated with the 'Classical' sonata. It remains briefly to indicate the lines which he laid down for the construction of the sonata as a whole. The number of movements he fixed at three [2]: an opening Allegro built on the plan which has been already described, an Adagio or Andante in some nearly related key, and a Finale of bright and cheery temper, written either in an extended dance-form or in a looser version of that employed for the first movement. Of the Finale there is little that need be said: it owed its character to the same convention which ended the Suite with a Gigue or some other such light-hearted number, and its plot was not sufficiently distinctive to require

---

[1] Made accessible by its inclusion in the *Trésor des Pianistes* (vol. viii).

[2] No doubt from reminiscence of the 'Italian' overture popularized by Alessandro Scarlatti, in which there is the same disposition of movements. The practice of prefacing the first Allegro with a short Adagio Introduction (rare in Bach, but more frequent among his successors) is in like manner derived from the 'French Overture' of Lully.

any detailed discussion. But in the slow movements Bach
allowed himself a free hand.   He selected his plan from among
any of the common and familiar types of the day :—the fugato,
the old Binary form, even the operatic scena :—and, no longer
occupied with complexities of design, allowed full play to his
delicate sentiment and his happy audacity of colour. It is
from these that we can best understand the estimate in which
he was held as a poetic composer:—the sweet and touching
elegy of the fifth Würtemberg Sonata, which begins :—

or the Andante from the first of the Sonatas inscribed to
Frederick the Great, a movement which is worth quoting entire
as an illustration both of sincere feeling and of melodious
phrase :—

Besides the sonatas he wrote voluminously in almost every conceivable kind of instrumental medium: over a dozen symphonies, over fifty concertos, a vast amount of miscellaneous chamber-music, several pieces for the organ, and at least a hundred smaller works—dances, fugues, fantasias, rondos—for clavier-solo. The symphonies are scored for all manner of odd combinations from string-trio to full orchestra (a sure indication that the term· was not yet precisely fixed): and for the most part vacillate between the form of the sonata and that of the current orchestral overture. They were probably composed for occasions of public display, and contain more of formal pageantry than of genuine artistic merit. The concertos and chamber-works are remarkable not only for the freedom of their form, but, in many cases, for their great melodic beauty and for their sense of balance and contrast. Indeed the two clavier-concertos in G major and D major, both of which have been edited by Dr. Riemann, are not only the most important works of their kind between J. S. Bach and Mozart, but are far more like the later master than the earlier. Bold and experimental in construction they are yet perfectly clear, they treat the solo-instrument with a· complete knowledge of its capabilities, and even handle the orchestral forces with some measure of individual freedom and character. The opening movement of the first is one of Bach's most vigorous and manly numbers: the andante of the second, an orchestral tune with rhapsodical interludes, is a fine instance of his tender and expressive melody.

Among his smaller clavier-forms the Rondo is the only one that requires any special consideration. The simplicity of its essential structure—a melodic stanza repeated three or four times with intervening episodes [1]—rendered it, in his judgement, unfit for the larger and more serious kinds of artistic composition: he seldom or never used it for any of his most

---

[1] Purcell's song, 'I attempt from Love's sickness to fly,' is a good example of the early Rondo-form.

important works, but relegated it to a place among his
Underwoods. At the same time, having once allowed it to
be planted, he was far too conscientious a forester to leave it
in neglect: indeed he seems to have tried every available
method of training its growth and enriching its foliage.
Some of his rondos are purely experimental, modulating into
the remotest keys, altering rhythm and tempo, substituting
variations for the exact restatement of the main theme, doing
all that the science of the day could suggest to prevent the
impression of a stiff and precise recurrence. His best known
example—that in E major with the graceful subject :—

seems, at first sight, as free as the most irresponsible fantasia.
The melody returns in F, in F♯, in C; the principal episode
given in B major at the beginning is repeated in G major towards
the end, the other intervening paragraphs are mainly rhapsodical or declamatory; the whole design, both in audacity of
key-distribution and in variety of phrase, has no parallel before
Beethoven. Yet the freedom is by no means that of anarchy
or lawlessness : the scheme, if a little exuberant, has a
definite and intelligible plan, and while it breaks away
altogether from established tradition helps to set a more liberal
tradition for the future. There is certainly some ground
for surprise that Bach should have undervalued a form which

he could employ to such good purpose, and which played so considerable a part in the subsequent history of the sonata.

The work begun by C. P. E. Bach was not to any serious extent furthered by his German contemporaries. The most capable among them was his brother Wilhelm Friedemann, whose best music, so far as we know it, belongs entirely to the old school. His sonatas and concertos are either dignified exponents of the contrapuntal methods which he had inherited from his father, or, as in the case of the Six Sonatas dedicated to Miss Dumerque, deplorable failures to adapt himself to an unfamiliar method. Indeed, it is mainly on works outside the sonata that his present reputation is founded: on the fugues and the polonaises, and above all the noble fantasias in which the inspiration of J. S. Bach is most clearly apparent. He made some interesting experiments in instrumental combination : a symphony in one movement for strings and flutes, three 'Ricercate' for string quartet and basso continuo, and best of all a sestet for strings, clarinet, and horns, the style of which is a curious anticipation of Haydn's early manner. But these appear to have been merely sporadic and incidental, written as the mood came and thrown aside as soon as the drudgery of the manuscript was over; they were hardly known in their own day and they are but now beginning to be rescued from oblivion. Of other German musicians, Hasse was occupying a distinguished position at Dresden, but he was far more occupied in conciliating the victor of Kesselsdorf with operas than in gathering the more secluded and academic laurels of instrumental composition : and apart from Hasse the only other men of considerable moment were gathered, with C. P. E. Bach, round the court at Berlin[1]. By an accident of history it happened that the next great genius arose not in Germany but in Austria, and there, under new racial conditions and amid new surroundings, carried on to a further stage the development of instrumental music.

[1] The sonatas of Christoph Nichelmann and of Georg Benda, who were both in Berlin at this time, show considerable traces of the influence of C. P. E. Bach.

CHAPTER VIII

THE INSTRUMENTAL FORMS (*continued*)

THE EARLY SYMPHONIES AND QUARTETS OF HAYDN

In the year 1749 Joseph Haydn, aged seventeen, was ignominiously expelled from the Choir-school of St. Stephen's, Vienna, and turned out to seek his fortune in the street. Seldom has a blessing presented itself in a more complete disguise. He had no money and no influence, he was in disgrace with the only authorities to whom his name was known, and as he spent his first night on a bench under the open sky the prospects of his future appeared sufficiently comfortless. But a few friends came to his aid : one offered him hospitality, another found him pupils, a third lent him 150 gulden until better times ; within a few days he was able to rent an attic and establish himself there with the two most precious of his possessions, a violin and an ' old worm-eaten clavier.' Vienna had then no distinctively poorer quarters: the city was confined within the circuit of the fortifications, and the same tall mansions sheltered wealth, competence, and poverty under one roof. On the ground floor lived Serene Highness, resplendent in Court apparel, overhead came the more dignified professions or the richer Bourgeoisie, and the staircase wound its length upward past the doors of the clerk and the petty merchant, until it reached its limit where indigence lay shivering under the tiles. By an odd chance Haydn selected for his place of abode the old Michaeler-Haus in the Kohlmarkt, two inhabitants of which were destined to play a considerable part in his career. The third étage was the lodging of Metastasio, from whom he obtained his first patronage in Vienna ; the lower part of the house was the town-residence of Prince Paul Esterhazy, who twelve years later appointed him to his office at Eisenstadt.

At the time, however, a more important ally was the good-natured publisher in the new Michaeler-Haus who lent him music which he was too poor to purchase : treatises of Fux and Marpurg, compositions of Werner and Bonno and Wagenseil, and above all the ' Frederick' and 'Würtemberg' volumes of C. P. E. Bach. On these Haydn fastened with all a student's enthusiasm. He read and re-read, copied and analysed, wrote voluminous exercises, strengthened his hand in composition, and devoted his leisure to taking pupils and to practising his violin until, 'though no conjuror,' he was ' able to play a concerto.' He is said to have worked for sixteen hours a day, training himself as hardly any other musician had been trained, and giving earnest of that ceaseless and untiring industry which distinguished him through his later life.

So passed five years of preparation : a quiet period diversified by few incidents. In 1751 appeared his first Mass and his first opera ; in 1753 Metastasio introduced him to Porpora, who carried him off for the summer to Männersdorf, and there gave him some rather intermittent instruction ; about the same time he added to his list of pupils the 'Wunderkind' Marianne Martinez. But in 1755 came the first great opportunity of his career. A certain Karl Joseph Edler von Fürnberg (son of an eminent physician who had been ennobled by Charles VI) had a country-house at Weinzirl near Melk, and, being an enthusiastic amateur, was in the habit of filling it with parties of musicians who spent their time in performing all manner of chamber-works. Through some unknown channel he heard of Haydn's reputation, and invited him down on a long visit. Haydn accepted with alacrity, packed up his violin, and, at the age of twenty-three, set out on a journey from which he was to return as the first instrumental composer in Austria. He found the usual ' country-house' orchestra of the time, a few strings, a couple of horns, a couple of oboes, and he at once set himself to illustrate in this larger medium the principles of design which the study of Bach had taught him at the clavier.

The whole nomenclature of instrumental music was still very fluid and indeterminate. Any work which was written 'for three or more instruments' could be called a symphony : sonatas could be written for clavier alone or clavier accompanied by strings or wind, or for two violins and a bass : and beside these were several more or less fantastic titles—Notturni, Serenades and the like,—which seem to have designated nothing more than a somewhat lighter style of composition. The eighteen works which Haydn composed in 1755-6, at Weinzirl, were called by him Notturni, Divertimenti, or Cassations [1], and were written for whatever instrumental forces happened to be available at the moment. There seems to have been a trustworthy viola-player, and he was therefore able to give some character and independence to his viola-part : the horns and oboes were not of proportionate merit [2], and he therefore wrote the majority of these compositions for the four strings alone. There is no evidence that he was consciously making any discovery or invention. He was simply applying to the needs of a miniature orchestra the forms which he had learned during his period of studentship.

The eighteen works in question are those printed in the Paris and London editions as the string quartets, Op. 1-3. At least three of them (Op. 1, No. 5 ; Op. 2, Nos. 3 and 5) were originally composed for strings and wind, and one of them (Op. 1, No 5) has every claim to be regarded as Haydn's first symphony. This title is usually bestowed, with insufficient reason, on the symphony in D major which he wrote at Lukavec in 1759. But a comparison of the two will show that there is no essential

---

[1] See Pohl, vol. i. p. 331.

[2] Until the latter part of the century the wind-players were not expected to keep in tune. See above, p. 8.

point of difference between them. They are scored for the same combination, strings, horns and oboes; each consists of three movements, the movements are in the same form and are almost identical in scale and length. It may be added that Op. 1, No. 5 is not included in Haydn's catalogue among the number of his quartets, and that it was published by Breitkopf with the wind-parts. We do not even know whether the composer sanctioned their omission when, in 1764, La Chevardière introduced Paris to the 'Six Simphonies ou Quatuors dialogués pour deux Violons, Alto Viola et Basse, composés par Mr. Hayden, Maître de Musique à Vienne[1].'

Throughout the first two opus-numbers Haydn is evidently feeling his way. Except the 'Symphony' all the works have five movements apiece; and two of the five are minuets, written in the tiny lyric-forms of which he was especially fond, and the duplication of which he might well cover under the modest title of Divertimento. But by the beginning of Op. 3 his method was fully established, and from thenceforward we find, with very few exceptions, the four movements which afterwards became traditional. The style, too, of the third collection is more mature than that of its predecessors; the themes are more definite and articulate, the treatment is more organic, and there is already some indication of that remarkable freedom and flexibility which were to signalize, in later times, the character of symphonic and concerted composition. No doubt there were still many conventions, but all art is in some degree conventional, and its true laws differ from their academic counterparts in their response to some psychological need, and in their almost unlimited capacity of growth and development. To write a quartet at the present day after the precise pattern of Haydn's early work would be to produce nothing more than a College exercise: but the forms which are appropriate to our

---

[1] In Venier's catalogue Haydn's early quartets are quoted 'avec cors et hautbois ad lib.'

use are as directly the descendants of his as they are the ancestors of others yet to come.

His opening movement is usually built on the 'three-canto' plan of C. P. E. Bach, embodying successively the principles of Duality, Plurality, and Unity in key-distribution. But the particular blend of his genius and his conditions enabled him to organize this general scheme more completely than had hitherto been possible. His imagination was essentially melodic, he was writing for the most melodic of instruments; he thus came to differentiate his exposition clearly into contrasted themes or subjects, while from the outset he saw the importance of securing the general balance of the movement as a whole by making the second subject the longer of the two. Thus, in his hands the mechanical scheme appears in its fullest shape as follows:—

Exposition.	Development Section.	Recapitulation.
1st subject : melody in the tonic, sometimes repeated. Transition : modulating to the contrasted key. 2nd subject : consisting of a series of melodic phrases or sentences in the contrasted key.	Thematic treatment of phrases from the exposition, modulating freely ; and usually, though not invariably, starting with an allusion to the first subject.	1st subject in the tonic. Transition, altered so as to lead to a cadence in the tonic. 2nd subject in the tonic.

Within this general outline there is obviously a wide field for option or alternative. But in Haydn's time the form was yet young, and before it could claim freedom it required some discipline and supervision. Accordingly, the natural laws of its growth were supplemented by a few purely artificial rules: adventitious supports to maintain the body until its bones were set and its muscles efficient. Thus the second subject was always, according to mode, in the dominant or the relative major:—the two keys to which Bach most naturally modulates:—the cadences, for fear they should pass unheeded, sometimes bid for recognition by the use of catchwords: and not only is the exposition repeated, but in most of these earlier works the other two cantos together. All these and similar rules, however, belong entirely to the custom of the time and may be paralleled in a dozen other schemes of art. The

Sonata form was slow in outgrowing them, but even while they surrounded it they did not seriously hamper its vitality, and in later and more experienced days they were successively discarded.

This structural type, the most complex and organic which Haydn employs, is used by him in a large majority of his elaborated movements, irrespective of their particular sentiment or character. Particularly suited, as it has proved to be, for the broad epic style of composition, it adapts itself without difficulty to light narrative pieces such as those which open the first two quartets, and to elegies such as the extremely beautiful adagio which stands at the beginning of the third[1]: many even of the minuets and other lyric numbers exhibit the same principles on a smaller scale. Indeed, it soon became customary that an instrumental work of any importance should contain at least one movement of this kind, since no other afforded the composer an equal opportunity of constructive skill; and there are not a few instances in which, with differences of style and treatment, this scheme of design underlies all four. But on the whole Haydn treated this question with a very free hand. Some of his lyric and elegiac movements are on the old Binary pattern, with two cantos, or stanzas, in exact balance: some of the minuets follow the common plan of the folk-song—assertion, contrast, reassertion; sometimes he writes an air with variations, once, in Op. 1, No. 3, the Finale is a rondo. In short, by the end of 1766, he had pressed into the service of the quartet every current instrumental form with the exception of the 'dramatic' rhapsody and the fugue; and both these he added later on. There was not much fear of academic stiffness in a scheme which, as he devised it, was very nearly coextensive with the art of music.

It remains to consider the nature of the contents which Haydn poured into these moulds. Throughout these early works he

[1] When Haydn uses it for slow movements he generally, though not invariably, omits the ' double-bar and repeat.'

shows, as may be expected, that in style as well as in structure
he is a follower of C. P. E. Bach: there are certain cadences,
certain turns of phrase, which, however much they came to be
common property, appear more frequently in these two masters
than in any of their contemporaries. Yet from the outset
Haydn speaks with his own voice. His imagination was more
vivid and concrete than that of Bach; he delighted in clear-cut
stanzas and epigrammatic sentences, sometimes brilliant, sometimes homely or humorous, but always neat, terse and pointed.
Even in his more extended melodies this characteristic is
noticeable: they have a gleam, a sparkle, which does not belong
to Bach's very delicate and beautiful enamel-work. Thus, for
example, the quartet in F (Op. 3, No. 5) opens with a bright
little dialogue:—

which is not in Bach's manner, while the principal theme of
the second subject:—

is almost crucial as to the difference between Vienna and Berlin, and prepares us for the further difference between Vienna and Eisenstadt. Another feature of Haydn's melody, almost certainly racial in origin, is his fondness for odd metres of three, five, seven, or nine bars, as distinct from the customary 'four-bar line' of the typical Western tune. Thus, the quartet in E♭ (Op. 1, No. 2) opens with the nine-bar theme :—

and the same tendency may be observed in his occasional habit of setting a melody across the bar 'per arsin et thesin': for instance, in the Adagio of the A major quartet, Op. 3, No. 6 :—

and though these metres are as yet sparingly employed their
presence even in a few numbers is significant, for they specially
mark the music of the Southern Slavs to whom Haydn belonged
by nationality, and whose folk-songs he was afterwards to lay
under such extensive contribution.

It is not to be expected that Haydn should yet exhibit much
fertility of thematic treatment. His development-sections are
usually somewhat shorter than the other two cantos, and, as
compared with his later work, are a little wanting in complexity
and distribution. The quartets of Op. 3 show, in this matter,
some advance upon their predecessors, the balance, at any rate,
is more even and the subjects are alternated with a freer hand,
but the pure lucidity of the music neither supplies nor requires
any very recondite devices of surprise or contrast. There is
more ingenuity in his handling of the recapitulation, where he
had a definite problem before him; yet even here, if we try him
by the highest standards, there is occasional evidence of prentice-
work. To say this, is in no way to disparage his genius. The
instrumental forms would not be worth having if all their
difficulties could have been completely solved at once, and the
few touches of weakness, here indicated, are marks not of
failure but of immaturity.

The slow movements are usually violin solos or duets, often
very beautiful and elaborate, with a simple accompaniment for
the lower strings. Two noticeable examples are the Adagios of
the quartets in D major (Op. 1, No. 3) and G major (Op. 1,
No. 4), in which the ornamental passages are all diffused melody,
living tendrils that twine and cluster in a hundred fascinating
curves. Sometimes there are special effects of colour[1]: the

[1] e. g. Adagio of Quartet in C, Op. 1, No. 6; Andantino of Quartet in E, Op.
3, No. 1. Compare also the Adagio of the Quartet in Eb, Op. 2, No. 3, in which
all the strings are muted.

melody veiled and muted hovers over light detached harmonies
or floats upon a murmuring ripple of sound: sometimes it soars
and poises and falls back in a plashing cadence, or eddies, circle
upon circle, over a broad and quiet expanse. And, throughout,
the whole sentiment is as pure and sweet as a spring landscape,
when all the world is breaking out into leaf and the woodland is
chequered with the April sun.

As the Adagios display Haydn's tenderness, so the Finales
illustrate his humour. Two of them (Op. 3, Nos. 5 and 6) are
marked 'Scherzando,' and almost all might well bear this
designation. Carefully exact in form they are extraordinarily
light-hearted in character, full of quips and jests, racing along
at break-neck speed, bubbling with laughter and gaiety and
high spirits. Here is a typical example from the quartet in
G major, Op. 3, No. 3 :—

We can imagine the effect of these gambols upon an audience accustomed to the court-manners of Bonno and Reutter and Wagenseil. No one had even dared before to play such tricks in the Presence-chamber: even the irony of Couperin and the incisive epigrams of Domenico Scarlatti are totally different in kind from this spontaneous outburst of boyish merriment. And, though now and then a hearer might shake his head and prate, as pedants have always prated, about the dignity of art, the majority of wholesome and sensible people acclaimed the innovation, and welcomed, as all true music-lovers since have welcomed, this appearance in chamber-music of the very spirit of pure comedy.

But it is in the Minuets that the true Haydn is most plainly and obviously revealed. This form, which, as we have seen, he added to the stated three movements of the Bach Sonata, was one in which he always took particular pleasure. 'People talk about counterpoint,' he said in his old age, 'but I wish some one would write a really new minuet.' Indeed, one reason why his wish was so difficult of fulfilment was that he had himself done so much to forestall it. In the first three volumes

of Quartets there are no less than six-and-twenty of these
dance-measures, each, according to usual custom, alternating
with a Trio, and in spite of their slender compass they show
a remarkable variety of rhythms, of melodic devices, and even
of structural forms. Occasionally, the phrase is reminiscent of
C. P. E. Bach :—

sometimes, even anticipatory of Beethoven :—

more often it is too distinctively Haydnesque to admit of any
doubt :—

in all cases the treatment is Haydn's own, and bears eloquent
witness to his lightness of touch and his fertility of invention.
As simple as nursery-tales they are yet extremely vivid and
ingenious, and they have in quintessence that charm of sheer
goodness and kindliness with which every page of his writing
is fragrant.

A few structural experiments were tried in these works and

afterwards discarded.   In Op. 2, No. 3 the 'Minuet and Trio'
form is combined with that of the air and variations : a device
which Haydn used later for some of his clavier-sonatas but
of which he made no tradition : in Op. 3, No. 2 the Finale,
which is in complete three-canto form, is followed by a quasi-
Trio and then repeated : in Op. 3, No. 4 there are only two
movements and they are in different keys [1].   All these variants
imply a certain looseness of organization which prevented their
survival : at the present stage of our history they are interesting,
for they indicate in some measure the range of selection out of
which the quartet was evolved.   There is probably no way of
representing proportion in musical structure which has not at
some time been attempted in the great 'Cyclic' forms; and
their record is almost as much one of elimination as one of
extension and development.   The next two years Haydn spent
at Vienna, teaching and composing, principally for the Countess
Thun.   In 1759 he obtained, on von Fürnberg's recommenda-
tion, his first official appointment, that of director to the private
orchestra of Count Morzin, a Bohemian noble who lived at
Lukavec, near Pilsen.   Here he found at his disposal a somewhat larger body of instrumentalists, probably from twelve to
sixteen, and for these he wrote symphonies and divertimenti
and other concerted works of a similar character.   Most of
these it is now impossible to specify ; but among them was
a 'divertimento a sei' for two violins, two horns, English
horn and bassoon, and the little symphony in D major which
Griesinger erroneously calls his first [2].   The latter is a short
unpretentious work ; the Andante scored for strings alone, the
Allegro and Finale for strings, horns and oboes ; and it is chiefly
interesting as evidence that the types of symphonic and
chamber composition were not even yet clearly differentiated.

---

[1] It is possible that this 'Quartet' consists of two separate fragments.   The
first movement contains some of Haydn's most melodious work, and, as Dr. Pohl
notes, has some curious anticipations of Mozart.
[2] See above, p. 208.

Still there can be no doubt that Haydn fully enjoyed this opportunity of experimenting in orchestral colour; and made such good use of it that, in 1760, Prince Paul Esterhazy, after hearing some of his compositions, forthwith invited him to take up his residence in Eisenstadt.

For the first five of his thirty years at Eisenstadt Haydn devoted himself almost exclusively to orchestral work : specially studying the wind-instruments and the various effects that could be produced by blending them with the strings. His symphony *Le Midi* appeared in 1761, and was followed in rapid succession by other symphonies, divertimenti, and cassations larger in scale and richer in treatment than any of his previous writings. In 1765 he composed the charming little quartet in D minor, afterwards published as Op. 42, and from thence to 1776 his music flowed in a continuous and abundant stream. To this period belong the eighteen quartets collected as Op. 9, Op. 17, and Op. 20; about fifty symphonies [1], many concertos and divertimenti, his first clavier-trio, and the first sixteen of his known clavier-sonatas : a remarkable record, considering that at the same time he was writing operas for the two theatres and a vast quantity of sacred music for the chapel. After 1776 there followed four years of comparative repose, the one brief interval in a laborious life; then, in 1781, Mozart arrived in Vienna and the two masters entered upon their decade of noble rivalry and unbroken comradeship.

In the symphonies before 1761, so far as we know them, Haydn shows far more stiffness and formality of style than in

[1] A few of these are included in Cianchettini's edition. There is also a collection of six early 'Haydn Symphonies' edited by Carl Banck and published by Kistner, of Leipsic. It contains *Le Midi*, the Symphonies in G major (Pohl 21), C major (Pohl 22), and B♭ major (Pohl 24), together with the overture to *Il Distratto*, and a Symphony in E♭ which is so inferior to the others that one would be glad to regard it as spurious. This last is not mentioned in Pohl's catalogue, though, by an odd coincidence, Pohl 23 is also in E♭. See, in addition, the catalogues of Breitkopf and Härtel.

his early quartets. Like Beethoven, in later times, he approached
the orchestra with some degree of hesitation, and until he had
mastered its technique, subdued his exuberant invention to
the requirements of his medium. The first symphony, that in
B♭, Op. 1, No. 5, is simply an exercise in C. P. E. Bach's least
successful manner: the only one, perhaps, among all Haydn's
works in which the character of the Zopf is predominant. It
opens with a bustling Allegro, which, for all its appearance of
vigour, has really nothing to say except scale-passages, or
sequences, or assertions, of some rudimentary harmonic progression : e. g.—

and again, the principal theme of the second subject :—

The Andante is more melodious, but it is spoiled by needless
italics :—

while the Finale—

is in lamentable contrast to that quoted above from the quartet in G major. In the 'Lukavec' symphony there is more life, the music has something of its composer's habitual serenity and good-humour, yet even here we feel that he is not fully at his ease, that he is still hampered by customary methods and conventional turns of phrase. But with *Le Midi*, the autograph of which is now in the library at Eisenstadt, he definitely broke away and declared his freedom. Possibly he was stimulated by his new office, possibly encouraged by his orchestra of picked virtuosi; at any rate, he turned his experience to good account in this finest and most imaginative of his early symphonic writings. The opening Allegro, prefaced by a short dignified Introduction, is wonderfully vigorous and forcible, its themes well contrasted, its development section varied and adventurous, its orchestration riper than any that the world had hitherto known. Indeed, through the entire work the instruments are treated with remarkable individuality: the parts for violin and violoncello are as salient as in a quartet, the oboes in the opening movement and the flutes in the adagio are counterpoised with a nice sense of discrimination; in the Trio of the minuet even the double-bass has its obbligato. There is no longer any question of straitened resources or of an enforced economy of ideas: every page is interesting and every melody significant. A particularly characteristic number is the dramatic recitative which leads into the slow movement: in form, perhaps, borrowed from Bach's second sonata, but in tone and feeling essentially Haydn's own. It is too long to quote, but its concluding bars may serve to illustrate that power of emotional expression

which, ten years later, he exhibited even more nobly in his
G major quartet [1] :—

Having thus brought all his forces into line Haydn maintained, during the next twenty years, a steady advance : writing almost continuously, gaining in facility and experience, and producing work after work not less remarkable for its variety of topic than for its evenness of quality. It is unnecessary to attempt here a detailed description of these numerous compositions; the work has been admirably accomplished by Dr. Pohl[1], and the general character of Haydn's music, with which alone we are concerned, will be more appropriately summed up in the next chapter. But one important point remains for consideration :—the change which he effected in serious instrumental composition by the introduction of the folk-song. We have already noted the conditions under which this practice arose[2] : it follows now to supplement that account with a few lines of example and illustration.

As far back as 1755 Haydn had shown his nationality by an occasional use of Slavonic rhythms and cadences : in his Eisen-

---

[1] See Pohl, vol. ii. p. 255 et seq.   [2] See above, p. 80.

stadt period these become so frequent as to be almost habitual. From no other source could he have devised the metres which, to mention a few instances alone, open the first movements of the quartets, Op. 9, Nos. 1 and 2; the Finale of Op. 17, No. 1, and all four movements of Op. 20, No. 3. But beside these indirect similarities he soon began to employ the actual songs and dances of the Croatian colony, in the heart of which he lived [1]. The symphony in D major (Haydn's catalogue, No. 4) sets out with the measure of the Kolo, a native dance of the South Slavonic peasants; the Cassation in G (1765) founds its first movement on a Croatian drinking-song; the Trio of the A major symphony (Haydn's catalogue, No. 11) on a Croatian ballad. The first Allegro of the quartet in D major, Op. 17, No. 6, the Finale of that in E♭, Op. 20, No. 1, the 'Rondo à l'Hongrie' of the third piano concerto, afford instances equally striking; and the list may be extended without a break through the compositions of Haydn's entire life [2]. It may be added that many of these melodies, which as folk-songs can be named and identified, are precisely those which a critic would select as specially characteristic of Haydn's maturer style. From 1762 onwards, his music is more and more saturated with their influence; he is in such close and intimate sympathy with them that, when he borrows, it is only as though he were coming by his own.

During the first twenty years of his Eisenstadt period he enjoyed, in his artistic realm, a position of undisputed supremacy. His fame was instant and widespread, his works were rapidly published and extensively circulated; in Vienna and Nuremberg, in Berlin and Frankfort, in Paris and Amsterdam and London, he was welcomed as an acknowledged leader. Bach wrote to him from Hamburg, 'You are the only musician

[1] The whole question is exhaustively discussed in Dr. Kuhač's monograph, 'Joseph Haydn and the Croatian Popular Songs': Agram, 1880. See also his collection of the South Slavonic Folk-songs: Agram, 1878–81.

[2] See in particular the Salomon Symphony in E♭, 'mit dem Paukenwirbel,' every movement of which is founded on a Croatian folk-song.

who understands me'; and, indeed, the development of Bach's later works, from the Reprise-Sonaten onwards, very probably owes something to his influence. 'He was the first man,' said the young Mozart, 'who taught me how to write a quartet': and though here again the master was not too proud to accept instruction from his pupil the relation between them was never forgotten. Austria called him 'der Liebling unserer Nation'; Yriarte, in Spain, devoted to him a canto of eloquent panegyric [1]; the King of Prussia sent him a commission from Potzdam, the Archduke Paul one from St. Petersburg. The same causes which kindled this blaze of contemporary reputation still avail to throw the central light of the time on his figure. He was famous not through idle fashion or caprice, but because in his work the whole progress of instrumental music was involved.

But to complete the record of events a brief mention must be made of the work accomplished, during these two decades, by other composers. Most of these attained no higher level than that of a respectable mediocrity, many are as unimportant as the poets of the Dunciad, and they are best left in the darkness from which only a malicious satirist would wish to drag them. Four men, however, stand out as honourable exceptions, not because much of their work has survived, but because they were at the time of some serious account, and bestowed their talents upon a better object than fulsome dedications and empty platitudes. The earliest of these was the Belgian Gossec (1733–1829) who published his first concerted piece in 1754—the year before Haydn's visit to Weinzirl—and is therefore sometimes described as the inventor of the Symphony. This title, of course, cannot be maintained. The Symphony was not invented; it grew by natural evolution from overtures and works for the chamber, as these in their turn grew from fanfares, and primitive dance-tunes, and the madrigals which were 'apt for viols and voices.' If we take the term in its loose

[1] See *La Musica*, canto v (1779).

eighteenth-century sense there were hundreds of symphonies before Gossec : if in its modern distinctive sense it becomes inapplicable. But though it is an historical error to fix any arbitrary point of inception, we may assign to Gossec a creditable place in the progress and development of the form. He was led to it, we are told, by observing the poverty of Rameau's operatic overtures ; and having some melodic invention and a remarkable sense of orchestral colour he succeeded in producing a series of works, some for full band, some for smaller combinations, which are not without historical interest and value.   The symphony called *La Chasse* was long popular in Paris, so were the string quartets which he began to publish in 1759 ; and he at least deserves our recognition for those experiments in scoring which presaged, and to some extent anticipated, the work of Berlioz.   Next to him follows Michael Haydn (1737–1806), who, though the bulk of his work was written for the Church, left his mark on instrumental music with about thirty symphonies and a number of smaller concerted pieces.   His best compositions, in this kind, are the three symphonies published in 1785, which contain some interesting experiments in the Rondo-form, and the fine string quintet in C which was long regarded as a work of his brother [1].   The third in order is Karl Ditters von Dittersdorf, an admirable violinist, who in later days used to lead at Vienna the quartet in which Haydn played second violin and Mozart viola.   He also is best known as a writer of vocal music, but his pleasant transparent style shows to good advantage on the strings, and he has the distinction of being the only Austrian composer, outside the great names, whose chamber work is still remembered and performed.

Last and most notable is Luigi Boccherini (1743–1805), a gifted and prolific composer who wrote no less than 366 instrumental works—125 of them string quintets. He was a famous violoncello-player, and after a very successful début in

---

[1] It is actually printed in some editions of Joseph Haydn as Op. 88.

Paris was appointed *virtuoso di camera* to the Spanish Infante, Don Luis. In 1785 he accepted the office of Chamber-musician to Frederick William II, of Prussia; on whose death his fortunes rapidly declined into an old age of extreme poverty. As nearly three hundred of his compositions were published during his lifetime it is difficult to understand the neglect of his later days: even the proverbial fickleness of public favour is hardly sufficient to account for so sheer a downfall. His work, in its slender and superficial kind, has real merit. The strings, and particularly the violoncello, are treated with sympathy and insight; the thought, though never deep or recondite, is usually simple, graceful and melodious ; the structure fairly exemplifies the traditions of the time. Indeed, there may be noted here a point of some historical interest. His earlier compositions (e. g. Op. 4) are all written in the old Binary forms which he had learned from his Italian masters: after he had found opportunity of studying Haydn he widens and organizes his design until, by Op. 11, the 'three-canto' form is firmly established.

There can be no doubt that he was influenced by Haydn in other respects beside structure. For obvious reasons he could not imitate his melody : but he evidently followed his scheme of decoration, and even copied, or at any rate reproduced, some of his most characteristic effects of colour. Thus, the Andante of Haydn's quartet in F (Op. 3, No. 5) begins as follows :—

and the Minuet of Boccherini's quintet in E as follows:—

Boccherini's texture is a little more elaborate, his colour, with the second violin shimmering across the melody, is a little softer and more sensuous, but in this, as in other similar instances, the method is that of Haydn.

It was no small matter to have dominated for twenty years the whole course of instrumental music throughout Europe, to have been not only the best-known and best-loved of all composers, but the master whose direction the others inevitably followed. And the man who did this was a self-taught peasant, simple, modest and retiring, with no knowledge of men and cities, no sense of ambition or intrigue, and not even that executive brilliance in which artists at the time found their readiest means of public display. Clad in a servant's livery, paid with a servant's wages, he gave his work to his patron and reaped in the opportunity of service his best reward. 'My Prince was always satisfied with my work,' he says, and again, with even greater *naïveté*, ' I was cut off from the world, there was no one to confuse or torment me, and I was forced to become original.' Critics at the present day profess to regard his music as old-fashioned; it seems thin and quiet beside our loaded scores and our thundering orchestras; but his fashion has outlasted many changes and will outlast many more. If his work ever becomes antiquated it will be not because we have advanced beyond it, but because our perceptions will have grown too blunted to do it justice : the craftsmanship is as delicate as that of a miniature, and as exquisite in colour and line. So long as men take delight in pure melody, in transparent style, and in a fancy alert, sensitive and sincere, so long is his place in the history of the art assured. Throughout its entire range there are few men to whom we owe a deeper gratitude : there is none for whom we feel a more intimate and personal affection.

CHAPTER IX

THE INSTRUMENTAL FORMS (*continued*)

HAYDN AND MOZART

The history of every art shows a continuous interaction between form and content. In their primitive origin they are twin-born :—the elk scratched on the cavern-wall, the praise of heroes by the camp-fire,—indeed, so close is the fusion between expression and symbol that the earliest music, we are told, is a cry and the earliest alphabet a row of pictures. But when art begins to grow self-conscious and intentional there gradually arises a discrimination between two ideals, and the artist finds himself confronted with a double problem : what is fittest to say, and what is the fittest manner of saying it. The balance between these two is rarely attained, and even when attained, commonly marks no more than a moment of unstable equilibrium : as a rule, one generation is mainly occupied with questions of design, another takes up the scheme and brings new emotional force to bear upon it, and thus the old outlines stretch and waver, the old rules become inadequate, and the form itself, grown more flexible through a fuller vitality, once more asserts its claim and attains a fuller organization. The Romantic drama follows upon the Classical, and in its turn gives birth to a fresh technique of dramatic construction : Schumann succeeds to Beethoven and Brahms to Schumann : throughout all artistic history we can trace these shifting alternations ; not, of course, set against each other in crude antithesis—as though one generation cared nothing for content and another nothing for form—but marked by varying degrees of emphasis or preference which are sufficient to indicate their respective characters.   The very few men whose work we can regard as final, Dante, for example, or Palestrina, stand outside the line of succession like a Cardinal Archbishop in a family-tree; the inheritors, not the transmittors, of ancestral virtues. Indeed, since our western scale was established there has been but one composer whose work is at once wholly perfect and vitally influential, and even J. S. Bach had to wait three-quarters of a century for recognition.

Now, by the year 1780, the year on which our last chapter closes, the structural types of sonata symphony and quartet had been as completely organized as the idiom of the time permitted. The genius of C. P. E. Bach, and still more that of Haydn, had so determined the general scheme that it seemed to require no further development until a fuller melodic or emotional content should press it to extend its bounds. For the next twenty years there is almost no structural modification at all: the plan remains practically uniform, and the whole advance is in architectural detail and embellishment.   Then, when the form could no longer bear the weight imposed upon it, came Beethoven who enlarged its base, widened its outlines, and gave it at once a new strength and a new beauty.

There is some significance in the fact that nearly all the most poetic compositions of Haydn and Mozart were produced after the year in which they first made personal acquaintance.   No doubt it may partly be explained by natural laws of growth and maturity, but in addition to this it is certain that they exercised on one another a strong and salutary influence.   There was no close tie of comradeship to connect them:—Mozart seems never to have visited Eisenstadt, Prince Esterhazy disliked Vienna and only brought his retinue there for a brief annual stay during the season :—but the admiration which each felt for the other was open and sincere.   Kozeluch, listening to a Haydn quartet, remarked in his dry sneering tone, 'I should never have written that passage in that way': 'nor I,' answered Mozart, 'neither of us would have had so good an idea.'

Haydn, when he accepted the most famous of musical dedications, turned to Leopold Mozart and said with genuine
emotion, 'I declare before God, as a man of honour, that your
son is the greatest composer of whom I have ever heard.'
From the time of their first meeting these two men may almost
be said to have worked in alliance. Vienna split round them
into cabals and parties: Joseph II was singular enough to
disapprove of Haydn, Salieri mean enough to intrigue against
Mozart, but amid all conflicts and rivalries they remained, like
the two princes of the Roman court, 'proximorum certaminibus
inconcussi.'

The whole career of Mozart impinges so closely on the
miraculous that to seek in it any precise relations of cause and
effect may well seem a needless pedantry. The musician who
wrote violin sonatas at seven and symphonies at eight[1], who
recalled, after twenty-four hours' lapse, a difference of half a
quarter of a tone, and who composed for a musical clock works
which are now used as virtuoso pieces for the organ, does not
appear very amenable to the laws which govern ordinary
humanity. Indeed, it is a matter of conjecture how and whence
he learned his first lessons of musical construction. His
teacher was, of course, Leopold Mozart; his models were
probably instrumental compositions of the Bachs, Jommelli,
Boccherini, and Stamitz, many of which were published in Paris
in 1763. At any rate, these early symphonies are little more
than boyish exercises in the prevalent style, bright, fresh and
sunny, foreshadowing even now that remarkable command of
rhythmic figure which was afterwards one of his distinguishing
characteristics, but in the main of biographical rather than
historical interest. The same may be said of his first string
quartet, written at Lodi in 1770—a tiny composition in three

---

[1] His first twelve sonatas were composed in Paris and London, 1763-4: his first
five symphonies in London and the Hague, 1764-5. It is worth noting that in the
third symphony he uses clarinets instead of oboes, and writes for them very much
as though they were akin to trumpets. See above, p. 45.

movements ending with the minuet [1]. That he found this
medium congenial we may infer from the fact that in the next
three years he wrote nine more works of the same kind, all
equally slight and unpretentious, all equally lucid and delicate
in style. The one most conspicuous achievement of these early
years was the string quintet which he wrote in Salzburg at the
beginning of 1768, about the time of his twelfth birthday,
a composition remarkable not only because it was larger in
scale and fuller in treatment than anything of the kind that
had ever appeared, but because Mozart himself thought so well
of it that, in 1780, he enlarged it into one of the noblest and
most masterly of his serenades [2].

We are told that he first made close acquaintance with
Haydn's work during a flying visit to Vienna in the summer
of 1773. At any rate, in August of that year, he wrote six
string quartets (K. 168–73) in which for the first time the
influence of Haydn is plainly apparent, and it is probably to
these that he specially referred when he spoke of him as his
master in quartet-writing. The Adagio of the third, which
begins :—

might well have come from Eisenstadt, and many other

---

[1] The Rondo, with which it now concludes, is far more mature in style and was
added later.
[2] The serenade for thirteen wind instruments, K. 361. It is interesting to
compare the treatment of the two works, especially in the Adagio.

instances could be quoted of similarity in phrase or treatment. Not, of course, that Mozart's individuality is in any way obscured or overlaid; but he was beginning to graduate in a higher school and to learn a lesson which Stamitz and Jommelli and even C. P. E. Bach had been unable to teach him. With these quartets we may mark the adolescence of his genius, and it is worth noting that immediately after them, on his return to Salzburg, he wrote his first really significant pianoforte concerto, the earliest true example of that form with which his name is most closely associated. To the same year is assigned the Symphony in G minor (K. 183), the poignant tone of which is totally unlike the gay irresponsible melody of Mozart's boyhood.

After 1774 there follows a curious gap in the history of Mozart's larger instrumental composition. No more symphonies until Paris (1778), no more string quartets until Vienna (1782); a few concertos, a few serenades[1] and divertimenti, make up the tale of a period which, in this field at any rate, is the least prolific of his career. It is possible, as Dr. Jahn suggests[2], that his growing discontent with his position at Salzburg and the increasing displeasure of the Archbishop, may have caused him to desist from writing works which would primarily be intended for performance at Court-concerts. Another hypothesis, that the symphonies of this period were composed *invita Minerva*, and afterwards destroyed, receives some confirmation from a passage in a letter of Leopold Mozart's (Sept. 24, 1778) which runs :—'When a thing does you no credit it is better forgotten. I have sent you back none of your symphonies because I feel sure that when you come to riper years and have a clearer judgement you will be glad to

---

[1] One of them being the famous Haffner Serenade, July 1776.

[2] Jahn, i. 298. But Dr. Jahn applies this remark solely to the absence of symphonies, and adds, 'most of the great serenades and concertos for violin and piano fall within these years': a statement which, except as regards the violin concerti, is not borne out either by the dates in Köchel or by those in Breitkopf and Härtel's edition.

forget them even if you are satisfied with them now.' In this outspoken assurance we may very likely find the solution of the problem.

At the same time the date of this letter is remarkable, for three months before it was written Mozart produced in Paris the finest symphonic work of his adolescence. He had gone there in the spring of 1778 hoping, it may be, for some permanent appointment or some commission like that which Gluck had received from the Académie, or at least for some renewal of the welcome which had greeted him on his earlier visit. At first he found more civility than assistance, and, in desperate need of patronage, was compelled to offer the Duc de Guines a concerto for flute and harp; two instruments which he particularly detested. But at the end of May, Le Gros asked him to write a symphony for the Concerts Spirituels, and in this opportunity he found compensation for many failures. He was obliged in some measure to adapt himself to his conditions. The orchestra prided itself on attack, and the composer was cautioned that he must lay special emphasis on the *premier coup d'archet.* There were to be no repeats: not because the Parisians could follow an exposition at a single hearing, but because they took no interest at all in construction and cared for nothing but epigrams in the dialogue. In a word, the whole composition was to be short, bright, and telling; not too recondite in thought, not too elaborate in treatment, not interposing too strong a personality between the players and the public. All these hints and restrictions Mozart good-naturedly accepted: began on a crashing unison, which was immediately received with applause, sprinkled his page with jests and phrases, and delicate effects of rhythm and scoring, played upon his hearers with every oratorical device and left them in the end convinced and satisfied[1]. The Paris symphony is, in

---

[1] After the first performance Le Gros complained that the Andante was too long and complex; whereupon Mozart withdrew it and substituted the exquisite Andantino which now appears in the current editions. 'Each is good of its kind,' he wrote to his father; 'on the whole I prefer the second.'

short, a brilliant and charming *pièce d'occasion,* perhaps the only true classic which was written throughout with an eye to practical requirements. Of course, Mozart was far too great an artist to degrade his work : there is not an unworthy bar from first to last ; but he seems to have treated the whole commission as a joke, and gleefully describes how he anticipated the points at which ' the audience would clap their hands.'

With the Paris symphony we may close the second period of Mozart's instrumental work. The three which he wrote at Salzburg, in 1779–80, are not particularly distinctive, though the third of them (' with forty violins and all the wind doubled ') had a great success in Vienna: in the winter of 1780 he was too fully occupied with *Idomeneo* to devote much time to other kinds of composition. Before entering upon the last decade of his career—the decade of his highest and most consummate achievement—it may be well to pause and consider what he brought to the alliance for which Haydn, through all these years, had been working in seclusion at Eisenstadt.

The catalogue of his writings, up to this time, includes thirty-four symphonies, thirty-one divertimenti and serenades, ten concertos for one or more claviers and eighteen for other instruments, two quintets and sixteen quartets for strings, one clavier trio, thirty violin sonatas, fifteen clavier sonatas, and a number of smaller pieces—variations, dances, and the like—both for solo instruments and for orchestra. Many of these are boyish efforts which it is no longer of any moment to discuss : the main historical interest begins with the six Viennese quartets of 1773, and continues through the various orchestral and chamber works which were written after that date. Apart from the concertos, which require a separate investigation, the reader cannot fail to be struck with the uniformity and even conventionality of the general structure. With hardly an exception the movements are of the orthodox number and kind ; not only is the main scheme of key-distribution invariable but

there are few incidental modulations; there is little development
of themes, little variation of treatment. Mozart was not
interested, as Haydn was, in problems of pure structure: he
mastered the form of the sonata as he mastered that of the fugue,
and no more thought of interfering with the one than the other.
It must be remembered that to call a scheme 'conventional'
merely means that it is accepted without question because it
happens to be current, and carries no implication as to its
inherent fitness or unfitness. It only becomes a term of reproach
when it suggests the unintelligent use of a method which has
served its purpose and has passed into the limbo of empty
ceremonial. Mozart found the established form sufficient for
his needs, and set himself to fill it with a most varied content
of melodic invention. In this respect his work may be
compared with a Greek drama. The Athenian audience knew
the plot from the beginning, for it followed the course of
a story with which they were already familiar: every one
expected that Clytemnestra would kill Agamemnon and that
Hercules would rescue Alcestis from the grave; but this only
allowed the attention to be more closely concentrated on portrayal of character and on beauty of verse and rhythm. So it
was with Mozart. He cared nothing that his construction ran
along familiar lines; indeed, he was writing for a generation which
could not have followed a more recondite scheme; he attains
his end by taste, by imagination, by warmth of colour, and
above all by that wonderful sanity and lucidity of style for
which among all composers he stands pre-eminent. The same
explanation may be given of another point on which he is often
held to be more open to criticism—his habit of detaching his
melodies and filling the interval with simple scale and harmonic
passages which do no more than emphasize a cadence or mark
a period. At a first hearing they often sound perfunctory, the
mere resource of indolence which is resting for a moment from
invention; but as we study more carefully we see that they are
really calculated, that they have the same purpose as the

Alberti bass or other such simple accompaniment figure on
which Mozart so often supports his melody. It was not
because he could write nothing better, for he was the greatest
master of polyphony between Bach and Brahms; it was not
because he was careless or impatient, or disdainful of his
art or his audience; the real reason is that he wished to
throw his high light on the melodies themselves, and that,
in the idiom of the time, this was the most natural way
of effecting his purpose. Take, for instance, the 'second
subject' theme from the Finale of the C major symphony
(K. 200):—

Here the second violin part is next to nothing, little more than
the blur of sound with which the tambura fills the accompaniment in a band of Slavonic peasants.   But its very insignificance is a point of art, for it leaves us free to give our whole
mind to the delightful swinging tune which courses above it.
No doubt a century of musical experience has taught us that
'to divide is not to take away': our delight in a melody of
Brahms is enhanced by the variety and ingenuity of its accompaniment or its context.   But it is no special pleading to point
out that the melodies of Mozart are sufficiently beautiful to
justify themselves, and that in relation to the history of the
time his treatment of them was inevitable.

A more disputable trait is his fondness for set phrases
and cadences:—the famous ' 6–4 followed by a shake on the
seventh,' the alternations of tonic and dominant which so often
constitute his opening theme.   The former of these is exactly
parallel to the use of stock-epithets in ballad or saga or epic:—
the swan's bath, the well-greaved Greeks, Hector of the
waving plume:—it is a *naïveté* of style accepted almost as
unthinkingly as the current conventions of accidence or syntax.

The latter, in any hands less skilful than Mozart's, would
inevitably risk monotony, and even with him does not always
succeed in avoiding it. Yet here it is only a superficial
criticism that condemns: the wonder rather is that Mozart
should have found so many different ways of stating this
simplest and most obvious of harmonic truths. It is a
sufficiently far cry from the almost crude juxtaposition of the
early symphony in C major (K. 162):—

to the more melodic opening of that in D major (K. 202):—

and from that again to the '*premier coup d'archet*' of the Paris symphony :—

There has been no other composer in the history of music who could move within so narrow a range of tonality, and repeat himself so seldom.

We have seen that Mozart visited Paris in 1778 with some hope of emancipating himself from the intolerable tyranny of Salzburg. He knew that there was no prospect of an independent career unless he could earn his living as a performer, and in order to lose no chances, gave concerts along the journey at Munich, Augsburg, and Mannheim. To these we owe the first six clavier sonatas (K. 279–84)[1] which he produced successively at these three cities, and probably also the six violin sonatas (K. 301–306) which he composed at Mannheim early in 1778. But a far more important result of his renewed interest in solo-playing is the development of the so-called 'Classical Concerto';—unquestionably his principal contribution to the history of instrumental forms. He was the first musician who ever played a clavier-concerto in public[2], he devoted to this kind of composition much of his most inspired work, and, what is more remarkable, he treated its construction with a freedom and an inventiveness wholly different from his usual acceptance of current methods.

The central idea of the Concerto,—the opposition between one or more solo instruments and a contrasting mass of larger volume and sonority,—has already been sufficiently indicated[3]. Its main problem is to dispose these unequal forces in such a manner as to secure for each its due measure of interest and beauty, to prevent the larger from being artificially subordinated, or the smaller absorbed through sheer weakness of tone. Somewhat the same problem confronts the operatic aria, which is, in a sense, a concerto for voice and orchestra: but the

---

[1] In a letter to his sister (Dec. 12, 1774) he speaks of some earlier clavier sonatas, but they are not in Köchel's catalogue.

[2] At the Tonkünstler-Societät, Vienna, April 3, 1781. See Pohl's *Haydn*, ii. 145.

[3] See vol. iv. pp. 161–4. See also Mr. D. F. Tovey's extremely interesting monograph on the Classical Concerto.

difficulty is here of less account, for the living voice has a special power of concentrating our attention, and of throwing its accompaniment into the background. This power is not equally shared by any instrument, *a fortiori* by any of those which are actually represented in the orchestral ranks, and it needs, therefore, a particularly acute sense of proportion and balance if the just relation is to be maintained. On the other hand, the concerto has its own peculiar opportunities. Though it is no more necessarily 'virtuoso-music' than a song is necessarily bravura, it may legitimately afford some scope for brilliance and dexterity, it can count on the soloist for a fuller and richer tone than that of any accompanying player, and, when written for a keyed instrument, has at its command a *timbre* different from those of strings or wind. It adds a new kind of protagonist to the play, a new kind of hero to the story; it holds our interest by tracing through event and circumstance the domination of a central character.

Such a principle is obviously compatible with almost any type of musical form, and hence it is that the early history of the name 'concerto' exhibits such a bewildering variety of usage [1]. The type, as established by Mozart, is a cross-texture with the old three-movement symphony for warp, and for woof the scheme of a solo with *ritornelli*; there is an opening Allegro in sonata-form, a short elegiac Andante or Adagio, and a light, loose-knit Finale, each of which is so organized as to set the solo-instrument and the accompanying 'tutti' in due balance and antithesis. Thus, in the opening Allegro, instead of mechanically repeating the Exposition Mozart gives its first statement as an orchestral *ritornello*, always in a designedly imperfect state of organization, and makes us wait for its full succession of themes and its full complement of keys until it is restated at the entry

---

[1] The Concerti published by Viadana, in 1603, are vocal pieces; those of Torelli are sonatas for two Violins and a Bass, accompanied by *ripieno* strings: some of J. S. Bach's are full Orchestral overtures in which the instruments, as Mr. Tovey says, 'split into whatever groups they please.'

of the soloist. In like manner each of the other two cantos is
introduced by the orchestra and elaborated by the solo player,
while toward the end of the Recapitulation the band stops and
then follows a short brilliant 'cadenza' (sometimes written by
the composer, sometimes left to the performer's improvisation),
after which, as in an operatic aria, a final *ritornello* brings the
piece to a close. In the elegiac movement, and still more in the
Rondo which by predilection Mozart employs for his Finale, there
is a wider freedom and range; sometimes the solo instrument
begins and the orchestra follows and corroborates it, sometimes
they alternate in passages of closer and more rapid dialogue,
but throughout all the main principle is the same—a basis of
symphonic structure traversed and cross-cut by this conflict
of unequal masses.

Mozart's greatest concerti were composed after 1781, but
even from these earlier works we may gain a clear insight into
his method. Among them the most important are the six violin
concerti written in 1775–6, and the six for one or more pianofortes which range in date from 1773 to 1780. As compared
with his symphonies or serenades they are remarkably rich in
themes and remarkably free and flexible in handling; it is no
unusual matter that a section should contain two or three
distinct melodies; indeed, however many are given to the *ritornello* the soloist nearly always receives at least one in addition ;
the range of keys is comparatively wide, the modulations are
often striking and sometimes unexpected. A treatise might be
written on the skill with which, especially in the opening 'tutti,'
Mozart subordinates the interest of the orchestral forces without
suppressing it : nothing short of actual presentation could do
justice to the beauty of the tunes, and the fitness of their
accompaniment. A noticeable point of pure structure is his
treatment of the Rondo-form, which he raises to a higher level
of organization by repeating the first episode, towards the end
of the movement, in the tonic key ; thus precisely anticipating
a constructive idea which is usually though inaccurately ascribed

to Beethoven[1]. But, apart from all technicalities, it is impossible to study these works without finding in them a fullness and mastery of detail to which even the best of his contemporary work does not otherwise attain. It is the Mozart of the early concertos, rather than the Mozart of the early symphonies and quartets, to whom we owe the imperishable masterpieces of the Viennese period and the influence which helped to mould successively the style of Haydn, of Beethoven, and of Schubert.

We have no actual record of the first meeting between Haydn and Mozart; but there can be no doubt that it occurred some time in the winter of 1781-2. The Grand Duke Paul and his wife had come to pay a ceremonial visit to the Emperor, a series of musical festivities was organized in their honour, and it was in the course of these that Haydn superintended the first performance of his ' Russian ' quartets (Op. 33) and that Mozart was set to his famous contest of skill with Muzio Clementi. The two men were widely different in state and fortune : the one protected by his office at Eisenstadt, the other recently emancipated from the galling servitude of Salzburg, and paying for his freedom by sheer poverty : the one saved from all petty anxieties, composing as the mood dictated and sure of a sympathetic hearing among his own people, the other compelled to seek for pupils, to perform at concerts, and to wear out hope and patience in the vain quest of an appointment worthy of his powers[2]. Nor was the distinction less

---

[1] Examples in which ' Beethoven's ' form is anticipated are the Finales of the Pianoforte Concertos in B♭ (K. 238), F (K. 242), C (K. 246), and E♭ (K. 365). A more remarkable experiment is that of the Pianoforte Concerto in E♭ (K. 271), the Rondo of which contains an interpolated Minuet, and recapitulates the second episode instead of the first.

[2] After Mozart's marriage, in 1782, this necessity became even more pressing. We have his own statement that, in 1784, he played at twenty-two concerts within six weeks, and if the number decreased later it was less from relief of need than from lack of opportunity. His only appointment in Vienna was the post of Kammermusiker to Joseph II, with a salary of £80 a year :—' too much for what I do, too little for what I could do,' as he wrote bitterly across the first quittance.

marked between their characters : Haydn, simple and easy-going, untravelled, inexperienced in life and manners, full of a racy peasant humour, yet on occasion holding himself with firmness and dignity: Mozart, rapid, alert, mercurial, varying from the deepest depression to the wildest spirits [1], witty, quick-tempered, often indiscreet of speech, but possessed of that personal charm which more than atones for indiscretion. Yet one point at least they had in common ; a high reverence for their art and an unfaltering loyalty to its pursuit.   Haydn brooked no interference even from Prince Esterhazy: ' Your Highness,' he once said in answer to an ill-timed criticism, 'this is my business.'   And Mozart, when Hoffmeister broke off a commission with the words, ' Write more popularly or I can neither print nor pay for anything more of yours,' blazed out in a flash of defiance, ' Then may the devil take me but I will write nothing more and go hungry.'

It is not altogether profitable to draw general comparisons between their styles of composition. We learn little from Dittersdorf's remark, that Haydn is like Gellert, Mozart like Klopstock, nor much more from the Emperor Joseph's reply, that Mozart is like a Parisian snuff-box, Haydn like one of London manufacture. It may perhaps be suggested that, of the two, Haydn's expression is a little more *naïf* and ingenuous, that whether he feels lightly or deeply he always speaks his mind without reticence, without modification, with no casting about for phrases ; while Mozart, to whom perfection of finish was as a second nature, is most concerned to present his thought in its most exquisite shape, and, whether he feels lightly or deeply, polishes his sentence until it shines like an epigram. Thus, for example, the Finale of Haydn's quartet in G, Op. 33, No. 5, is an air for variations which begins as follows :—

---

[1] A good example of the latter may be seen in the MS. of the Horn Concerto written in 1782 for Leutgeb, of Salzburg. It is scrawled all over with the most extravagant jests and mock-directions :—' A lei Signor Asino . . . ma intoni almeno una (at a repeated high note) . . . ah termina ti prego,' and so on.

while that of Mozart's, in D minor (K. 421), written in the next year, turns to more artistic account a very similar theme :—

On the other hand, Haydn is often the more poignant of the two. It was, for instance, a common idiom of the time to open a movement with an incisive phrase in unison, and to follow this immediately by a strongly opposed answer in rich or striking harmony. Mozart is usually contented with the pure delight of the contrast, as in the Trio of the G major quartet (K. 387):—

Haydn strikes with it a note of tragedy, as in that of the C major quartet, Op. 54, No. 2 :—

Nor does this hold good only during the earlier days of their intercourse. Haydn's Salomon symphonies are frank and ingenuous as ever, and even such a magnificent outburst of passion as Mozart's G minor quintet is not more remarkable for its depth of feeling than for its consummate mastery of technical resource.

But it is of greater moment that we should note some of the ways in which those two artists stimulated each other. And first, the very catalogue of names and dates is significant. Between 1781 and 1791 Mozart wrote his ten best string quartets[1], the seven piano trios[2], the two piano quartets[3], the piano quintet[4], the seven last and finest of his symphonies[5], his last seventeen piano concertos[6], including those in D minor (K. 466), A major (K. 488), and C major (K. 503), the great string quintets[7], the clarinet quintet, and the clarinet concerto[8]. During the same period, Haydn wrote twenty-four symphonies, including the twelve for Paris[9], the eighteen string quartets from Op. 50 to Op. 64[10], and, what is more noticeable, the earliest of his concerted works for the pianoforte which it has been thought suitable to republish[11]. To these, for the sake

[1] Six dedicated to Haydn, 1782-5; the single quartet in D major, 1786; three dedicated to the King of Prussia, 1786 and 1790.

[2] The first in 1782, the others in 1786-8.

[3] G minor, 1785; E♭ major, 1786. They were to have formed part of a set of six, but Hoffmeister stopped publication on the ground that they were too difficult.

[4] Written for piano and wind in 1784. ' I regard it,' said Mozart, ' as one of my best works.'

[5] Haffner, 1782; the two Linz symphonies, 1783; the Prague Symphony, 1786; the last three, 1788.

[6] Produced successively at Mozart's concerts in Vienna from the winter of 1782-3 to that of 1790-1.

[7] The C minor, adapted from a serenade, 1782 ; the others, written in 1787, 1790, and 1791.

[8] Both written for Stadler : in 1789 and 1791 respectively.

[9] Commissioned for the *Concerts Spirituels* in 1784 : the first six, written in 1784-6, the last (of which only five can be identified), 1787-90. The so-called ' Oxford Symphony ' is one of this last set.

[10] Op. 50 (dedicated to the King of Prussia), 1784-7; Op. 54, 1789; Op. 55, 1789 ; Op. 64, 1790.

[11] The first fifteen clavier trios (excluding the four early efforts) were written in 1785, 1788-9, and 1790. The early piano-concerto in F major (1771) was

of completeness, may be added the chief instrumental works composed by Haydn after his departure for England in 1790 : the twelve Salomon symphonies [1], the string quartets from Op. 71 to Op. 103 [2], and a considerable number of solo and concerted pieces for the clavier [3]. It is not by multitude alone that this list challenges attention. If we except some of Haydn's early quartets, the Paris Symphony, and a few of Mozart's early concerti and sonatas, we shall find in it all the pure instrumental compositions of both masters which still form an efficient part of our musical inheritance.

The interrelation between them is not so well illustrated by similarities of phrase as by more general similarities of idea and method. It is true that many examples might be found of melodies which, on internal evidence, a critic would hesitate to assign, as, for instance, the following :—

printed by Le Duc in Paris ; but the only one of Haydn's piano-concerti, which is at present currently accessible, is that in D major, which was written, evidently under the stimulus of Mozart, in 1784. Pohl mentions another in G major, printed ' in London, Paris, and Amsterdam.' the date of which is 1785.

[1] The first six in 1791-2 : the last six in 1793-5.

[2] Op. 71 and Op. 74, in 1793 ; Op. 76, in 1797 ; Op. 77, in 1797-8 ; Op. 103, left unfinished at Haydn's death.

[3] It is not at present possible to assign all these to their precise order of composition. The fine ' Andante with variations ' in F minor was written between the dates of Haydn's two visits to London, i. e. between 1792 and 1794 ; and the last eleven clavier-trios were all published after 1795. It may be remembered that Haydn's closing years were mainly occupied with *The Creation* and *The Seasons*.

but we feel instinctively that such examples are not of the
highest relevance, and that, in such a question as this, theme
is of less account than treatment. Far more striking is the
first of the two Linz symphonies, that in C major (K. 425).
The Adagio introduction, the characterization of the minuet,
the counterpoint of the finale, are all saturated with Haydn;
and so, to take widely divergent instances, are the finale of the
D major quartet (K. 499), and the opening movement of the
symphony in E♭ major (K. 543). On the other hand Haydn,
though, as an older man, he naturally adapted himself more
slowly to a change of style, seems unquestionably to have
learned from Mozart's music a fuller and rounder tone, a wider
range in development of themes, and a greater freedom in the
combination of rhythmic figures. Such a passage as the following (from the quartet in B minor: Op. 64, No. 2):—

is not to be found in his earlier work, where the part-writing, as a rule, is either formally contrapuntal or determined by the simplest considerations of harmonic mass: while in his larger use of episodes and in his growing sense of orchestral colour he follows, with a somewhat uncertain tread, the direction and leadership of his comrade.

Yet it would be erroneous to suppose that either of them in any real sense dominated the other. Each maintains throughout his own individuality of character, his own sense of beauty and fitness: their mutual debt was no more than that of Addison and Steele, the intercommunication of a method which each could employ for his appropriate end. Their most distinctive tunes are not more widely dissimilar than are their ideas of humour, of pathos, of the whole emotional range which it is one function of music to express. But in their treatment of the instrumental forms we can trace, in some measure, the working of a common purpose, and this it now follows that we should consider in detail.

It has already been said that from 1781 the main structural outlines remain unchanged until the time of Beethoven. The number of movements, their general character, their schemes of key-relationship were uniformly accepted by a working convention, and the composer claimed little option except to determine how often he should employ the 'three-canto' form, and whether the minuet should follow or precede the adagio. But it is not true that all cruciform churches are built in the same style; and within these outlines there was plenty of scope for architectural variety and invention:—the relative length and importance of the subjects, their rhythm and stanza, their treatment in the development section, the degree of exactitude in their ultimate restatement, and in a hundred other points which belong rather to the content of the work than to its form in the strict and technical sense. And here we may begin by noting a curious touch of atavism, a survival from an earlier stage of organization, which appears not infrequently among the compositions of this period. The 'first subject and transition' of the normal Sonata-form follow somewhat the same method of phraseology and modulation as the first half of the old Binary movement, and the correspondence is specially close when, as often happens with Haydn and Mozart, the transition ends with a full-close in the dominant key. And just as the old Binary movement then proceeded to assert in the dominant the initial theme of the piece, so in a certain number of cases Haydn and Mozart allow the second subject to set out with the same melody as the first, thus contrasting the two main centres of the exposition in key alone. As a rule this device appears rather meagre and parsimonious, e. g. in Mozart's B♭ piano-trio, and in the finale of Haydn's 'Rasirmesser' quartet: it becomes more effective if, on its reappearance, the theme is varied or modified or subordinated to some striking counter-subject, as, for example, in the very ingenious ' Vivace assai ' of Haydn's B♭ quartet, Op. 55, No. 3. But though, as Beethoven abundantly testifies, some recurrence of phrase in the exposition aids to organize and unify the whole canto, we feel that the opening of the second subject is not the most fitting place for it; that at so sensitive a crisis in the plot we need the inter-vention of a new character.

As a general rule, Mozart's expositions are richer in melodic invention than Haydn's. Not only does he make each of the two principal themes essentially tuneful, but he follows the second with a retinue of episodes and cadence-phrases, which atone for their moments of ceremonial formality by passages of admirable beauty and significance. A famous example is the first movement of the Jupiter symphony; others, not less remarkable, may be found in almost any of the pianoforte concertos, where the predominance of the soloist is nearly always marked by a peculiar lavishness of theme and idea. Haydn weaves with fewer strands. In his quartet-writing he is often content with a single chief melody : even in the Paris symphonies his second subject is more frequently a series of interconnected phrases than an organized melodic stanza. When he writes a great tune it touches a deeper emotion than any of Mozart's [1], but he does so more rarely and with a more sparing hand.

It is, however, in point of thematic treatment that the com-position of this period is most noticeable. 'The working-out section,' as Dr. Jahn says [2], 'is the centre of gravity ': the pivot on which turns the main structural interest of the move-ment. In sonatas and other smaller pieces it is still somewhat light and perfunctory ; at most it never approaches the limitless

---

[1] The best instances are late : e. g. the Andante of the seventh Salomon symphony, and the slow movements of the quartets in C, Op. 76, No. 3 ; and F, Op. 77, No. 2. [2] Jahn, *Mozart*, iii. 10.

opulence of Beethoven, but as a stage in the development of
the musical idea its importance can hardly be overestimated.
In every symphony, in every concerto, in every quartet there
are some differences of method, the intrigue is never precisely
repeated, the adventures never recur in the same shape.
Sometimes the section is built on a single theme, sometimes on
two or three in succession: in one instance the subjects of
the exposition suffice, in another they are combined with new
subordinate episodes; now the phrases are bandied in loose
alternate dialogue, now compressed into the closest of polyphonic textures: there is no device germane to the idiom of
the time which is not employed to add variety or to heighten
interest.   We may take an illustration from the first movement
of Mozart's G minor quintet.   Its exposition is built mainly
on two themes: the one a charming little stanza with a rising
triad and a fluctuating downward scale:—

the other a broad expressive melody, which begins as
follows:—

Through the development section Mozart treats these successively, the first in loose texture, the second in close polyphonic imitation:—

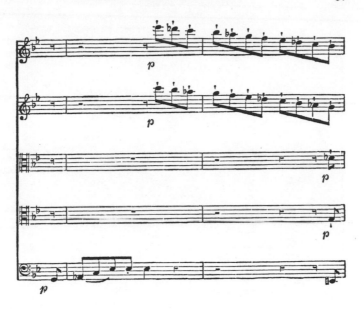

Apart from the wonderful drawing of this passage, and apart
from its deeper qualities of eloquence and passion, it well
exemplifies that delight in pure colour which is characteristic of
the later eighteenth century. Some indications of this have
already been observed in the music of C. P. E. Bach (who, it
may be remembered, was living and composing up to 1788),
but Bach's range is narrower and his command of resource
weaker than that of Mozart and Haydn. Yet in this respect
also, the methods of the two Viennese composers are different.
Haydn usually makes his richest point of colour by sheer, abrupt
modulation, as, for instance, in the Largo of his quartet in
G minor, Op. 74, No. 3[1]; Mozart by iridescent chromatic
motion within the limits of a clearly defined harmonic sequence.
The one, in short, takes a whimsical pleasure in an effect of
sudden surprise; the other prefers to charm by the richness and
transparence of the colour itself.

Yet it is on a point of colour that Mozart has most directly
challenged critical opinion. The famous introduction to the
C major quartet was an enigma in his own day, it remains an
enigma in ours. Technically, no doubt, it is easy of explanation:

[1] See also the Fantasia of his quartet in E♭, Op. 76, No. 6.

it aims, for once, at obscuring tonality, in order that the key
when established may stand more salient by contrast; it effects
this by playing upon two notes which are, for many purposes,
harmonically interchangeable. But the direct result is a false
relation[1] which, even after a century of experience, it is easier to
understand than to enjoy, and of which our safest judgement is the
verdict of Haydn, that 'if Mozart wrote thus he must have done
so with good reason.' Far too much coil has been raised over
a few bars which, whether we like them or not, are evidently
intentional, and of which the momentary harshness only
enhances our pleasure in the radiant melody that follows them.

Such, however, was not the attitude of contemporary Vienna.
Sarti convicted the passage of barbarism, Count Grassalcovich
tore up the parts, as Romberg afterwards did to those of the
first Rasoumoffsky; even the publisher's reader sent back the
manuscript with sarcastic annotations about its 'obvious mis-
prints.' The fact is that Mozart was beginning to employ an
idiom which stood wholly out of relation to that in customary
use, and he was met with that unintelligent persecution which
is often the destiny of the artistic pioneer. When he produced
a new concerto at the Tonkünstler-Societät his own share in the
performance gained him respectful attention and applause:
when the charm of his personality was withdrawn Vienna turned
its back on his work and preferred the empty commonplaces of
Vanhall. and Martin and Kozeluch and Adalbert Gyrowetz,
whose symphonies 'were much admired at the. Imperial
concerts.' Indeed, we meet with Gyrowetz at every turn of
the story. Salomon engaged him for the Hanover Square
Rooms, where public taste had been formed by a dozen years
of J. C. Bach and Abel; Paris so confused his work with
Haydn's that he was compelled to distinguish them by an
action for copyright; and in Vienna his compositions won
a popular success which they fully merited by their neatness,

---

[1] The opening triad gives us the erroneous impression that the key is A♭ major,
an impression somewhat rudely dispelled by the A♮ of the first violin.

their facility, and their entire lack of ideas. No doubt there were other less creditable reasons at work. The Augarten was as full of intrigue as a Byzantine court; the theatres bore a record of dishonesty from Affligio to Schikaneder; the great virtuosi, like Stadler, too often showed themselves incapable of common honesty or gratitude. But Mozart's genius was not to be repressed by discouragement. Throughout these years of poverty and misrepresentation he maintained his ideal untarnished, holding to his art through good report and evil report, delivering with each successive number a fuller, deeper message, until he found his reward in that supreme achievement of eighteenth-century instrumental music, the G minor symphony.

It has been called his ' swan-song,' and though he wrote fine music after it he wrote none more fine. Even the magnificent counterpoint of the Jupiter is cold beside this delicate and tender colouring, exquisite in tone, perfect in phrase, touched with pathos and humour and a love of all things gentle and beautiful, turning by divine alchemy its very sorrows into fragrance and delight. It is of the art which neither age can wither nor custom stale, it is as fresh to-day as when the ink was wet on its page; so long as the joy of music remains so long will it carry from generation to generation its angelic youth and immortality.

With this work we may fitly conclude our survey of Mozart's instrumental composition. It follows to describe briefly the career of Haydn from that day in December 1790 when he bade farewell to his friend for the last time and set out upon the conquest of London. He was then fifty-eight years of age, he knew no word of English, and he had never been farther than Lukavec from his native village. But Salomon's offer came at an appropriate moment, for the Eisenstadt Kapelle had, on the death of Prince Esterhazy, been recently disbanded; its terms were sufficiently liberal [1], and it brought

---

[1] On the occasion of his first visit he received £500 for six symphonies, and £200 for twenty smaller works, besides a benefit concert which brought him about £350. For a complete account of his stay in this country the reader should consult Dr. Pohl's admirable volume, *Mozart und Haydn in London*.

with it the assurance of a cordial welcome. Indeed, the highest expectations were far surpassed by the event. Haydn's two visits to this country—in 1791-2 and in 1794-5—were of the nature of a triumphal progress; his London audiences acclaimed him with enthusiasm; Oxford awoke from academic slumbers to decorate him with an honorary degree [1]; and the *Morning Chronicle*, that accredited organ of wit and fashion, exhausted its fullest eloquence upon his 'agitating modulations' and the captivating quality of his 'larmoyant passages.'

The twelve symphonies which he wrote for Salomon are not only the greatest of his orchestral works, but those also in which we can most clearly trace the effect of his intercourse with Mozart. Dr. Pohl specially notes the influence of the Jupiter symphony both in the richer orchestration and in the freer use of episode and incident. Nor is the debt less evident in the later string-quartets, composed from 1793 onwards, especially in the two noble examples with which his chamber-music attained its consummation. Here, for instance, is a passage from the quartet in F major, Op. 77, No. 2, the colour of which is more in Mozart's manner than in Haydn's :—

[1] July 6-8, 1791. Haydn composed a symphony for the occasion, but as there was insufficient time for rehearsal, he substituted that in G major, from the second set written for Paris, with which the band was already familiar. It is now commonly known as the 'Oxford Symphony.'

Yet in many ways these last works are among his most distinctive. The minuets, far different from Mozart's courtly dance-measures, have all his old rustic drollery and humour, the rhythms have all his old incisiveness of touch, the folk-tunes that he loved grow thick along the wayside, the melodies of his own sowing are unmistakeable in hue and shapeliness. And the music is all suffused with a sense of mellowness and maturity, of long experience and an old age honourably won ; it is too serene for passion, too wise for sadness, too single-hearted for regret; it has learned the lesson of life and will question its fate no further. When the French attacked Vienna, in 1809, a shot fell near his house, and his servants in terror fled to his room for protection. 'Children,' he said, ' there is no need to be frightened : no harm can happen to you while Haydn is by.' It is not a fantasy of interpretation which bids us find in his music the quiet unquestioning confidence of one who, throughout his seven and seventy years, remained ' in wit a man, simplicity a child.'

CHAPTER X

THE INSTRUMENTAL FORMS (*continued*)

BEETHOVEN

In studying Haydn's chamber-music we are often surprised by a note of presage, a hint or suggestion, not yet wholly articulate, which seems to be waiting for corroboration or fulfilment. During the middle period of his life it was, indeed, a matter of occasional conjecture on whom the mantle of his inspiration would fall. Of his Eisenstadt pupils none was sufficient to wear it: Pleyel, a meritorious composer, never redeemed the promise of his early years [1], the two Webers were amateurs whose reputation has long been eclipsed by that of their younger brother, the rest are hardly known to us even by name. According to the common expectation of human life he might well have looked to Mozart for the continuance and completion of his work : this hope was extinguished by Mozart's death in 1791. Thus when, in the course of the next summer, he started to return homeward from his first London visit he bore with him the sorrow not only of a personal bereavement, but of a loss to Art which appeared, at the time, wholly irreparable.

On the way back he broke his journey at Bonn, and, while there, good-naturedly consented to look over a cantata recently written by the sub-organist of the Elector's Chapel. Interested

---

[1] 'Some quartets have just appeared by a man named Pleyel: he is a pupil of Joseph Haydn. If you do not already know them try to get them, it is worth your while. They are very well and pleasantly written and give evidence of his master. Well and happy will it be for music if Pleyel is ready in due time to take Haydn's place for us.'—Mozart : letter to his father, April 24, 1784.

in the work he made enquiries about its composer; learned that his name was van Beethoven, that he was the son of a tenor in the Chapel choir, that his master, Neefe, spoke highly of his clavier-playing, and that, a few years before, while on a flying visit to Vienna, he had even won a few words of approbation from Mozart. It was probably this last fact which turned the scale. Haydn sent for the young man, gave him warm encouragement, and offered without hesitation to take him back to Vienna as a pupil. The offer could not be immediately accepted, for the Elector was away at Frankfort, taking part in the coronation of Francis II: on his return the necessary permission was obtained, and by the middle of November Beethoven[1] was established in the city which was thenceforward to be his home.

The lessons were not altogether successful. Haydn was a careless teacher, Beethoven a self-willed and refractory pupil; for one reason or another the exercises appear to have often gone uncorrected. But the relation remained intact until Haydn's second visit to England, and to the end the two men seem to have been on terms as friendly as their extremely. antagonistic temperaments would allow. There is no doubt a legend, narrated on the authority of Ries[2], that Haydn heard Beethoven play his first three pianoforte trios from manuscript and advised him to publish the first two, but not the third, which is incomparably the finest, that Beethoven resented this advice as a mark of incompetence or jealousy, and that an open quarrel ensued. But this legend may, without scruple, be relegated to the ample domain of musical mythology. In the first place, there is no intelligible reason why Haydn should have censured the C minor trio, which is a living embodiment of the freedom

---

[1] He dropped the prefix from the time of his residence in Vienna: apparently for fear of its being confused with the German ' von.'

[2] See *Thayer*, i. 284. Ries was, at the time, a child of ten, living in Bonn. He did not come to Vienna until 1801, when he brought a letter of introduction to Beethoven and became his pupil.

for which he always protested [1] ; in the second place there was
evidently no quarrel, for Beethoven played at Haydn's next
concert and dedicated to him his next composition; in the third
place, the sketches for these trios appear in Beethoven's note-
book during the winter of 1793, and continue, on the back of
counterpoint-exercises for Albrechtsberger, during the spring
of 1794: they were published in July 1795, and from January
1794 to August 1795 Haydn was in London. He may
possibly have seen the first tentative drafts : he cannot
possibly have seen the MS. as it was prepared for the printer.

The three pianoforte trios, though catalogued as Op. 1, are
by no means the earliest of Beethoven's known compositions.
Before Haydn discovered him he had already written a trio
for strings (Op. 3), the Serenade trio (Op. 8), the Bagatelles
(Op. 33), the two boyish sonatas (Op. 49), the two rondos for
pianoforte (Op. 51), and several sets of variations, one of which,
on Righini's 'Venni Amore,' gave him, in Vienna, his first
opportunity of public display as a pianist. To these he added,
in the course of the next three years, the pianoforte concertos
in B ♭ (Op. 19), and C (Op. 15), a rather weak trio for oboes
and corno Inglese (Op. 87), and several songs and smaller
pieces including the *Opferlied* and *Adelaide*. It was eminently
characteristic that he should keep all these in reserve, and hold
back from publication until he could approach it with a
masterpiece. In all the works above-mentioned there are signs
of immaturity, some slightness of texture, some vacillation of
touch, some mark of the trial-flight and the uncertain wing.
The gift which he selected for his first offering contains at
least one composition of unerring genius and of flawless workmanship. It is worth while to devote some special attention
to the C minor trio, for in it much of Beethoven's later
manner is foreshadowed. The opening phrase, for instance,
turns a customary formula to entirely new account:—

[1] See Grove's *Dictionary*, vol. i. p. 718 *b*, first edition ; vol. ii. p. 582, third
edition.

We have already seen the uses to which Mozart and Haydn
put this device [1]; Beethoven raises it to a higher plane of
interest by shifting his principal figure a semitone along the
scale, as he does afterwards in the *Appassionata,* and thus not
only challenging our attention in a novel and ingenious manner,
but so preparing our ear that when this phrase recurs it can
carry without the slightest effort the most extreme and recondite modulations.   In this way, by means so simple that they
almost pass unnoticed, the plan is laid for a scheme of accessory
keys which enriches the structure with point after point of
glowing colour, and yet never allows its essential character to
be obscured.   Thus, the development section begins :—

[1] See above, p. 249.

and there is another equally striking instance at the beginning
of the recapitulation. Again, the second subject opens with
a graceful and flowing melody, the precursor of a hundred
similar examples, and then breaks into a cry of tenderness and
passion such as no man but Beethoven can utter :—

So it is with the rest of the movement :—a plot so masterly
that every incident appears strange until we learn to see that it
is inevitable, a texture so close that not a strand in it could be
spared or altered, above all a kind of emotional expression to
which even Mozart and Haydn could not attain. For the first
time since Bach we realize the mystery of music—the 'in-
articulate unfathomable speech which leads us to the edge of
the Infinite and lets us, for moments, gaze into that.'

For the Andante Beethoven writes an Air with variations, in
which, again, some of his most essential characteristics are
already apparent. *A priori* it would be easy to conjecture that
the variation form is unsatisfactory. It affords little scope for
structural organization, little for episode or adventure, it seems
to have no higher aim than that of telling the same story in the
largest possible number of different words. Indeed, composers

before Beethoven are often in evident straits to maintain its interest[1]. Haydn when he has a tune as good as that of the Emperor's Hymn can afford to repeat it through an entire movement with mere changes of harmony or counter-subject: elsewhere, though he can sometimes treat the form with a strong hand, as in the well-known Andante for clavier, he more often evades its main difficulty either by introducing topics that are really irrelevant or by seeking adventitious aid from such extraneous forms as the minuet and the rondo. Mozart again seldom put his best work into variation-writing. On a few rare occasions, e.g. the string quartet in A major, he showed a true appreciation of its problems: as a rule he was content to draw his theme into graceful filigree, which differs from that of Kozeluch or Clementi rather in purity of metal than in any intricacy of design. But with Beethoven the principle itself is changed. His variations stand to the current methods of the *salon* as the *Ring and the Book* stands to the reiteration of a traveller's tale. They are independent studies, not only of the theme but of its whole basis and environment; they rise in gradually heightening degree of interest until they concentrate the issue upon its final climax. Not, of course, that Beethoven attained at once to a full command of his resources. There is a long step from the C minor trio to the *Kreutzer*, and from this again to the variations written for Diabelli. But in the earliest of these there is a clear indication of the coming style: as each number succeeds the accessory figures grow in value and prominence, the restatement becomes less and less obtrusive, until, in the last variation, the little limpid chromatic scale takes the height of our attention, and the theme, though it has been felt throughout as a unifying force, appears as it were the harmonic accompaniment of its own counter-subject.

The Minuet exhibits, within its tiny compass, Beethoven's favourite devices of surprise and contrast, of feigned hesitation

---

[1] For an exhaustive history of variation-form see Sir C. H. H. Parry's article in Grove's *Dictionary*, s. v.

and calculated effect. We can almost see him watching his
audience while the tune pauses and vacillates and puts forward
its perplexed and tentative suggestions. We know that it is
bound to reach its goal at the double-bar : meantime we follow its
fortunes with the same humorous sympathy which is aroused
in us by a comedy of adventure. Not less characteristic is the
stirring finale, now foreshadowing that Titanic vigour which
inspires the Sonata Pathétique, and, with still greater power,
the Fifth symphony :—

now issuing into a broad, suave melody, perfect in curve and
rhythm, of which the cadence is purposely delayed, both to

heighten its beauty at the moment and to provide for a dramatic crisis later on :—

It is not, of course, contested that the issues here are slighter than those with which Beethoven dealt in the maturity of his genius. The C minor trio is the work of a young man, it is *A Midsummer Night's Dream* beside *The Tempest, Richard III* beside *Othello;* indeed the parallel may be carried a step farther, for Shakespeare began under the influence of Marlowe, and in Beethoven's early writing may be found many traces of the style and phraseology of Mozart [1]. But though this work is still somewhat restricted by the narrow experience of youth and pupilage it is nevertheless a child that is father of the man. With it Beethoven definitely set his foot on the path that was to lead to his highest attainment and addressed himself to the task which, in the whole range of his art, he found most congenial. It is not for nothing that the first thirty-one of his published compositions are all written in the larger instrumental form, and that the style so moulded and matured affected the whole course of his subsequent work.

---

[1] A very noticeable instance is the first pianoforte sonata. Its opening phrase is almost identical with that of Mozart's early symphony in G minor (K. 183), throughout the adagio, though the sentiment is Beethoven's the style is often reminiscent of Mozart, while the great episodical tune, interpolated in the finale, contains a quotation, too close for coincidence, from the second subject of Mozart's pianoforte sonata in D major (K. 284).

From the outset, then, it is possible to trace in living germ the
two most essential of his qualities.   First, his supreme mastery
over the whole architectonic scheme of musical design.   Not
only is the balance perfect—it is often perfect in Haydn and
Mozart—but it attains its perfection through a fullness and
wealth of detail which in their best work they never commanded.
There is no 'clattering of dishes at a royal banquet': there are
no intervals of rest to relieve attention that it may take up the
thread where the interest recommences; every bar, every phrase
is relevant to the main issue, and the canvas is crowded with
figures and incidents all significant and all indispensable.   To
let the mind flag for a moment is to risk losing some point
of vital importance: the actor who crosses the stage may be
carrying the key of the plot, the modulation thrown out with
studied carelessness may be the explanation of the whole organic
scheme.   No doubt in this matter Beethoven, like all great
artists, was *felix opportunitate vitae*.   'It was his good fortune,'
says Sir Hubert Parry [1], 'that the sonata-form had been so
perfectly organized and that the musical public had been made
so perfectly familiar with it, that they were ready to follow
every suggestion and indication of the principle of form; and
even to grasp what he aimed at when he purposely presumed
on their familiarity with it to build fresh subtleties and new
devices upon the well-known lines; and even to emphasize the
points by making progressions in directions which seemed to
ignore them.'   His favourite methods of stimulating, baffling,
and finally satisfying the curiosity of his hearers would have
been impossible, because unintelligible, in the Vienna of 1781.
But he took his opportunity as no man of lesser constructive
skill could have taken it, and dominated the higher musical
intelligence of his day with wide sympathy and penetrating
insight.

Second, and complementary to the first, is the immense
vigour and vitality of his emotional expression.   Born of the

---

[1] *Art of Music*, ch. xii.

tenacious northern stock he was by temperament inclined to feel deeply and indelibly. Educated through a boyhood, the tragedy of which was not less bitter for being sordid, he learned early the lessons of concentration and of a rugged self-dependence. Writing in a period of revolution, himself an ardent revolutionary, he broke in upon the politeness of the Austrian court with an eloquence as tempestuous as that of Mirabeau or Danton. The very process of composition was often with him a physical agony—an outburst of volcanic force from which he would emerge, after hours of labour, as if from the throes of bodily conflict. Brilliant in improvisation he was hardly ever satisfied with the first inception of his thought, but laid it white-hot on the anvil and moulded it again and again with sledge-hammer vehemence. In the sketch-books [1] we may often find seven or eight different versions of a theme, successively tried and discarded until by sheer strength and constraint the intractable metal is beaten into obedience. Nor is this in any sense a mere selection of phraseology. It is as far removed from the *curiosa felicitas* of Chopin as from the logical precision of Cherubini. The successive presentations actually increase in meaning and significance: not the word only but the idea itself grows at every stroke more vivid, more distinct, more full of import and value. Hence in his best pages—and they far outnumber the weaker exceptions—there is not a commonplace sentence, there is hardly a formality. ' His chromatic scales,' said Schumann, ' are not like those of other people ': his simplest utterance can be as pregnant and as memorable as a line of Shakespeare.

To these may be added, as accessory, the higher level of executive skill which Beethoven attained and exacted. At the beginning of his career Vienna was much interested in feats of

[1] Among salient instances may be noted the first two movements of the *Eroica* symphony and the opening themes of the *Hammerclavier* sonata in B♭. The whole question of the sketch-books has been fully discussed in the excellent editions and commentaries of Nottebohm. See *Ein Skizzenbuch von Beethoven*, *Beethoveniana*, and *Zweite Beethoveniana*.

dexterity, and indeed was somewhat inclined to confuse the artist with the virtuoso. The soundest and most musicianly school of pianoforte teaching was then in England: established by Muzio Clementi, for whose sonatas Beethoven had a high regard, and whose *Gradus ad Parnassum*—a set of one hundred progressive studies—is still valuable as a textbook. The excellence of his method may be gauged by the career of his two most famous pupils, J. B. Cramer, the only British member of Schumann's Davidsbund, and John Field, whose nocturnes anticipated and influenced those of Chopin. Apart from this the pianists of the time seem to have devoted themselves almost exclusively to the mere rhetoric of execution. Dussek (1761–1812) was a composer of undoubted gifts, but he was too idle and shiftless to work out his ideas, and all his sonatas, even 'L'Invocation,' are full of purposeless scales and of passages that lead to nothing. Steibelt was a mere charlatan of talent whose highest aim was to astonish his audience: Woelfl is said to have been brilliant in improvisation, but there is little in his work of any lasting quality: behind these followed a miscellaneous crowd, all skilful, all industriously trained, and all equally devoid of any artistic meaning. The air was full of rivalries and competitions. Steibelt openly issued a challenge from the keyboard: Woelfl published a sonata with the title 'Non Plus Ultra,' implying that any work more difficult would require to be played by four hands: Dussek responded with a 'Plus Ultra' which was even harder and yet could be performed by two: in short, pianoforte music seemed to be degenerating into a contest of speed and endurance, which could only be justified by a liberal interpretation of Plato's maxim that gymnastic equally with music is for the good of the soul.

Beethoven beat these men on their own ground. In sheer dexterity of hand his only serious rival was Woelfl; in every other respect he stood alone. Tomaschek, an able and discriminating musician, heard every great pianist from 1790 to 1840, and in his estimation Beethoven was the greatest of them all [1]. The difference indeed was one not of hand but of brain, the only difference which even to the executant is of any real importance. Virtuosity is always suicidal, for its very difficulties when once they are surmounted become trivial and commonplace. 'The so-called concertos of the virtuoso-composers,' says Mr. Tovey [2], ' are easier than any others, since whatever types of passage they employ are written on poor and obvious harmonies, so that they can in time be mastered once for all like the knack of spinning a peg-top: whereas the great composers' passages never take your hand where it expects to go, and can be mastered by the muscle only in obedience to the continued dictation of the mind.' It is the same with Beethoven's treatment of the violin. The quartets, for instance, most of which he wrote for his old master Schuppanzigh [3], require, even for the bare notes, a good deal more than mere suppleness and accuracy: it needs constant and alert intelligence to follow their movement and to thread their intricacies. In short he developed his own *technique* as he developed his own conception of structure, and in both cases the enlarged resource was the natural organ and vehicle of an intenser thought.

It is customary to divide his work into three periods: a division which is really serviceable and illuminating if we do not lay pedantic insistence on exact lines of demarcation. The basis cannot be precisely chronological, for the simple reason that Beethoven did not master all his media simultaneously, and that he could treat the pianoforte with entire freedom at a time when he was still somewhat hampered and restricted by the

[1] He calls him 'Der Herr des Clavierspiels,' and ' Der Riese unter den Clavierspielern.' See *Thayer*, ii. 31, and the account of Tomaschek in Grove, vol. iv. pp. 132-3, first edition.

[2] *The Classical Concerto*, p. 24.

[3] Schuppanzigh (who taught Beethoven the viola) was the leader of a famous quartet-party which met every week during 1794-5 at Prince Carl Lichnowsky's. The Prince or Sina played second violin, Weiss viola, and Kraft or Zmeskall violoncello. In 1808 he founded the ' Rasoumoffsky' quartet, with Mayseder, Weiss, and Linke, and devoted it to a special study of Beethoven's compositions. See Grove, vol. iii. p. 425, first edition : vol. iv. p. 687, third edition.

orchestra. Thus the Second symphony (Op. 36) is in style and character earlier and more immature than some of the pianoforte sonatas, e. g. Op. 27, Op. 28, and Op. 31, which actually preceded it in point of date: while the string quintet in C major (Op. 29) and the violin sonata in C minor (Op. 30, No. 2) stand, with the C minor concerto [1] (Op. 37), somewhere about the point of transition. Yet if we compare works in the same medium the change is often sufficiently apparent. No one can doubt that there is a general difference of character between the first six string quartets and the three dedicated to Count Rasoumoffsky, or between the first two symphonies and the *Eroica,* while the opening movement of the so-called 'Moonlight' sonata, and still more that of the sonata in D minor, Op. 31, No. 2, is of a more subtle and recondite beauty than any of the preceding pianoforte compositions. Between the second and third periods the lines can be drawn with a more approximate accuracy: the Eighth symphony (Op. 93) may fairly be classed with the second, the transition to the third begins with the F minor quartet (Op. 95), the G major violin sonata (Op. 96), and the pianoforte trio in B♭ (Op. 97); though here again it is worth noting that, in actual date, the pianoforte trio was the earliest of the four [2]. The periods, in fact, merge into each other, as stages in a continuous line of development. The earlier works, e. g. the scherzo of the First symphony, often contain direct predictions of a subsequent method; the later, e. g. the sonatina Op. 79, occasionally recall an almost forgotten idiom; but at least the problem of internal evidence is not more difficult here than in the plays of Shakespeare, and is far easier than in the dialogues of Plato.

To the first period belong almost all Beethoven's experiments

[1] 'In the finale of this work we almost surprise the change of style in the act of being made,' Grove, vol. i. p. 202 note, first edition; vol. i. p. 304, third edition. Beethoven himself spoke of the three sonatas, Op. 31, as 'in a new style.'

[2] Lenz (*Beethoven et ses trois styles*) includes all these works in the second period, and begins the third immediately after them.

in combination of colour[1]; all the trios for string or wind-
instruments, the clarinet trio, the quintet for pianoforte and
wind, the septet, and the sonata (Op. 17), which in a sardonic
moment, he inscribed ' Für Pianoforte und Horn, oder Violine,
oder Bratsche, oder Violoncell, oder Flöte, oder Oboe, oder
Clarinette.' Beside these it includes all the violin sonatas
except the *Kreutzer* and the ' G major,' the first eleven pianoforte sonatas—all, that is, which were originally composed 'for
pianoforte or harpsichord '—the two violoncello sonatas, Op. 5,
the six string quartets, Op. 18, the first two symphonies and the
other works, of varying account, which have been already
mentioned[2]. In most of these, though the voice is the voice of
Beethoven, the idiom is still more or less that of the eighteenth
century. The first string quartet, for instance, uses words with
which Haydn was familiar: the two first concertos testify to
a close and accurate study of Mozart. The topics are different,
the eloquence is more vivid, more nervous, more full-blooded,
there is a far greater use of rhythmic gesture, a far more
intimate and telling appeal to emotion, but in point of actual
phraseology there is little that could not have been written by
an unusually adult, virile, and self-willed follower of the accepted
school. It is eighteenth-century music raised to a higher power.

With the second period there gradually comes a change not
less astonishing in its way than that which, in another field,
separates the age of Wordsworth and Keats from that of
Cowper and Thomson. If we compare the beginning of
Mozart's quintet in C :—

---

[1] The only exceptions are the wind sestet, Op. 71, and the sestet for strings
and horns, Op. 81, *a*, both somewhat unsuccessful. The wind octet, Op. 103, is
simply an arrangement (after Mozart's plan) of the early quintet for strings, Op. 4.

[2] See above, p. 270.

with that of the first Rasoumoffsky quartet :—

we shall see that they belong to alien worlds : not only are
they different in balance but the whole conception of Beethoven's
theme is of another age and generation. There has come into
music the element of the incalculable : the phrase seems to have
an initiative and a personality of its own, and the artist is but
the envoy through whom it delivers its message. So it is with
the opening of the Fifth symphony, of the *Appassionata*, of the

violin concerto : so it is with a hundred other instances and examples. The magician has woven his spells until, by some more potent alchemy, he has elicited from the crucible a spontaneous and independent life.

Thus in the most characteristic work of Beethoven's second period there is a force and vitality, predicted no doubt in his earlier writing, but even there not fully realized. It has all the attributes of a vigorous, well-rounded manhood, which ' sees life steadily and sees it whole ' : capable alike of strong passion and of a deep serene tranquillity, thoughtful or tender or humorous by turn, interpreting every noble feeling in human nature, holding them with a firm hand in just balance and equipoise. There is no music at once so many-sided and so complete ; no music which touches so many keys with so masterly a hand. We may grant a few inequalities and a few mannerisms :—the finale of the *Waldstein* falls short of its promise, the third Rasoumoffsky quartet, except in one melodious number, ranks below its fellows :—yet these, even if judgement of them pass unchallenged, are but flecks in the sun. There is assuredly no lack of achievement in the decade which has given us the pianoforte sonatas from Op. 27[1] to Op. 90, the symphonies from No. 3 to No. 8, the *Kreutzer* and the violin concerto, the string quartets Op. 59 and Op. 74, the violoncello sonata in A major, and five of the greatest concerted works for pianoforte that have ever been written.

Before we proceed to the consideration of the third period it may be well to discuss certain points of structure and treatment which belong to the first and second together. Of these the most obvious is the greater scale and expanse of Beethoven's work as compared with that of Mozart or Haydn. His pianoforte sonatas are often laid out on as large a canvas as they use for a quartet, his concerted and symphonic works are of proportionate grandeur. Indeed, it is notorious that Vienna,

[1] Lenz would include the ' Funeral march ' Sonata, Op. 26, which indeed among the pianoforte compositions may be said to stand at the frontier-line.

at a first hearing, treated some of them with a mixture of
bewilderment and impatience; just as the wits of our Restoration sneered at 'the old blind schoolmaster's tedious poem on
the fall of man.' Not, of course, that grandeur is a matter
of size: Blake on a few inches of paper could paint the
morning stars with a touch worthy of Michael Angelo,
Beethoven in such a marvel of concision as the Fifth symphony
could set an entire epic upon the page; but given the epic
quality there is no paradox in holding that in the wider field it
commonly finds the wider scope and opportunity. And the
whole of Beethoven's work is in 'the grand style': it is large,
free, elemental, lacking the ingenuousness of Haydn and the
daintiness of Mozart, but compensating for both by its heroic
breadth and dignity. It is this same grasp of first principles
which enables him to discard as obsolete many of the regulations
and restrictions that were current in his day; the number of
movements in a sonata is determined by the character of the
work, the formal 'repeat' is made optional, the whole scheme
of key-distribution is emancipated once for all and allowed to
select any tonal centre which affords the requisite contrast and
antithesis[1]. He was far too deeply concerned with the essentials
of musical construction to let himself be fettered by its accidents.

In the development of his themes he follows mainly the lead
set by the larger symphonic and concerted works of Mozart.
There is no device, not even the great episode in the *Eroica*,
which can be assigned to him as its inventor: yet his method
of development is in a very real sense his own, for no man has
ever solved its problems with so inexhaustible a fertility of
imagination. The tiniest figure becomes important, the most
obvious progression becomes new; at one moment the intrigue
is so wayward that we hold our breath in anticipation, at
another so involved that the knot appears wholly inexplicable.

---

[1] It is noticeable that, like all the great classics, Beethoven instinctively avoids
the subdominant for his second subjects. The mediant and submediant he uses
freely, always with some special ingenuity of balance in the recapitulation. See
for instance the sonatas in G major, Op. 31, No. 1, and in C major, Op. 53.

And so the interest grows and gathers until the development-section has fulfilled its due course, when with one magical stroke we are recalled to the main issue and emerge upon the inevitable solution.   Among all the structural devices of which Beethoven is the consummate master none is more striking than the ease with which he unravels this Gordian entanglement.   The unexpected modulation in the 'Pastoral' sonata, the horn-call in the *Eroica* symphony, the conflicting voices of the E♭ trio, are familiar examples of his mature method, yet even these yield for sheer simplicity and beauty to the ringing challenge with which, in the most exquisite of his early quartets, the melody re-enters :—

There remain two points of structure, in the larger sense of the term, which are illustrated by the work of both these periods. The first is Beethoven's use of the introductory adagio, which, ultimately derived from the old 'French overture,' could on occasion be employed by way of prologue. Before his time it bore very little organic relation to the music that followed it, but served its purpose mainly as an announcement or preparation. C. P. E. Bach, in one of his pianoforte concertos, tries the experiment of repeating it in place of the romance; Haydn, who uses it far more frequently than Mozart[1], now and then recalls it at the close of the first movement[2]: as a rule it stood detached and separate, at most emphasizing by contrast the character or tonality of the succeeding allegro. Beethoven employed it as he chose, and made it perform whatever function was suitable to the topic which he had in hand. Sometimes it is a call to attention, as for instance the beautiful phrase which heralds the F$\sharp$ major sonata; sometimes it designedly obscures tonality, as in the quartets Op. 59, No. 3, and Op. 74; sometimes, as in the Seventh symphony, it anticipates an integral portion of the plot, or, as in the Sonata Pathétique and the E$\flat$ trio, fulfils Horace's advice to the chorus and plays the part of an actor. Here again we may see evidence of the same vitalizing spirit, the same disregard of mere formula, the same determination to make every line in the composition true and significant. Beethoven, in short, uses his introductions as Shakespeare uses his prologues, and with the same variety of resource and intention.

Second, and even more important, is his treatment of the coda or epilogue. In its origin this device was simply determined by the rhetorical need of a peroration, especially in movements of which, by the convention of the time, the last

---

[1] It is hardly too much to say that Mozart only uses it in works more or less directly influenced by Haydn: e. g. the symphonies in C and E$\flat$ (K. 425 and 543), and the C major string quartet (K. 465).

[2] e. g. the symphony in E$\flat$, 'mit dem Paukenwirbel.' But this is rare.

half was formally repeated[1]. To avoid the bald inconclusiveness of ending on a mere restatement, it became customary
to round off the music by adding a few final bars of emphasis
or corroboration (e. g. the Finale of Haydn's quartet in E,
Op. 17, No. 1); then it appeared that this device could be
employed in all movements alike, and that it could serve, like
the 'envoy' of a novel, to sum up the final situation or bid
farewell to the characters. Interesting examples may be found
in the opening movement of the first Salomon symphony and
in the Finale of the Jupiter, the former of which deliberately
omits an entire scene from the story in order to keep it for the
envoy, while the latter reserves for the peroration its highest
flight of eloquence and rises through it to a climax for which
all the rest of the symphony seems to have been preparing.
But with Haydn and Mozart the coda is comparatively infrequent, and when it appears is seldom of great structural
importance[2]; with Beethoven it is habitual, and often plays
so large a part that it is no more an epilogue but an entire act,
no more a peroration but a culminating argument. In the
Eroica it is almost as long as the recapitulation ; in the 'Adieu'
sonata it outbalances the rest of the allegro put together; in
the 'Harp' quartet it continues the plot to an entirely unforeseen issue; in the *Appassionata* it introduces, with perfect
artistic fitness, the most incisive theme of the whole movement.
It is maintained by some theorists that this practice makes no
alteration in the essential structure : one might as well argue
that the ground-plan of a house is not changed by the addition
of a new wing. No doubt there are many cases in which

[1] See Sir C. H. H. Parry's article on Form : Grove, vol. i. pp. 547-9, first
edition ; vol. ii. p. 276 sq., third edition. It was no doubt for this reason that
Corelli so often, at the close of a movement, reiterated his last phrase. See
the examples quoted above, pp. 189-90.

[2] In slow movements of the ordinary 'romance' type (assertion, contrast,
reassertion) Haydn and Mozart sometimes use the coda to restate the clauses of
contrast in the tonic key. See, for an extremely beautiful instance, Mozart's
quartet in B♭ (K. 458). Beethoven, after his manner, extends and amplifies this
usage, as may be seen by comparing the slow movements of his first four pianoforte
sonatas.

Beethoven's coda is but a brief and telling rejoinder to the question raised by some previous melody or modulation : there are some in which it simply moralizes on the catastrophe like the few concluding lines of chorus in a Greek play ; but the examples above quoted are not isolated exceptions, and they are sufficient to show a growing dissatisfaction with the limits of the established form.

If he appears more conservative in his concerti, that is because the scheme laid down by Mozart affords a wider range of precedents. The C minor contains some experiments in the direction of symphonic form, but they are tentative, and are not repeated later : the concertos in G and E♭ open with the pianoforte instead of keeping it until the close of the ritornello, but this so-called 'innovation' had already been anticipated both by Mozart (K. 271) and by C. P. E. Bach. Beside these are the triple concerto for pianoforte, violin, and violoncello, an interesting though not wholly successful attempt to adapt an antique principle to modern conditions, and, greatest of all, the superb concerto for violin, which still holds among all works of its kind its uncontested supremacy. Yet even this is content to follow the accustomed scheme, and though it suggests a new method of treatment, both in its use of episodes and in its distribution of solos, rather approaches the frontier than crosses it.

In his overtures there is much the same acceptance of tradition. Originally indistinguishable from the symphony[1] the overture came, in Mozart's hands, to consist of a simple allegro movement, in free symphonic form, usually, though not invariably, preceded by an adagio introduction. To this plan Beethoven adhered throughout, from *Prometheus* and *Coriolan* down to *König Stephan* and *Zur Weihe des Hauses*. Of his overtures four were written for his opera *Fidelio*, the others either at the behest of a playwright or for some special occasion of public pageantry; and though, like all his work, they

---

[1] Some of Haydn's operatic overtures are catalogued among his symphonies : e. g. ' Il Distratto,' ' Ritter Roland,' and ' Roxelane.'

contain some magnificent music, they are not comparable as
landmarks to his achievement in the stricter forms. To the
critic they afford inexhaustible opportunities of study : to the
historian they but fill, nobly and sufficiently, the interval which
elapses between Mozart and Weber.

As an example of the second period we may take the pianoforte sonata in D minor, Op. 31, No. 2. It is an early instance :
the adagio, indeed, contains one melody which directly recalls
the influence of Mozart—

but the general character of this movement, as well as that of the
first and last, is unmistakable. The opening phrase of the first—

is pure Beethoven, nor less so are the petulant agitation of its
second theme and the sharp interchange of dialogue in the
episodes which follow it. The music constrains us like the
course of a rapid exciting drama, and indeed grows almost
articulate when, at the beginning of the recapitulation, Beethoven
breaks his first theme with an expressive piece of recitative :—

We have already noted examples of this device both in C. P. E.
Bach and in Haydn: it is used here with particularly striking
effect, as it is afterwards in the A♭ sonata, in the A minor
quartet, and, we may add, in the Choral fantasia and Choral
symphony.

The finale, apart from its intrinsic beauty, is interesting in
two ways. There is a legend that its measure—

was suggested by the beat of a galloping horse, and this if true
illustrates the manner in which Beethoven allowed his music to
be affected by external impressions. Like all the greatest
musicians he seldom attempted any direct representation of
scenes or sounds in nature: the Pastoral symphony comes
nearest, and this, as he himself said, was 'mehr Ausdruck der
Empfindung als Malerei.' In place of that artistic error, which
is commonly known by the nickname of 'programme-music,'
he prefers as here to represent not the external scene but its
psychological analogue or counterpart: the measure is not that
of a gallop, but it calls up the same impression of haste and
urgency. Yet even so slight an equivalence is far more in-

frequent in his work than the vaguer, more indeterminate emotion, as in the allegretto of the Seventh symphony, where the music speaks for itself and needs no interpreter.

Again, he broke through the convention that certain musical forms belonged by right to certain kinds of content or treatment. Before his time it was almost prescriptive that the rondo should be gay and cheerful—a lilting ballad measure through which the music should attain to a happy ending—just as with Haydn the scherzo was always a good-humoured jest [1] to lighten the interval between two more serious movements. At the touch of Beethoven this observance crumbled away. His scherzos are as various in character as they are in structure [2]: that of the Fourth symphony is an outburst of high spirits, that of the Fifth is as eerie as a ghost story, that of the Sixth a village holiday, that of the Seventh a whirlwind. In like manner he can make the rondo subservient to any mood he pleases [3]: in one sonata it is merry, in another wistful, now it is serious and reflective, now as gallant as a cavalry-charge. And it was assuredly through such broadening and deepening of the emotional content that he acquired his flexibility of form. From beginning to end he was essentially a Tondichter, whose power of expression grew in response to the poetic need.

The first part of Goethe's *Faust* is the tragedy of mankind as it lives and acts and suffers upon the stage of our own world. Some things in it repel, for we cannot all bear to see the soul unveiled, some elude our vision, for the innermost recesses lie open to the poet alone : but through its alternations of joy and sorrow, of love and sin and repentance, it holds our sympathy in a warm human grasp. The second part carries us to a different plane of thought where we can hardly climb for the

---

[1] See Haydn's six quartets, Op. 33, commonly called ' Gli Scherzi.'

[2] In the E♭ pianoforte sonata, Op. 31, No. 3, the scherzo takes the structural form of the slow movement and the minuet its elegiac character. See also the symphony in F, No. 8.

[3] The variation of mood may easily be illustrated by a comparison of the sonatas in E♭ (Op. 7), D (Op. 10, No. 3), C major (Op. 53), G (Op. 79), and E minor (Op. 90).

steepness of the ascent, or breathe for the rarity of the atmosphere. We grow dizzy and bewildered ; we lose our sense of
direction ; we are sometimes tempted to lay the book aside in
despair and to leave the throng of characters and the intricacy
of dialogue : Manto and Chiron, Helena and Phorcyas, the
scenes of court and field and laboratory, the voices that mock
and plead and baffle our comprehension. Yet all the while we
feel that the riddle could be solved if only we knew how, that
the immense complexity has a purpose and an end : if we hold
to our point there is hardly a page that does not bear some
message of deep import or some line of haunting music, until
we are brought at last onward and upward to the Mater
Gloriosa and the mystic chorus.

Beethoven's last period is like the second part of *Faust*.
There is no music in the world more difficult to understand,
none of which the genius is more unearthly, more superhuman.
It contains passages to which we can no more apply our
ordinary standards of beauty than we can to the earthquake or
the thunderstorm; it contains phrases, like the moments of
cynicism in Goethe, which, till we comprehend them better,
we can only regard as harsh or grim or crabbed; at times it
rises into melody, the like of which the world has never known
and will never know again. To criticize it in detail would need
an exhaustive survey of every work which it includes : all that
can be here attempted is to note its historical bearing and to
gather a few generalities which may serve as prolegomena to
some future criticism.

And first, since the bare dates are of importance, we may
briefly sketch the order of the compositions. In 1815 Beethoven wrote the two violoncello sonatas Op. 102, transitional
works of somewhat less account than the others; then follow
the last five piano sonatas and the Diabelli variations (1817–23),
then, in 1823, the Choral symphony [1], then from 1824 to 1826

---

[1] The Choral symphony is separated from the Eighth by an interval of eleven
years, during which Beethoven's only 'symphonic' work was the 'Battle of

the last five string quartets. In this succession there is an odd
exactitude and symmetry which is not wholly without significance: at any rate it may be said that the Choral symphony
presupposes the sonatas and is itself presupposed by the
quartets. Through each of these media in turn—the pianoforte,
the orchestra, and the four strings—Beethoven set himself to
work out the problems with which his closing years were
principally occupied.

One of these is an immense enlargement and extension of
the structural forms. It is no doubt still technically possible
to analyse the movements into first and second subject, into
exposition, development, and recapitulation, but the whole
centre of gravity has so shifted that the terms themselves appear
almost irrelevant. The music is fused and unified until it no
longer needs these formal distinctions : where it is more sharply
divisible, as in the opening movements of the E major and
C minor sonatas, it seems to admit a new principle and to
promulgate a new law. For the old close-wrought paragraph
in which many melodic sentences gather round a single key,
Beethoven often substitutes one incisive phrase, such as—

from the quartet in B♭, or—

from that in A minor: phrases which dominate the multitude
of surrounding voices as a word of command dominates an
army. Again, Beethoven no longer begins by formally putting
forth his themes, to wait for development until their complete
presentation is accomplished : he often sets them on their career
of adventure from the moment at which they enter the stage,

Vittoria ': one of his very few compositions which it is better to forget. See
a complete account of the history in Grove's *Beethoven and his Nine Symphonies*,
pp. 310–21.

so that we should think the whole work one vast fantasia but
for the firm and masterly vigour with which its plot is determined and its moments of successive climax ordained.   In
short the whole scheme of formal structure has passed into
a new stage of organic evolution, as different from that of the
Pastoral or the *Waldstein* as they are different from the
earliest quartets and symphonies of Haydn ; yet nevertheless
derived from its origin by continuous descent, and bearing
through all divergencies the heritage of many generations.

Another problem which occupied Beethoven during these
later years was that of a freer and more varied polyphony
which should assign to each concurrent voice its utmost
measure of individuality and independence.   The following
example, from the *Hammerclavier* sonata—

illustrates a new method of dealing with the resources of the
pianoforte; its texture wholly unlike that of the old counterpoint,
yet made up of strands almost equally distinctive.   In quartet-
music the change was, for obvious reasons, more gradual, since
the style which it implies is more essentially polyphonic; and
the adagio of Op. 74, to mention no other instance, is
sufficient to show that Beethoven had already learned to handle
the strings with extraordinary freedom.   Yet here also the
change is apparent: the andante of the quartet in B♭, the
variations of that in C♯ minor, are shot and traversed with an
interplay of part-writing more intricate than had been woven at
any earlier loom.   To this is largely due the sense of combined
movement and volume which essentially belongs to Beethoven's
maturer style: it is music at the full flood, brimming its banks
with the increase of a hundred tributary streams.   There is
little wonder if, at a first plunge, we may sometimes find the
current too strong.

It cannot be questioned that the ideal at which Beethoven
was here aiming, is one of the highest value to musical art.
The resources of polyphonic treatment are wider than those of
pure harmony, which, indeed, they include and absorb; they
carry with them a special power of varying and co-ordinating
effects of rhythm.   But though in the vast majority of cases
he attains his end beyond cavil or dispute, there are nevertheless
two subsidiary points in regard of which we cannot feel ourselves
wholly convinced.   First, he sometimes elaborates a phrase until
the ordinary human ear can no longer adjust itself to his
intention.   The graceful dance-tune which opens the Vivace
of the F major quartet loses its charm when it reappears in
double counterpoint: the reiterated figure of the 'trio' is
carried almost beyond the limits of physical endurance.   Again,
in the slow movement of the A minor quartet the Choral is
introduced by a few simple notes of prelude, which we
feel to be entirely appropriate to its character: at each recurrence they are bent with syncopations or broken with new

rhythms until they are hardly recognizable. No doubt Beethoven does this not for scholastic ingenuity but for deeper expression,—the most complex of the variants is specially marked 'mit innigster Empfindung'—but in this process of sublimation some of the material beauty seems to have evaporated, and it may be that we can here trace some effect of his growing deafness. Secondly, though in his adoption of the fugal principle he undoubtedly adds a new resource to the sonata, and though the magnificent example in C minor (Op. 111) is a triumphant vindication of his purpose, yet he approaches the fugue itself from the outside, and sometimes exhibits an almost uneasy desire to propitiate it with academic devices. Thus the finale of the *Hammerclavier* sonata would be a vigorous and forcible piece of eloquence if it would ever allow us to forget that it is a fugue: we can hardly catch its meaning for the strettos and inversions and other laborious artifices of the counterpoint-school. This is no matter of accident. It is not by accident that a man writes his theme cancrizans or in augmentation; it is a deliberate sacrifice at a shrine long since deserted. Yet we may well be content to reserve judgement until we find a more penetrating truth behind these apparent exhibitions of professorial learning. They are but enigmatic utterances of the Sphinx on the Pharsalian Plain, and we answer, as Heine answered, 'You cannot touch them: it is the finger of Beethoven.'

For among all Beethoven's melodies those of the last years are the most profound and the most beautiful. Not that we can even hope to exhaust the meaning of the great tunes which he wrote in early manhood,—the violin concerto, the *Appassionata*, the adagio of the Fifth symphony,—but even they deal with truths of less divine import than he learned to utter in the fullness of his age. Such a melody as the following[1]:—

---

[1] From the sonata in E major, Op. 109. For other examples see the Cavatina of the quartet in B♭, the adagio of the *Hammerclavier* sonata, than which there is no greater work in the literature of the pianoforte, and the rondo of the quartet in A minor.

seems to be transfigured with a sort of spiritual beauty, its infinite pity and tenderness are from some 'ideal world beyond the heavens.' Music is irradiated with a new light, and the joys of song pass into the awe and rapture of the prophetic vision.

High above the other works of this period there towers, like Mont Blanc over its Alpine chain, the Choral symphony. It was, indeed, the slow-wrought masterpiece of Beethoven's whole career: a setting of Schiller's *Ode to Joy* had occupied his attention as far back as 1792 [1]: in 1808 he wrote the Choral fantasia, which is not only a study for the form of the Finale

---

[1] See a letter of Fischenich to Charlotte von Schiller: Thayer, vol. i. p. 237.

but an anticipation of its treatment[1]; by 1816 the actual
sketches had begun to appear in the note-books; by the autumn
of 1823 the score was completed.   In its colossal proportions
all his music seems to be contained: an entire life of stress
and labour, an entire world of thought and passion and deep
brooding insight; it touches the very nethermost abyss of
human suffering, it rises 'durch Kampf zum Licht' until it
culminates in a sublime hymn of joy and brotherhood.

The music begins with an ominous murmur, like the
muttering of a distant storm, which suddenly bursts in levin
and thunderbolt:—

and battles with a fierce elemental energy from horizon to
horizon.   Now and again there opens a space of quiet tender
melody, as the sky may show through a rift in the tempest;
now and again, by a miraculous effort of genius, Beethoven
commands the whirlwind itself, and bids it be still:—

[1] Nohl (Beethoven's Leben, iii. 925) states, on the authority of Sonnleithner
and Czerny, that as late as June or July, 1823, Beethoven still hesitated whether
to make the Finale choral or instrumental.   The only evidence adduced is that in
the sketch-book of the time there appears a melody in D minor marked 'Finale
Instrumentale.'   This is the melody which, two years later, Beethoven transposed
and employed for the exquisitely tender and reflective rondo of the A minor
quartet.   It seems incredible that he can ever have meant it for the climax of a
symphony so wholly different in character.   See Grove, Beethoven and his Nine
Symphonies, p. 330.

and so through alternations of peace and conflict the great
movement surges onward to its climax of sheer overwhelming
passion. The scherzo, which follows next in order, is the
longest and greatest example of its kind, a wonderful outburst
of rhythmic speed which sets the blood coursing and tingling.
Its trio has one of Beethoven's happiest melodies, distributed after
his later manner [1] between two different instrumental voices :—

and in both numbers it affords a masterly example of the point
to which can be carried the organization of simple figures. Not
less admirable is the contrast between its lightness of touch and
the tremendous depth and earnestness of the adagio. Two

[1] Other instances may be found in the andante of the B ♭ quartet, and in the
Air for Variations of the C ♯ minor.

bars of yearning prelude, in which, as Grove says, 'the very heart of the author seems to burst,' and there follows a lament which expresses and spiritualizes the sorrows of all the world :—

It is answered by a second theme which, though grave, is of a serener cast, a responsive voice of comfort and resignation :—

and of these two, in varying converse, the entire movement consists. Complexity of plot would be out of keeping with the utterance of truths so mystic and so sublime.

It was on the Finale that Beethoven expended his chief labour, and indeed he may well have doubted how most fitly to bring so great a drama to its triumphant conclusion. For a few moments the orchestra seems to share his anxieties: tragedy reaches its climax in crashing discords and passages of wild unrest, themes of preceding movements are tried and rejected: at length there tentatively emerges the tune devised for Schiller's Ode :—

which, with a shout of welcome, the music seizes and carries shoulder-high. When the chorus enters it is as though all the forces of humanity were gathered together : number by number the thought grows and widens until the very means of its expression are shattered and we seem no more to be listening to music but to be standing face to face with the living world. To ask whether ‘Seid umschlungen, Millionen’ is beautiful is not less irrelevant than to ask for beauty in the idea which inspired it.

The first performance of the Choral symphony took place in the Kärnthnerthor Theatre on May 7, 1824, with Umlauf as conductor and Mayseder as leader of the violins. The concert included the overture *Zur Weihe des Hauses* and the *Kyrie, Credo, Agnus,* and *Dona* of the Mass in D. At its end the audience rose in salvo upon salvo of such enthusiasm as had never before been aroused by any musical composition, and we are told that when the applause had reached its full volume one of the singers touched Beethoven on the shoulder and motioned to him that he should turn and see the manner of his reception. He had heard nothing.

CHAPTER XI

THE INSTRUMENTAL FORMS (*continued*)

SCHUBERT AND THE LATER CONTEMPORARIES OF BEETHOVEN

It has often happened that the followers or associates of a great master, unable to comprehend the full import of his teaching, have carried onward, each in his own direction, some imperfect part of the message which it contains. To his eye alone shines the lustre of the entire jewel: they catch the light from one or other of its facets and reveal, through the medium of their own temperament, so much of its beauty as they have the power to interpret. At most there is one disciple, a Plato or an Aristotle, a Giotto or a Raphael, who can share the intimacy of the master's thought, and the very genius which gives him understanding will at the same time teach him independence. The rest are outside the dynasty; courtiers and ministers, not princes in the line of succession; and the utmost that they can achieve is to bear some part in the administration until a new monarch ascends the throne.

So it is with the Viennese period of musical history. We have seen the line of descent pass from Haydn to Mozart and from Mozart to Beethoven; we shall see it pass to one more hand which, though of weaker grasp, was unquestionably of the blood-royal; meantime we may consider some men of lesser account who hold subordinate positions in the record and annals of the realm. Spohr and Hummel both called themselves followers of Mozart: Cherubini, though, with the exception of Sarti, he acknowledged no actual master, shows evident traces of the same influence; and without a brief survey of their work the study of Viennese instrumental music would therefore be incomplete.

The career of Hummel (1778–1837) has a certain historical interest. For seven years, from 1804 to 1811, he was Prince Esterhazy's Kapellmeister at Eisenstadt, holding the office which Haydn had filled during the period of his greatest activity: he was then for some time resident in Vienna, where ill-advised friends treated him as the serious rival of Beethoven: in one of his many concert-tours he visited Warsaw, and taught Chopin for the first time what pianoforte-playing really meant. There can be no doubt that he was a great player: all contemporary accounts are agreed as to his dexterity, his neatness, and his purity of touch; but the qualities in which he excelled at the keyboard were the only ones which he carried into the higher fields of composition. His published works, over a hundred in number, include several sonatas and concerted pieces for the pianoforte, of which the best known are the concertos in A minor and D minor, the sonatas in F♯ minor and D major, and the septet for piano strings and wind. At the present day they have little more than an academic value. Sometimes they exhibit the charm which may belong to cleanness of style, as for instance the dainty little rondo which begins:—

in almost all cases they are useful for purposes of technical study, and they have at least the negative merit of never falling below a true standard or sincerity and refinement. But of genius in the true sense of the term they have hardly a trace. With little inventive power, little passion, and almost no humour, they are like the smooth mellifluous verses of Hoole or Tickell, which never offend, never disappoint, and rarely please.

To the same category belong the writings of Beethoven's pupil Carl Czerny (1791–1857), one of the kindest, most amiable and most industrious of men, who was universally beloved by his contemporaries, and now only survives as the natural enemy of the schoolroom. Like Hummel he was an admirable pianist and a sound teacher: indeed we are told that his lessons often occupied him for ten or twelve hours in the day and that he was usually obliged to defer composition until after nightfall. When to this it is added that his catalogue of works approaches the portentous number of a thousand, we shall have no difficulty in understanding why they have made so little mark on musical history. There is but one master whose power of improvisation seems never to have failed him, and he did not bring to the work a tired hand and an overwrought brain.

In strong contrast, though in its way not less academic, is the prim, laboured, and unattractive chamber-music of Cherubini. His strength lay in Mass and opera; under the stimulus of great ideas or dramatic situations he could often express himself with true eloquence: it is in the narrower field and the more restricted palette that we can most clearly detect Berlioz's 'pedant of the Conservatoire.' His first quartet was written in 1814, his second, adapted from a symphony, in 1829, then from 1834 to 1837 came four more in successive years, and in the last year a quintet for strings as well. Only the first three quartets (E♭, C and D minor) were published during his lifetime: those in E, F, and A minor appeared posthumously. In a sense they are remarkably well-written: the parts clear and independent, the rhythms varied, the forms always lucid and perspicuous. But the music is entirely cold and artificial; there is not a heart-beat in the whole of it; only a stiff and arid propriety which knows the formulae for passion and can unbend into gaiety when occasion requires. Here, for example, is a melody, from the slow movement of the quartet in E major, which Cherubini has marked ' dolce assai' and ' espressivo '—

There can be no doubt that it clinches its point with extreme logical aptitude: but one would as soon think of going to Barbara Celarent for poetry. So it is with the others. The allegro movements are everything except stimulating, the largos everything except pathetic, the scherzos are like Swift's famous jest on Mantua and Cremona, too admirable for laughter. And yet when all is said we go back to the workmanship, to the finale of the quartet in E♭, to the first movement of that in D minor, and sincerely regret that a hand so practised and so skilful should have failed for want of a little human sympathy. It is the more remarkable from a man who, as we have already seen, had in vocal writing a real gift of dramatic presentation.

The general character of Spohr's music has already been discussed, and it but remains to trace the adaptation of his

style in the particular medium of instrumental composition.
Despite his voluminous industry this is no very difficult task.
It is true that he wrote as many symphonies as Beethoven, as
many quartets as Beethoven and Mozart together, chamber-
works for every combination of instruments from two to
nine, four concertos for clarinet and seventeen for violin,
beside a vast number of miscellaneous works which range
from *sinfonie concertanti* to pots-pourris on the themes of
Jessonda. But through all this apparent variety his manner
is so consistent and uniform that almost any work might be
taken as typical of the whole. Schumann [1] pleasantly compares the 'Historical Symphony' (in which Spohr attempts
to imitate the styles of different musical periods) with the
Emperor Napoleon's presence at a masked ball:—a few
moments of disguise, and then the arms are folded in the
well-known attitude, and there runs across the room a murmur
of instant recognition. Much more, then, do the mannerisms
appear when Spohr is addressing the audience in his own
person. Whatever the form which he employed, whatever the
topic with which he dealt, he spoke always in the distinctive
but limited vocabulary which he was never tired of repeating.

The violin he treated with a complete and intimate mastery.
Less astonishing than Paganini, he was, as a player, almost
equally famous; and we are told that in his firmness of hand
and in the broad singing quality of his tone he remained to the
end of his life without a rival. Hence the remarkable prominence which in almost all his instrumental works is assigned to
the first violin. The concertos in particular separate the soloist
widely from his accompaniment, and even the quartets, many
of which bear the disheartening title of 'Quatuor brillant,' too
often exhibit the same inequality of balance. But the violin-
writing, considered simply in point of technique, is invariably
excellent, and if it indulges the selfishness of the virtuoso at any
rate it supplies an adequate test of his capacity.

[1] Gesammelte Schriften, vol. iv. p. 82.

The style, though never robust, is always melodious and refined. Indeed, Spohr seems to have so dreaded vulgarity that he shrank even from manliness. He honestly disliked the Fifth and Ninth symphonies of Beethoven: they seemed to him noisy and uncouth, barbarous outbreaks of elemental passion which ought to be moderated or concealed. In his own work there is assuredly no such passion, but hints and *nuances* and discreet half-tones which hide their meaning under a polite phrase, and would think it indelicate to speak plainly. 'Be his subject grave or gay, lively or severe,' says Mr. Hullah, 'he never if he can help it leaves a tone undivided or uses an essential note when he can put an altered one in its place.'

As might be expected from one whose main preoccupation was colour, he was particularly attracted by experiments in combination. The nonet, unusually equal in distribution of interest, is scored for five wind instruments and four strings: the octet for clarinet, a couple of horns, and string quintet with two violas. Besides these are four 'double-quartets,' which are really quartets with *ripieno* accompaniment, a nocturne for wind and percussion instruments, a septet for 'piano trio' and wind, a sestet for strings alone, probably the first ever written, and a concerto for string quartet and orchestra. One of his oddest experiments is the Seventh symphony (Op. 121), entitled 'Irdisches und Göttliches im Menschenleben,' which requires two separate orchestras, the larger representing the human element in life and the smaller the divine. But like everything else this turns to a concerto at his touch, and except for a few passages in the finale, the human orchestra has no function but that of accompanist.

In the name of this last work we may find another point for consideration. Spohr was essentially a classic, following the forms of Mozart with little attempt to modify or supersede them. But of all composers outside the Romantic movement he was the most concerned to make music as far as possible representa-

[1] The *History of Modern Music*, p. 185.

tive of some actual scene or mood. His Fourth symphony, 'Die Weihe der Töne,' was deliberately intended to represent in music a poem of Pfeiffer: indeed he left instructions that the poem should be publicly read wherever the symphony was performed. In like manner his last symphony is called 'The Seasons,' his most famous violin concerto is 'in Form einer Gesangscene,' and the inclination clearly stated in these examples is in many others almost equally apparent. No doubt this is curiously discrepant with the narrow range of colour and feeling which he actually achieved, and it is probably by this failure to serve two masters that we may explain the disregard into which most of his work has now fallen. Of his quartets the G minor (Op. 27) alone has passed into any familiar use, three, or at most four, of his symphonies are occasionally given as curiosities, and though the concertos still form a necessary part of every violinist's equipment, they are yearly growing of less interest to the audience than to the performer.

It is worth while to contrast his method of violin-technique with that of Paganini, who was his exact contemporary [1], and almost his exact antithesis. In Spohr's temperament there was nothing of the charlatan and very little of the innovator: he took the accepted manner of bowing, as established by Rode and Viotti, and on it built a solid, clear-cut, *cantabile* style, capable of great execution but wholly free from any kind of rhetorical device. Every phrase had its full value, every note, even in his most rapid staccato, was firmly marked by a movement of the wrist, every stroke was of entirely honest workmanship which, like all true art, recognized the limitations of its medium. Paganini had a thin but expressive tone, made free use of the springing bow, a device which Spohr particularly detested, and by natural gift and untiring practice attained a miraculous dexterity which he did not scruple to enhance by every trick that his mercurial imagination could invent. Thus

---

[1] They were both born in 1784.

in his E♭ concerto there are passages which, on the page, appear literally impossible: he evaded them by a special method of tuning his violin; and in almost all his works may be found pizzicatos for the left hand, extravagant harmonics, and other equally unworthy feats. Yet it would be unfair to regard him merely as a charlatan of genius. There must have been some sound musicianship in a man who was the first among great violinists to appreciate Beethoven, and a part of whose work has been immortalized by Schumann and Brahms.

The artists here considered represent a wide variety of purpose and idea. Each in his way memorable, each is nevertheless imperfect and incomplete, one oppressed by circumstance, another failing through lack of the divine impulse, another checked by timidity or diverted to the pursuit of a side-issue. There remains the work of the one great genius who inherited in full measure the Viennese tradition and who closed its record of splendid and supreme achievement. It is of course impossible that there should be found in Schubert's work any conspicuous trace of Beethoven's third period: Beethoven died in 1827, Schubert in 1828, the one in the full maturity of manhood, the other little more than thirty years of age. But with the more romantic side of Beethoven's genius Schubert was as well acquainted as he was with the style and melody of Mozart, and it was in these together that he found both his artistic education and his point of departure.

By an odd coincidence the history of his instrumental work falls naturally into two divisions; one on either side the year 1818, the year of his twenty-first birthday. Almost all the examples written before that date are marked by a boyish immaturity of character: the style, mainly influenced by Mozart and early Beethoven, is clear and lucid, but with little profundity, the themes, though wonderfully fresh and spontaneous, lack the intensity and expression of the later years, the whole workmanship is rather that of a brilliant and skilful craftsman than that of ' le musicien le plus poète qui fût jamais.' After

1818 the influence of both masters becomes less apparent, the
genius grows riper and more individual, there is a new meaning
in the melodies, a new sense of beauty in their treatment.
Indeed, the distinction between the two periods may be
indicated by the single fact that, except for the Tragic
symphony, every instrumental work by which Schubert is intimately known to us belongs to the second.

The first, then, in point of instrumental composition, may
be taken as a time of pupilage, during which he was learning,
by study of the great models, to control his medium and to
form his style. It covers a lapse of but little more than four
years [1] (1813–1817), yet within these narrow limits it includes
the first six symphonies, the two 'Overtures in the Italian
style'—good-natured satires on the growing worship of Rossini;
four string quartets in B♭ (Op. 168), D, G minor, and F;
a string trio; a concerto, three sonatinas (Op. 137) and a
sonata (Op. 162) for violin; and ten pianoforte sonatas, of
which, however, three alone are of serious account [2]. Up to
1816 they show hardly any change or development: there is
always the same frank buoyancy of tone, the same lightness
of touch, the same lavish melody, and the same frequency of
reminiscence or adaptation. Thus the finale of the quartet in
G minor (1815) opens with a tune which reaches back to Haydn
himself :—

---

[1] A few schoolboy compositions have been omitted. For practical purposes
Schubert's instrumental work begins, with his first Symphony, in October 1813.

[2] E♭, Op. 122; B, Op. 147; A minor, Op. 164: all written in 1817. It must
be remembered that Schubert's Opus-numbers are of no assistance at all in
determining the order of composition. The pianoforte trio in E♭, Op. 100, was
published about a month before his death, and all works bearing a higher number
are posthumous.

The andante of the First symphony (1813) is, except for its
shortened metre, curiously reminiscent of Mozart :—

while in the opening movements of the first two symphonies we
may find familiar themes of Beethoven but slightly disguised :—

Yet all the while Schubert wears his rue with a difference.
These works are in no sense imitations : they have as coherent
a personality as Mozart's own early quartets, and but exhibit
that vivid and alert receptiveness which is one of the sure marks
of adolescent genius. At the same time their historical value
consists partly in their indebtedness, for it is through them that
Schubert's kinship to the Viennese dynasty can most readily be
observed.

The structure, though generally conforming to the established

tradition, is marred by one sign of weakness which seems to
have grown on Schubert through the whole of his career:—the
habit of building an entire musical section on variants of a single
melodic or rhythmic phrase.   This is particularly noticeable in
the expositions of the more elaborate 'three-canto' movements,
where we often find the same figure maintained with uniform
persistence from the entry of the second subject to the double-
bar.   A salient example occurs in the opening allegro of the
Third symphony, another in that of the B♭ quartet: indeed
there is hardly an instrumental work of Schubert from which it
would be impossible to quote an illustration.   In all probability
this was due to his rapid and extemporaneous method of writing :
the melody once conceived took his imagination captive, the
passage once written was allowed to stand without recension.
But, whatever the cause, it usually gives an unsatisfactory
impression of diffuseness, and in the long run approaches
perilously near to the false emphasis of reiteration.

With the Tragic symphony (No. 4) written in 1816 there
came a premonitory change of style.   The principal theme of
the slow movement

strikes a deeper note, the vigorous finale is drawn with a stronger
hand, there is more use of distinctive harmonies and accompani-

ment-figures. In other words, Schubert is beginning to find his true form of expression, to pass beyond the care of his teachers and to face the problems of art in his own way. A further stage is reached in the andante of the 'little symphony' (No. 5 in Bb)[1], and another again in the works of 1817, the C major symphony (No. 6) and the pianoforte sonatas. Much of Schubert's later technique is here clearly apparent; a preference for 'rhyming' melodies, a close alternation of major and minor mode, a fondness, which he never lost, for distant modulations and remote accessory keys. Take, for instance, the following passage from the B major sonata (Op. 147) :—

Beethoven would hardly have written as abruptly as this in a development-section: Schubert places it at the outset of the movement and further obscures the key-system in the next bar. It must be remembered that, like Beethoven, he was addressing an audience already familiar with the principle of the sonata and could therefore allow himself an almost unlimited freedom in its treatment. But it is interesting to observe that he uses his opportunity less for purposes of dramatic coherence than for those of gorgeous colour and pageantry. As a rule we are little concerned with the development of his plot: our

---

[1] See in particular the change from C b major to B minor and the string figure on which it is carried: pp. 17, 18 in Breitkopf and Härtel's edition.

attention is rather concentrated on the beauty of isolated characters or the splendour of particular scenes.

During 1818 he was occupied partly with his Mass in C, partly with his first appointment as music-teacher to the family of Count Johann Esterhazy, and in this year alone there are no important instrumental compositions. The interval of quiescence undoubtedly aided to mature his thought, for it was followed in direct succession by the whole series of imperishable masterpieces on which, in the field of instrumental music, his reputation is established. First among them comes the pianoforte quintet (1819); then in 1820 the Quartettsatz; in 1822 the 'Unfinished' symphony; next year the piano sonata in A minor, Op. 143; in 1824 the octet, the string quartets in E♭, E, and A minor, and the piano sonatas for four hands; in 1825 the solo sonatas in A minor (Op. 42), D (Op. 53), and A major (Op. 120); in 1826 the Fantasie-sonata in G, and the string quartets in D minor and G major; in 1827 the two pianoforte trios and the fantasie (Op. 159) for pianoforte and violin; in 1828 the C major symphony [1], the last three piano sonatas, and the string quintet. To them may almost certainly be added the vast majority of his other works for pianoforte, the fantasias, the impromptus, the ' Moments musicals,' and the more important marches and dance-forms. The dates of their composition are not accurately known, but if internal evidence have any value they may safely be assigned to this later period.

If we seek for one central idea, by the light of which this music can be understood and interpreted, we may perhaps find it in the term ' fancy ' as commonly employed by our English poets. Analogues between different arts are proverbially dangerous, but

---

[1] Called No. 7 in Breitkopf and Härtel's edition; No. 10 in Grove's *Dictionary*. We have seven completed symphonies of Schubert, namely the first six and the famous one in C major. Beside these there is a sketch in E major dated 1821, and the 'Unfinished symphony' (two movements and the fragment of a scherzo) dated 1822. There is also evidence that Schubert composed another C major symphony while on a visit to Gastein in 1825, but of this work no copy has yet been discovered. See Grove, vol. iii. p. 344, first edition; vol. iv. p. 608, third edition.

music and poetry have at least this in common that their very
language has often a special power of touching the emotions or
enchanting the senses. When Keats tells of

> Magic casements, opening on the foam
> Of perilous seas in faery lands forlorn,

it is not the picture alone which gives us delight: each word
has a charm, a colour: the exquisite thought is crowned with
a halo not less exquisite. And much of Schubert's melody
is in the very spirit of Keats. The themes of the Unfinished
symphony, of the first pianoforte trio, of the octet, are the
incarnation and embodiment of pure charm : every note, every
harmony, every poise of curve and cadence makes its own appeal
and arouses its own response. Not less magical is the opening
of the A minor quartet :—

where the rhythm stirs and quivers round the melody like the
voices of the forest round the nightingale.   Again in Schubert,
as in Keats, there is an indescribable, mesmeric attraction which
takes us wholly out of the work-a-day world and sets us in
a land of dreams.   *The Tempest* is a fairy-tale, *The Eve of
St. Agnes* a romance, yet Ferdinand and Miranda and even
Ariel are nearer to human life than the entranced and vision-
ary passions of Madeline and Porphyro.   The 'Belle Dame
sans merci' wanders by no earthly meads, her elfin grot lies
in the remote and moonlit kingdom of fantasy.   And, in
like manner, when we listen to music such as that which
begins :—

we seem to pass altogether from the realm of living flesh and blood, we sit spell-bound before the enchanted mirror and surrender our senses to its control. So potent is this mood that the rare occasions on which Schubert deserts it are generally those in which he is least a poet. The scherzo of the string quintet, for instance, has a rough and roystering gaiety which is out of keeping with the ethereal beauty of the rest, and in some of his pianoforte works there are passages which aim at strength and achieve violence. But in his own kind he is supreme. No artist has ever ranged over more distant fields, or has brought back blossoms of a more strange and alluring loveliness.

With less general power of design than his great predecessors he surpasses them all in the variety of his colour. His harmony is extraordinarily rich and original, his modulations are audacious, his contrasts often striking and effective, and he has a peculiar power of driving his point home by sudden alternations in volume of sound. Every one who has heard the G major quartet will recall the electric impulse of the following passage from its andante :—

and the devices here used to such masterly purpose may be found in a hundred similar examples. In the pianoforte quintet also, and in both the pianoforte trios, he invents many new and ingenious ways of contrasting the *timbre* of the keyed instrument with that of the strings : indeed the finale of the first trio is, in this matter, a study of the highest value. His polyphony never approaches that of Beethoven, and he therefore lacks the particular kinds of colour which polyphonic writing alone can give. But the quality of his harmonic masses does not require this, and in fact hardly admits it. He paints on the flat surface, and uses the rainbow itself for his palette.

By customary judgement his greatest work is held to be the C major symphony, 'in which,' as Schumann said, 'he added a tenth to the nine Muses of Beethoven.' And when we remember the romantic circumstances of its discovery and the wonderful beauties which it undoubtedly contains we should feel little wonder at the enthusiasm which assigns to it the highest place in his art. Yet after all it may be doubted whether he shows to best advantage upon so large a canvas. His genius was lyric rather than epic, expressive rather than constructive ; as we have already seen his manner of writing rendered him specially liable to repetition and diffuseness. It is true that the manuscript has some unwonted marks of recension : but they amount to little more than three inspired afterthoughts—the change in the opening theme of the allegro, the interpolation in the scherzo, and the second subject of the finale. At any rate it is possible to maintain that each of the first two movements would have gained something by compression, and that in so gaining they would have prepared us better for the flying, coruscating splendour of the last.

The lyric quality of his genius gives a special character to his use of the smaller instrumental forms. His variations are always distinctive, not like those of Beethoven, by architectonic power, but by a lavish melodic freedom in detail and ornament. He occasionally builds them on themes taken from his own songs :—*Die Forelle, Der Tod und das Mädchen, Der Wanderer, Sei mir gegrüsst*[1] ;—in every case he adorns them with brilliant colour and dainty carved-work, with mosaic of rhythmic figures and with clusters of jewelled melody. Of even deeper historical interest are the six tiny pieces which he collected under the title of '*Moments musicals*': for these exhibit in actual process the transition from classical to romantic ideals. They are not, like the dances of Mozart or the *Bagatellen* of Beethoven, chips thrown aside from a great workshop, but close-wrought miniatures, in which, perhaps for the first time, the direct influence of the sonata is not paramount. To them, and to the tendencies which they represent, may be attributed the prevalence through the nineteenth century of short lyric and narrative forms in pianoforte music :—the *Lieder* of Mendelssohn, the *Novelletten* of Schumann, the *Caprices* and *Intermezzi* of Johannes Brahms.

Schubert therefore stands at the parting of the ways. The direct inheritor of Mozart and Beethoven, he belongs by birth, by training, by all the forces of condition and circumstance, to the great school of musical art which they established. In the peculiar quality of his imagination, in his warmth, his vividness, and we may add in his impatience of formal restraint, he points forward to the generation that should rebel against all formality, and bid the inspiration of music be wholly imaginative. Yet there can be no doubt to which of the two periods he belongs. Schumann uses colour for its emotional suggestion, Schubert for its inherent loveliness ; Berlioz attempts to make the symphony articulate, Schubert will not allow it to be descriptive ; Liszt accentuates rhythm, because of its nervous force and stimulus, Schubert because it enhances the contour of his line. Possessing in full measure all the artistic gifts which we commonly associate with the mid-century, he devoted them, at their highest, to the loftier ideals of its beginning.

[1] Pianoforte quintet : string quartet in D minor, pianoforte fantasia in C, fantasia for pianoforte and violin.

Like Mozart, whose influence upon his work is noticeable to the very end, he meant his music to be independent of all adventitious aid or interpretation, he never assigned to any composition a picturesque or poetic title, he never gave any indication of specific meaning or content. It is true that he did little to extend or deepen the great symphonic forms; and that in some respects he may even have prepared for their disintegration. Nevertheless his strength lay not in revolt against a method but in loyalty to a principle. The laws of his kingdom were the laws of pure beauty, and in their service he found at once his inspiration and his reward.

CHAPTER XII

SONG

IT is not difficult to divine, from a study of Schubert's instrumental writing, that his genius would find its natural outlet through the medium of song. The composer in whose hands the symphony itself becomes lyric sufficiently indicates the central purpose and predilection of his art ; the singer whose highest gift is that of expressive melody must needs gain both impetus and guidance from the poet's collaboration. Colour, which in a quartet or a sonata delights by its sheer beauty, acquires a special value and significance when it is used to enhance the spoken word ; devices of rhythm and modulation, which in pure music arouse some vague indeterminate emotion in the hearer, grow big with actual tragedy when the poet has shown us how to interpret them. Again in this collaborate form of song it is the poet rather than the musician by whom the general scheme is set forth and determined : by him the outlines are drawn, the limits ordained, and the function of music is not so much to construct as to illuminate and adorn. Here then arose a special opportunity for an artist of Schubert's temperament : an opportunity which the very forces of circumstance conspired to bestow upon him. His imagination, always sensitive and alert, rendered him keenly susceptible of poetic suggestion ; he was born at a time when German song, matured through half a century of noble achievement, offered itself in full measure for his acceptance. With such material to his hand it is little wonder that the most romantic of classical composers should have risen through the most romantic of musical forms to his height of supreme and unchallenged pre-eminence.

The development of artistic song, during the period which we are here considering, is almost exclusively confined to Germany and Austria. It is, no doubt, a matter for comment that the form which is most readily intelligible and most universally beloved should have remained, through the majority of European nations, virtually stagnant and unprogressive; that France, Italy, and England, to name no others, should for a hundred years have contributed little or nothing to its advance; whatever the reason, and there are many that could be suggested, the fact holds that two of these countries produced no lyric masterpiece on either side, and that the third left Burns and Scott to be set by German composers. But before tracing the history along its most important field of production we may turn aside for a moment to these outlying districts and gather from them such scanty harvest as they were able to afford.

Of the three countries here specified Italy bears, in this matter, the most barren record. From Scarlatti to Rossini the land of the *bel canto* produced hardly a song which it is of any value to recollect. The old traditions of the seventeenth century appear to have been forgotten. Italian science buried itself in counterpoint, Italian melody trilled and postured upon the stage; between the two are a few airs of Gasparini, Cimarosa, and Mercadante, which are as trivial in theme as they are slight in workmanship. It is the more remarkable, since the beauty of many operatic arias is enough to show that the gift of pure vocal melody was still living and effective: but with all the best talent devoted to the service of the Church or the theatre there was little room for the more solitary and self-contained expression of lyric feeling. No doubt there were *canti popolari*, folk-songs of the vintage and the trysting-place, but of them our evidence is as yet imperfect, since most of the collections belong to the nineteenth century and bear traces of Gordigiani and his generation. In any case they were disregarded by the more prominent composers, and in their neglect we may perhaps find a concomitant symptom of the national weakness and apathy.

The history of French music shows an intimate connexion between song and dance, the natural outcome of a temper by which musical art is almost as much determined by gesture as by tone. Indeed, we are told that in early days if a branle or a minuet became popular it was customary, as the phrase went, to 'parody' it—that is, to adapt it to words if it had none already [1]; and we may match this on the other side by the 'Gascoigne roundelay' to which Sterne found the peasants dancing 'on the road between Nismes and Lunel.' By the eighteenth century several of the old forms were still surviving; —the *chanson*, gay, light-hearted or satirical, the *romance*, a love-song in dainty couplets, the *brunette*, tender and playful, the *Vaudeville*, carrying in its name its origin from the city streets [2]; all expressing in their several degrees the primitive unsophisticated emotions of simple folk. But in eighteenth-century France, as in contemporary Italy, song lay somewhat outside the domain of serious and official art. Rousseau, who steadfastly endeavoured to call his countrymen into Arcadia, wrote a few naïve and pleasing melodies, of which the most famous are 'Le Rosier' and 'Au fond d'une sombre vallée': he was followed by Monsigny, Rigel, Favart, and some other members of the Bouffonist party; but in the main France continued its allegiance to more artificial forms, until the Revolution swept them away to the tunes of 'Ça ira' and the Marseillaise. It was not until 1830 that French song began as an artistic force with Montpou and Berlioz, Hugo and Gautier, and the story of its development belongs not to this period but to the romantic movement which came after.

With England the case was somewhat different. Between 1750 and 1830 there was, apart from Arne, a good deal of 'slim and serviceable talent' expended upon song-writing. The ballads of Arnold and Dibdin, of Shield and Storace, of Hook

---

[1] See Wekerlin's *Échos du temps passé*, iii. 136; also the article on Song in Grove, vol. iii. p. 592, first edition; vol. v. p. 6, third edition.

[2] Some derive it from Olivier de Basselin's 'Vaux de Vire,' but 'voix de ville' seems more probable.

and Davy and Horn, possess genuine melodic feeling : the glees
of Webbe and Stevens exhibit the same characteristics and
occupy a similar station in the outer courts of the art.   With
the music of Arne English song rises for a brief moment to
a higher level. ' Rule Britannia ' has a certain bluff manliness—
as though Henry Fielding were proposing a national toast—
and the Shakespearian songs, though they fall far short of their
subject, are pure and melodious.   But at its best our native art
was restricted within narrow limits.   Based on the folk-song it
raised a superstructure little higher than its foundation, and
though sound and truthful contributed no monument that should
be visible to the distant view.   In its choice of topics there
was neither subtlety nor range : only the obvious praise of
love and wine, the obvious expressions of patriotic sentiment, or,
in a further flight of fancy, some Chelsea-ware pastoral of
Chloe or Phillis.   To our own countrymen it is valuable as
a stage of preparation and promise : to the world at large
it was of no account until the fullness of time should bring it to
fruition.

About the middle of the eighteenth century German
literature began to gather its forces and to raise its national
standard. When Frederick the Great came to the throne in 1740
French influence was still paramount, and the king himself set
the fashion of depreciating his countrymen and declaring
that outside of Paris there could be neither taste nor genius.
An amusing conversation [1], which he held on the subject with
Gellert, exhibits his point of view with surprising frankness.
' I understand,' he said, ' that you have written fables.   Have
you read La Fontaine ?'   ' Yes,' answered Gellert audaciously,
' but I have not followed him. I am original.' ' So was he, '
said the king, ' but tell me why it is that we have so few good
German authors.'   ' Perhaps,' said Gellert, ' your Majesty is
prejudiced against the Germans, or,' pressing his point as
Frederick hesitated, ' at least against German literature.'

[1] Quoted in Dr. Hahn's *Geschichte der poetischen Litteratur der Deutschen*, p. 153.

'Well,' said Frederick, 'I think that is true.' And when, at the royal request, Gellert recited his fable of ' Der Maler ' the king broke out in astonishment, 'Why, that flows. I can follow it all. The other day Gottsched was trying to read me his translation of the *Iphigénie*, and though I had the French in my hand I could make nothing of it.'

It was under these discouraging circumstances that Gellert began the work of reconstruction which, with the aid of a fortunate alliance, places him historically in the forefront of German song. In 1757 he published his famous collection of *Geistliche Oden und Lieder*, one of the finest volumes of sacred poetry in the German language, containing, among other numbers, the hymns ' Für alle Güte sei gepreist ' and ' Die Ehre Gottes in der Natur.' These fell at once into the hands of C. P. E. Bach, who had already written a few ' Oden mit Melodien ' to words by Kleist, Gleim, and other poets, and in 1758 the *Gellert'sche Lieder* were printed by Winter of Berlin. ' Mit diesem schönen und edlen Werke,' says Dr. Bitter, ' ist Em. Bach der Begründer und Schöpfer des deutschen Liedes in seiner jetzigen Bedeutung geworden [1].' The preface, which, after the fashion of the time, introduced the music to its audience, explains clearly enough Bach's principle of song-composition. The plan is not to be that of a ballad with the same melody for each stanza, still less that of the formal ' da capo ' aria which was artificially maintained by operatic convention : ' Bei Verfertigung der Melodien,' he writes, ' habe ich so viel als möglich auf das ganze Lied gesehen.' The tone is modest and tentative, for the path had yet to be opened : but there can be no doubt as to its purpose and direction.

Meanwhile the ranks of German poetry were receiving year by year fresh recruits and accessions. After Gellert, Klopstock, and Wieland led the way, there came the Göttinger Hainbund of Voss, Hölty, and Miller, then the philosophic romanticism of

---

[1] *C. P. E. Bach*, vol. i. p. 143. Dr. Reissmann (*Geschichte des deutschen Liedes*, p. 86) calls Bach ' der Vater des durchcomponirten Liedes.'

Lessing and Herder, then the period of revolution which took
its name from Klinger's wild tragi-comedy 'Sturm und Drang,'
and after revolution the triumvirate of Goethe, Schiller, and
Jean Paul.   With these later movements of revolt and reconsti-
tution Bach appears to have had little sympathy; they
outstripped his resources, they passed beyond his horizon;
but short of them he followed the literary progress of his age,
and bore no inconsiderable part in maintaining its cause.
In 1774 he published a set of psalms to words by Cramer, and
beside these wrote in all nearly a hundred secular songs on
lyrics selected from Hölty, Gleim, Lessing, Haller, and others
among his contemporaries.   An interesting example of his style
may be found in the refrain of the *Nonnenlied*[1] (No. 5 of the
volume published posthumously in 1789) :—

There is an odd touch of formality in the opening phrase,
but we cannot fail to be moved by the beauty and pathos with
which the melody sinks upon its cadence.

For nearly thirty years Bach remained among German song-
writers, without a rival and almost without a comrade.   The
lyrics of Graun and Agricola, of Marpurg and Kirnberger, are
of little historical account; even Gluck's music to the odes
of Klopstock is singularly dry and uninteresting.   But the

[1] Quoted in Bitter's *C. P. E. Bach*, vol. ii. p. 78.

appearance of Goethe's lyrical poetry opened a new world and gave a new inspiration. In 1780 Reichardt published his first volume of *Songs from Goethe*, which he supplemented by a second in 1793, and by a more complete collection in 1809 : his example was followed by Zelter and Eberwein, whose melodies, now wholly forgotten, were preferred by Goethe to those of Beethoven and Schubert. The beacon kindled at Weimar aroused answering fires from every height in Germany: from Tieck and the Schlegels, Brentano and von Arnim, von Kleist and Werner, Hölderlin, von Collin, and Hebel, Arndt and Körner, Rückert and Uhland: until at the last there soared from its remote and solitary peak that 'spire of audible flame' which was lighted by the hand of Heine. Never perhaps in the history of literature has a single generation witnessed the outburst of a passion so widespread and so overwhelming.

It would be interesting to conjecture the probable effect on German music had Mozart shown any interest in song-writing. His tunefulness, his lucidity of style, his skill in accompaniment-figures, his power of expressing a dramatic scene or situation would here have found ample opportunity, and might even have forestalled by half a century some of the most characteristic work of Schubert. But it is evident that he regarded this form of composition as little more than the recreation of an idle moment. Of the forty-one songs attributed to him in Köchel's catalogue only five[1] appear to have been printed in his lifetime : the rest, with one exception, are but charming trifles, thrown off like Beethoven's canons, for the entertainment of his friends, and in no way intended to be representative of his more serious art. There remain, therefore, six alone which it is of any moment to consider : *Das Lied der Freiheit*, a capital folk-song with a good swinging German

---

[1] 'Das Lied der Freiheit,' ' Das Veilchen,' ' Trennung und Wiedervereinigung,' ' An Chloe,' and ' Abendempfindung.' Even of these the two last are doubtful. See Jahn's *Mozart*, ii. p. 371, and notes Köchel, pp. 523 and 524.

tune; *An Chloe,* playful, tender, and as vocal as an Italian
canzonet; *Abendempfindung,* with something of the quiet
of evening in its melody; two love-songs; *Trennung* and
Unglückliche Liebe, of a more tragic tone; and, most perfect of
all, *Das Veilchen,* in which, for the one occasion of his life,
Mozart joins hands with Goethe.   Nowhere else has he so
clearly shown the power of music to entrance and heighten
a true lyric poem.   The little story, which might be told
to engage the sympathies of a child, grows instinct with human
feeling and passion, as a fairy-tale may sometimes startle us
with a touch of nature :—

Veil - chen,   es war ein her - zig's Veil - chen.

Yet though *Das Veilchen* is perfect of its kind, it is too
slender and fragile to bear any weight of artistic tradition.
And this is true of all Mozart's songs. Had they been left
unwritten we should be the poorer for the loss of some exquisite
melodies, but the course and progress of musical composition
would not have been appreciably altered. Compared with
those of Beethoven, and still more with those of Schubert, they
are 'as wild-roses to the rose and as wind-flowers to the roses
of the garden.'

A somewhat different cause debarred Haydn from bearing
his full share in this lyric movement. There is no reason
to think that he took song-composition lightly: indeed most of
his examples are carefully, even elaborately, written with
polished melodies, long *ritornelli*, and almost symphonic
accompaniments. But the fact is that he took no interest
in the new poetry.   Remote, secluded, unlettered he sat in his
quiet study beside Eisenstadt church, and made his music
without any regard to the controversies and achievements
of the sister art.   In no single case did he choose words by any
German poet of eminence; even Gellert, with whom he was
so often compared, was left by him wholly neglected; and
nearly all the songs of his Eisenstadt period are marred by the
formalism or triviality of the verse.   In his first volume
(*Zwölf Lieder*, Artaria, 1781) there is a spirited setting
of Wither's 'Shall I wasting in despair,' a translation of
which must have floated to him on some unexpected wind: in

his second (*Zwölf Lieder*, Artaria, 1784) are a few songs of graver mood — *Am Grabe meines Vaters*, *Gebet zu Gott*, *Das Leben ist ein Traum*—which contain passages of serious and lofty import; but with a few exceptions the style is antiquated and artificial, very different from the spontaneous melody of his symphonies and quartets. We feel throughout that he is unequally yoked, and that he finds collaboration not a stimulus but an impediment.

Shortly after their publication these volumes were brought over to London and adapted by Shield and Arnold to English words. In consequence of their success Haydn, on his first visit to this country, was besieged with further applications, and responded by composing some half-dozen English ballads, and the famous twelve canzonets on which his reputation as a song-writer mainly depends. Though unequal in value they far surpass any of his earlier work in the same kind : indeed as examples of graceful and flowing melody, some of them may take rank with the best of his inventions. The tunes of ' My mother bids me bind my hair,' of the *Mermaid's Song*, of *Recollection*, can still be heard with delight; while the *Wanderer*, if somewhat impaired by its strophic form, carries the stanza to a dramatic climax of real force and intensity. With them the distinctive style of eighteenth-century song attained its close : with Beethoven the old order changed and gave place to new.

Beethoven's earliest known songs are contained in the volume numbered as Op. 52, and belong for the most part to the time of his residence at Bonn. They are slight, boyish experiments, barely redeemed by a pretty setting of Goethe's *Mailied,* and showing but little promise of his maturer style. But on his arrival in Vienna there followed a remarkable alteration of method. We have already seen that he came with the avowed intention of writing for the stage, and although this intention was only partially fulfilled it left a significant mark on his vocal writing. For the next eighteen years all the greatest of his secular songs are distinctly influenced by dramatic treatment, following the various suggestions of the words by entire changes of style or tempo, lacking the homogeneity of the lyric, and substituting for it the more direct representation of an operatic song or scena. *Adelaide* was published in 1796, *Ah! perfido* in 1804, *An die Hoffnung* in 1805, *In questa tomba* in 1807, *Kennst du das Land*, with other songs from Goethe, in 1810. Indeed during this whole period the only works which are at once of lyric character and of first importance are the six sacred songs from Gellert (including *Die Ehre Gottes* and *Das Busslied*), which were published in 1803 as Op. 48; and it is not less noticeable that in 1810 he attempted a setting of Goethe's *Erlkönig* and laid it aside as unsuitable to his genius[1]. These facts would seem to admit of but one interpretation. With the old simple melodic type of song he was no longer satisfied, or at best relegated it to his more slender and unimportant works : to the fused and molten passion of the modern lyric he had not yet attained, the metal of which it should be wrought was still lying in the furnace: meantime he set himself to inspire and vivify song, by taking it openly and frankly on its dramatic side. Whatever the degree of direct influence which these works had upon Schubert they represent beyond question the stage of artistic endeavour from which he was to emerge.

And we may go further than this. In the songs which Beethoven published between 1810 and 1816 we may catch the very point of transition, where to the diffused force of dramatic presentation there succeeds the concentrated emotion of the lyrical mood. It appears in the first of his four settings of Goethe's *Sehnsucht* :—

---

[1] It was finished by Becker and published in 1897.

it appears in the second of the Egmont songs, the opening phrase of which might almost have been written by Schubert :—

han - gen und ban - gen in schwe - ben - der Pein

it is not less evident both in the form of the *Liederkreis* and in the exquisite and touching melody with which the cycle begins and closes :—

Auf dem Hü - gel sitz' ich späh - end in das

blau - e Ne - bel - land, nach den fer - nen Trif - ten

seh - end, wo ich dich . . Ge - lieb - te fand,

In these three examples song is speaking a language entirely
different from that of Mozart and Haydn : it has begun to glow
with that peculiar warmth and fervour which we designate by
the name of romance.   And it may be remarked that after
these Beethoven wrote no more songs of any account.   The
torch was lighted and the hand that should receive it from him
was ready.

A few months before Beethoven composed the *Liederkreis* [1],
Schubert, then a boy of eighteen, brought down to the Convict-
school his setting of *Erlkönig*.   We have a vivid picture of
the scene : Schubert still white-hot with the excitement of
Goethe's poem, his comrades gathering round the piano, half-
fascinated, half-incredulous, Ruzicka, good easy man, endeavouring to explain by rule and measure the utterance of a new
genius.   On that winter evening a fresh page was turned in the
history of German song, a page on which was to be recorded
the most splendid of its achievements.   Hitherto the lyric
element in musical composition had been subordinated to the
epic and dramatic, henceforward it claimed its rights and
asserted its equality.

Schubert's activity as a song-writer extends over a period of
seventeen years, from *Hager's Klage*, which is dated 1811, to
Die Taubenpost, which he composed in October, 1828, a few
weeks before his death.   No musician has ever worked with less
of external stimulus and encouragement.   It was not until 1819
that a song of his was publicly performed ; it was not until
1821 that any were printed : through his brief career of stress
and poverty Vienna treated him with unpardonable neglect, and
only awoke at its close to a half-hearted and tardy recognition.
Yet the number of his songs, apart from sketches and fragments,
is considerably over six hundred : in the year 1815 alone he
composed a hundred and thirty-seven, eight of them in one day,
and the two years which followed were hardly less prolific.

---

[1] ' Erlkönig' was written either in December, 1815, or January, 1816: the ' Liederkreis ' in April, 1816.

His genius was, as Vogl says, *clairvoyant*; wholly independent
of condition or circumstances: with a volume of poems and
a pile of music paper, he could shut his door upon the world
and enter into the kingdom of his own creations. We are told
that a visitor once asked him some questions as to his method
of work. 'It is very simple,' he answered, 'I compose
all the morning, and when I have finished one piece I begin
another.'

His lyric gift was from the first wonderfully mature. Before
he was twenty years old he had written nearly all the finest of
his songs from Goethe, a collection which by itself would be
sufficient to win his immortality. But as in his instrumental
music the approach of manhood brought him a firmer hand, so
in song it enriched him with an even deeper and more intimate
expression. In the earlier compositions we have an extremely
vivid illustration of the poet's theme—Gretchen at her spin-
ning-wheel, the father and child galloping through the haunted
night, restless love beneath the pelting of the pitiless storm—
and the same power of pictorial suggestion is apparent in the
great mythic odes—*Ganymed, An Schwager Kronos, Gruppe
aus dem Tartarus*—with which he was at this time much
occupied. The later work penetrates more closely to the
centre, and instead of confirming the poet speaks, as it were,
in his actual person. In the *Schöne Müllerin* (1823), the songs
from Scott and Shakespeare (1825-7), the *Winterreise* (1827),
and the *Schwanengesang* (1828), the fusion between the two
arts is complete: they are no longer two but one, a single,
indivisible utterance of lyric thought. No songs of Schumann
and Heine, of Brahms and Tieck, have attained to a more perfect
and indissoluble unity.

One of the chief problems which confronts the composer of
song-music is that of adjusting the balance between melodic
form and emotional meaning. The scheme of melody is a
continuous and sweeping curve where each note depends for its
value on those which precede and follow it, and the unit of

appreciation is the entire line or phrase. Poetry, on the other hand, because it deals with the articulate word, can at any moment arrest our attention without risking the loss of continuity: the *mot juste* by sheer force of colour or association drives home its point, and yet leaves us free to follow the general tenour of the verse unhindered. No doubt in some types of song this difficulty is not apparent: a simple ballad may be purely melodic, a dramatic scena may be purely declamatory; but the greatest musical lyrics rise between these two extremes to a height of co-ordinate perfection which is beyond the scope of either. There is no paradox in holding that it is easier to write a good tune or to follow a close-wrought poem than to attain both these ends at the same time.

It is one secret of Schubert's greatness that he solved this problem with an unerring mastery. In the first place he had an extraordinary power of constructing his melody out of short expressive phrases, each appropriate to the poetic idea which it was set to embody, yet all together giving the effect of unbroken tunefulness. He can even enhance this by echoing each phrase as it comes with a tiny instrumental *ritornello,* often but two or three notes in length, which not only emphasizes and corroborates the voice, but, far from interrupting, carries our ear onward to its next utterance. An example may be quoted from the beginning of *Liebesbotschaft* :—

Rau - schen-des Bäch - lein, so sil - bern und hell,

and there are equally familiar instances in *An Sylvia* and the *Ständchen*. Again he realized, as no composer before him had realized, the manner in which an emotional point could be enforced by a sudden change or crisis in the harmonization. The strident discords in *Erlkönig*, the sigh at the words ' Und ach! sein Kuss' in *Gretchen am Spinnrade*, are examples which have become historically famous : not less wonderful is the sudden flash of livid colour which breaks upon the cold and bleak harmonies of *Der Doppelgänger* :—

In his earlier songs he often made this effect by unexpected
and remote modulations, a device which on one or two occasions
(e. g. Mayrhofer's *Liedesend*) he carried to an extreme of
restlessness. In his later works the general key-system is
more clearly defined, and the points of colour lie within a more
determinate scheme of tonality. The alternations of major and
minor mode, intimately characteristic of his instrumental
writing, are, as might be expected, of frequent occurrence
in his songs, either bearing their obvious emotional significance as in *Gute Nacht*, or suggesting a more subtle
distinction as in the song from *Rosamunde*. Allied to the last
of these, though technically different in reference, is the wonderful change of a semitone which in *Du bist die Ruh* recalls the
melody to its key.

Another important accessory is his use of rhythmic figures,
employed sometimes to indicate actual sound or movement—
the murmur of the brook, or the rustle of leaves in the forest

—sometimes, as in *Die Stadt,* to support an emotional mood, and always with the additional purpose of binding and unifying the accompaniment into an organic whole. Their design covers an astonishing range of variety and invention : the most intractable curves grow plastic, the simplest effects of arpeggio or recurrent chord are vitalized, now by an ingenious progression, now by a well-placed point of colour. The pianoforte part of *Geheimes* is not too light to be interesting, that of *Suleika* is not elaborate enough to be obscure, while those of *Ungeduld, Die Post, Wohin,* and *Frühlingsglaube,* contain effects which in Schubert's time were absolutely new, and which remain in our own day marvels of tact and certainty.

Yet after all his supremacy in German song depends far less on his command of detail than on the imagination, at once receptive and creative, by which his general conception of his art was inspired. His vocal music is saturated with that quality which painters call atmosphere ; that limpidity of touch by which hues are blended and outlines softened and the receding distances grow faint and mysterious. When we listen to the two songs from Shakespeare, or the *Litanei,* or *Sei mir gegrüsst,* we feel that the melody is, in a manner, etherealized : that we hear it through a translucent veil as we see the colours of dawn or sunset. From horizon to zenith they merge and tremble and change, and the light that kindles them shines across the liquid interspaces of heaven.

Critics have reproached him for a want of literary discrimination ; and there is no doubt that he could sometimes catch the hint or suggestion that he needed from verses of which the rhyme is poor and the style commonplace. But in the words of all his best songs there is the germ of a true poetic idea : in the vast majority of them he joined alliance with poets who were worthy of his collaboration. Over seventy are taken from Goethe, over fifty from Schiller, others again from Scott and Shakespeare, from Klopstock, Hölty and Claudius, from Körner and Wilhelm Müller and Schlegel and

Heine.   Among lesser men some, like Mayrhofer and Schober,
were his personal friends, others, like Seidl, Rellstab, and
Kosegarten, were in vogue during his day: and if they
sometimes dragged him to their level it is little wonder if
he oftener lifted them to his own.

For his emotional moods, despite their range and variety,
were, each as it came, altogether whole-hearted and sincere.
'I never force myself into devotion,' he says, speaking of
his *Ave Maria*, 'or compose prayers or hymns unless I am
absolutely overpowered by the feeling': and the same is true, in
corresponding measure, of his entire art.   His temperament,
extremely sensitive and sympathetic, vibrated like an Aeolian
harp to every breath of passion: the verse which aroused
his imagination took at once complete possession of it and
struck a responsive note that quivered into music.   His
favourite themes are those of all true lyric poetry—songs
of the brookside and the woodland, songs of adventure, of
romance, of human love and religious adoration, of every
issue to which spirits can be finely touched.   He takes the
heightened and quickened movements of our life, and by
very keenness of vision reveals in them an unwonted and
unsuspected beauty.

The songs of Schubert bring the Viennese period to its
historical conclusion.   The latest of them—those which we
know by the title of *Schwanengesang*—he composed in the
autumn of 1828; in November of that year he died; in
1830 began simultaneously the careers of Schumann and
Berlioz.   Thenceforward the course of musical art passed
into new fields of action and accepted aims and methods
which it is beyond the scope of this volume to consider.
Yet through all extremes of diversity and revolt much of
the old influence remained.   The freedom which the romantic
movement claimed as a right it received as a heritage, won
through long years of steady and patient advance.   Our
debt to the Viennese masters is not summed up in the delight

with which we contemplate the monuments of their genius : the very possibility of later progress is in great measure due to the tradition which they set and to the principles which they established. They gave dramatic truth to opera and poetic truth to song; they developed the great instrumental numbers through which music finds its purest expression ; they first taught men how to blend the voices of the orchestra and the quartet ; they emancipated style from formalism and melody from artifice; they bore their message upward to those mystic heights where the soul of man communes with the Eternal. ' From the heart it has come, to the heart it shall penetrate,' said Beethoven : and in these words he not only crowned the labours of a lifetime but held aloft the noblest ideal for the generations that should follow after him.

INDEX

ABEL, 39, 264.
Académie de Musique, 95, 96, 118, 236.
ADOLFATTI, 89.
AFFLIGIO, 265.
AGRICOLA, 329.
AGUJARI, 26-7.
Alberti Bass, 63.
ALTARRIBA, 181.
ANFOSSI, 98.
ANTONIOTTI, 22, 39.
ARNAUD, 99.
ARNE, 104, 144, 327.
ARNOLD, 144, 176, 326, 333.
ARNOULD, Sophie, 28, 44, 95.
ARTEAGA, 86.
ATTWOOD, 141, 176-7.
Austrian National Anthem, 81, 161.

BACH, C. P. E., 6, 10, 51, 52, 66, 182, 195-204, 224, 232.
—— Influence on style, 68-79.
—— Influence on Haydn, 79, 210-3.
—— Oratorios, &c., 69-72, 144-8.
—— Sonatas: *Frederick*, 69, 201, 207; *Würtemberg*, 69, 196, 198, 201, 207; *Reprise*, 69, 77, 198, 225; *Kenner und Liebhaber*, 70, 200.
—— Songs, 328-9.
—— *Wahre Art*, 51, 55, 69.
BACH, J. C., 52, 67, 264.
BACH, J. S., 6, 39, 51, 55, 57-9, 62, 63, 70, 177, 183, 192, 193.
BACH, W. F., 10, 53, 66-7, 205.

BACKERS, 52.
BAILLOT, 30, 32.
BARTHÉLÉMON, 26.
Baryton, 41.
Bassoon, 43-4.
BATTISHILL, 176.
BEETHOVEN, 15, 18, 51, 74, 116, 269, 276, 344.
—— Three periods, 279, 281, 293.
—— Use of folk-songs, 82.
—— Influence on Schubert, 311-3, 334-7.
—— *Christus am Oelberge*, 151.
—— *Fidelio*, 124-33.
—— *Ruins of Athens*, 125.
—— Masses, 166-75, 303.
—— Chamber-music, 269-75, 279-98.
—— Concertos, 289.
—— Overtures, 289, 303.
—— Sonatas, 51, 56, 61, 83, 280-98.
—— Songs, 333-7.
—— Symphonies, 82, 280-303.
—— Choral symphony, 83, 298-303.
BENDA, 30, 205.
BERLIOZ, 326, 343.
BERNACCHI, 21, 25, 28.
BERTEAU, 39.
BERTON, 100.
BESOZZI, 22, 43.
BISHOP, 141.
BOCCHERINI, 10, 39, 226-9, 233.
BÖHM, J., 30.
BÖHM, T., 43.
BOIELDIEU, 135.

BONNO, 89, 207.
BORTNIANSKY, 144, 157.
BOUCHER, 31.
BOYCE, 176.
BRAHMS, 322.
BRIDGETOWER, 31.
BRÜHL, Count, 137, 140.
BURNEY, 8, 9, 21, 92.
BUXTEHUDE, 57.

CABO, 178, 180, 182.
CAFFARELLI, 25.
CALZABIGI, 91, 93.
CANNABICH, 32, 47.
CANOBBIO, 113. .
CARTIER, 32.
CATHARINE II, 12, 113.
Cecchina, La, 97-8.
CHABRAN, 30.
Chalumeau, 44.
CHERUBINI, 42, 304.
—— Operas, 118-24.
—— Masses, 163-4.
—— Instrumental works, 306-7.
CHEVARDIÈRE, LA, 209.
CHOPIN, 52, 278, 305.
CIMAROSA, 114, 143, 325.
Clarinet, 44-5.
Clavichord, 49.
Clavier, 47-53, 55-6.
CLEMENTI, 52, 246, 273, 278.
Coda, 287-9.
Concerts Spirituels, 122, 136, 236.
Conservatorio, 20-2.
Contrapuntal and harmonic styles, 59-63.
CORELLI, 29, 33, 182, 184-91.
Cornetto, 45.
COUPERIN, 48, 58, 182, 216.
CRAMER, J. B., 278.
CRAMER, W., 32, 47.
CRISTOFORI, 49-51.
CUZZONI, 26.
Cymbalom, 51.
CZERNY, 306.

D'ARTOT, 32.
DAVID, 32.
DAVY, 326.
DENNER, 44.
DIBDIN, 141, 326.
DIDEROT, 91, 94.
DITTERSDORF, 30, 108, 149, 226.
DÖBBERLIN, 137.
DORN, 136.
Double-bass, 40.
DRAGONETTI, 40.
DUNI, 94.
DUPORT, 39.
DURAND, 30.
DURANTE, 21, 97.
DURAZZO, Count, 91.
DUSSEK, 278.

EBERWEIN, 330.
ECK, 32.
EISEL, 39, 40, 42, 43, 44.
EISENSTADT, 41, 79, 219, 265, 305.
English Church Music, 176-8.
ESTERHAZY, Count Johann, 15, 316.
ESTERHAZY, Prince Nicholas, 14, 41, 232, 265.
ESTERHAZY, Prince Paul, 207.

FABER, D., 49.
FARINELLI, 13, 25-8.
FAUSTINA, 26.
FAVART, 94, 326.
FERDINAND IV, 41.
FERRANDINI, 22, 28.
FIELD, 278.
FISCHER, 44.
Folk-songs, influence of, 79-83, 224.
FRANCISCELLO, 39.
FREDERICK THE GREAT, 3, 11, 29, 43, 56, 225.
FUENTES, 179.
FÜRNBERG, VON, 207.
FUX, 207.

GALUPPI, 10, 12, 21, 156.
GARCIA, 181.

GASPARINI, 325.
GASSMANN, 110, 116.
GAVINIÉS, 32.
GELLERT, 327.
GEMINIANI, 22, 35, 36.
GIARDINI, 30, 36.
GINGUENÉ, 99.
GIORNOVICHI, 9, 33.
GIZZIELLO, 26.
GLUCK, 10, 12, 24, 85-104, 137.
—— Early operas, 86.
—— Transitional operas, 89-90.
—— *Orfeo*, 43, 90.
—— *Pilgrims of Mecca*, 91.
—— *Alceste*, 43, 44, 91.
—— *Paride ed Elena*, 92.
—— *Iphigénie en Aulide*, 93.
—— *La Cythère assiégée*, 96.
—— *Armida*, 99.
—— *Iphigénie en Tauride*, 100.
—— Odes, 329.
—— Preface to *Alceste*, 91-2.
GOETHE, 113, 329-38, 342.
GOSSEC, 21, 44, 121, 123, 144, 157, 225.
GRASSALCOVICH, Count, 264.
GRAUN, 10, 23, 58, 137, 148, 156, 329.
GRÉTRY, 9, 10, 94, 109, 119-20, 123.
GRIMM, 94.
Guerre des Bouffons, 93-4.
GUSTAVUS III, 12, 113.
GYROWETZ, 264.

HANDEL, 38, 42, 43, 142, 149.
Harpsichord, 46, 48.
HASSE, 10, 12, 23, 70, 89, 137, 148, 205.
HAYDN, Joseph, 13-5, 23, 24, 40, 41, 73, 206, 232, 233, 246-7, 265-70.
—— Influence on Mozart, 234, 250.
—— Use of folk-songs, 79-81, 223-4.
—— Concertos, 40, 41.
—— Divertimenti, 41, 208, 218.
—— Masses, 154, 156, 160, 163.

HAYDN, Joseph, Operas, 105.
—— Oratorios : *Tobias*, 43, 149 ; *Creation*, 150; *Seasons*, 151.
—— Quartets, &c., 208-18, 219, 246, 248-9, 263.
—— Sonatas, 219.
—— Songs, 332-3.
—— Symphonies, 208, 218-23, 251, 265-6.
HAYDN, Michael, 13-15, 156.
—— Masses, 157-8.
—— Instrumental works, 226.
HEBENSTREIT, 51.
HIERONYMUS, Archbishop of Salzburg, 14-15.
HILLER, J. A., 108, 141.
HIMMEL, 137.
HOFFMEISTER, 247.
HOGARTH, G., 87.
HOOK, 327.
Horn, 42.
HORN, C. F., 327.
HUMMEL, 304-6.

IFFLAND, 137.
ITALY, influence of :—
—— Musical education, 20-2.
—— Singing, 22, 24-9.
—— Violin-playing, 29-31, 35-8.
—— Pianoforte, 50-2.
—— Style, 63-6, 75-7.
—— Operatic convention, 86-8.

JOACHIM, 30.
JOMMELLI, 7, 12, 37, 89, 96, 143, 157, 233.
JOSEPH II, 3, 12, 161, 233, 246.
JULIÀ, 179.

KAUNITZ, 4.
KEISER, 23.
KELLY, M., 2, 28, 104, 141.
Keyed instruments, 47-53, 55-6.
KIRNBERGER, 74, 329.
KÖLBAL, 42.

Kolo, 224.
KOZELUCH, 232, 264, 273.
KREUTZER, 32.

LA HARPE, 99.
LARRIVÉE, 95.
LECLAIR, 30, 32.
LEGROS, 95, 236.
LEO, 21, 97.
LÉONARD, 122.
LESUEUR, 123, 134, 144.
LIDON, 180.
LINKE, 279.
Lira da bracchio, 40.
LOCATELLI, 31, 35.
LOGROSCINO, 97.
LOLLI, 31, 36.
LULLY, 47, 93, 200.

Mannheim Orchestra, 8, 45, 46, 47.
MARA, 28-9.
MARENZIO, 60.
MARIA THERESA, 3, 12.
MARIE ANTOINETTE, 95.
MARMONTEL, 94, 96, 98.
MARPURG, 9, 74, 207.
MARTIN, 264.
MARTINEZ, Marianne, 207.
MARTINI, Pardre, 21, 180.
Mass Music, 154-6.
Masses:
—— Haydn, 154, 156, 160, 163.
—— Mozart, 158-60.
—— Beethoven, 166-75, 303.
—— Cherubini, 163-4.
—— Schubert, 165.
MAYSEDER, 279, 303.
MÉHUL, 121-3.
MELZI, Count, 85.
MENDELSSOHN, 148, 153, 322.
MERCADANTE, 325.
METASTASIO, 89, 205, 206.
MINGHOTTI, Regina, 26.
MONSIGNY, 94, 326.
MONTESINOS, 180.
MONTPOU, 326.

MORZIN, Count, 218.
MOZART, Leopold, 41, 233, 235.
MOZART, W. A., 9, 10, 15, 16, 47, 51, 73, 149, 177, 225, 232-3, 268, 269, 289.
—— Influence on Haydn, 162, 250.
—— Influence on Beethoven, 275, 289.
—— Influence on Schubert, 311-3, 323.
—— Masses, 158-9.
—— Requiem Mass, 43, 45, 159-60.
—— Operas: early, 106, 109; *Idomeneo*, 10, 29, 107-8, 237; *Die Entführung*, 24, 109; *Der Schauspieldirektor*, 110; *Figaro*, 110-2; *Don Giovanni*, 43, 110-2, 126-8; *Così fan tutte*, 110-2; *La Clemenza di Tito*, 112; *Die Zauberflöte*, 43, 45, 112-3.
—— Oratorios, 149.
—— Quartets, &c., 233-5, 248-9, 254-64.
—— Serenades, 10, 234, 235.
—— Sonatas, 243.
—— Songs, 330-2.
—— Symphonies, 10, 45, 235-7, 239, 241-2, 252, 255, 265.

NAPOLEON I, 123-4.
NARDINI, 30.
NAUMANN, 12, 113, 149.
NEBRA, 180.
NICHELMANN, 205.

Oboe, 43.
Oboe d'Amor, 44.
Oboe da Caccia, 44.
OLEG, Prince, 113.
Opera, 7, 64-5, 85-8.
—— Gluck, 86, 89-104.
—— Piccinni, 97-9, 104.
—— Haydn, 105.
—— Hiller, 108.
—— Mozart, 109-13, 126-7.

Opera, Sarti, 114.
—— Paisiello, 115-6.
—— Salieri, 104, 116-7.
—— Cherubini, 118-24.
—— Grétry, 94, 119-20.
—— Gossec, 121.
—— Méhul, 121-3.
—— Beethoven, 124-33.
—— Schubert, 133-4.
—— Lesueur, 134.
—— Boieldieu, 135.
—— Spontini, 135-41.
—— Spohr, 137-40.
—— Weber, 140.
—— English, 104, 141.
Oratorio, 10, 142-4.
—— C. P. E. Bach, 69-72, 144-8.
—— Mozart, 149.
—— Haydn, 149-51.
—— Beethoven, 151.
—— Schubert, 152.
—— Spohr, 152-3.
Orchestras, 46.
ORTES, Abbate, 10.
OSPEDALI, 20.

PACHELBEL, 57.
PACHKIEVICH, 113.
PAGANINI, 4, 29, 310.
PAGIN, 7.
PAISIELLO, 10, 12, 23, 97, 115-6, 123, 143.
PARADIES, 75.
PARKE, 44.
PEREZ, 104.
PERGOLESI, 88.
Pianoforte, 50-2.
PICCINNI, 10, 97-9, 104, 143.
PISTOCCHI, 21.
PLEYEL, 268.
PONS, 178, 181.
PORPORA, 21, 25, 143, 207.
PRIETO, 181.
PUGNANI, 30.
PURCELL, 58, 203.

QUANTZ, 12, 43.

RAAFF, 28.
RABASSA, 179.
RAMEAU, 24, 93, 226.
RAPPOLDI, 30.
REICHARDT, 9, 137, 330.
REUTTER, 5, 89, 92, 207.
RIES, 32, 269.
RIGEL, 326.
RIPA, 180.
RODE, 32.
ROMBERG, A., 32.
ROMBERG, B., 40, 264.
Rondo, 203, 211.
ROSSINI, 134, 312.
ROULLET, 93.
ROUSSEAU, 94, 96, 141, 326.
ROVELLI, 32.

SACCHINI, 10, 21, 97, 104, 114.
SALIERI, 23, 104, 116-7, 143, 233.
SALOMON, 30, 265.
SARASATE, 30.
SARTI, 10, 12, 21, 22, 97, 113-4, 157, 264.
SCARLATTI, A., 58, 200.
SCARLATTI, D., 12, 23, 57, 216.
SCARLATTI, G., 12.
Scherzo, 215.
SCHIKANEDER, 112, 265.
SCHRÖTER, 50.
SCHUBERT, 15, 17, 74, 117, 165, 311, 322, 323.
—— Operas, 133-4.
—— Oratorios, 152.
—— Masses, 165.
—— Instrumental works, first period, 311-4; second period, 314-22.
—— Songs, 337-43.
SCHUMANN, 73, 321, 322, 343.
SCHUPPANZIGH, 32, 279.
SEDAINE, 94, 120.

SINA, 279.
Singspiel, 88, 108.
SOLER, 180.
SOMIS, 22, 29.
Sonata-form, 184–321.
—— Corelli, 184–95.
—— J. S. Bach, 193–4.
—— C. P. E. Bach, 195–204.
—— Haydn, 209–18.
—— Mozart, 237–64.
—— Beethoven, 270–5, 283–9, 294–303.
—— Schubert, 313–21.
Song, 325–43.
—— Italy, 325.
—— France, 326.
—— England, 326.
—— C. P. E. Bach, 328–9.
—— Mozart, 330–2.
—— Haydn, 332–3.
—— Beethoven, 333–7.
—— Schubert, 337–43.
Spanish Church Music, 178–82.
SPOHR, 32, 137–40, 165, 304.
—— Operas, 138–40.
—— Oratorios, 152–3.
—— Instrumental works, 307–10.
SPONTINI, 135–40.
STADLER, 265.
STAMITZ, A., 32.
STAMITZ, J. K., 8, 32, 233.
STAMITZ, K., 39.
STEIBELT, 278.
STEIN, 51.
STORACE, 141, 326.
STRAUS, 30.
STREICHER, 51.

TARTINI, 22, 23, 33.
Théâtre Favart, 122.
Théâtre Feydeau, 122.
Theorbo, 40.
TOMASCHEK, 278.
TRAETTA, 7, 12, 21, 97.

Trombone, 43.
Trumpet, 42.

UMLAUF, 108, 110, 303.

VANDINI, 22.
VANHALL, 264.
Variation form, 272–3.
VENIER, 209.
VERACINI, 31, 33, 35.
VERDI, 115.
VESTRIS, 95.
Viennese Hofkapelle, 43.
Viola, 38.
Viola da Gamba, 39.
Violin-playing, 31–8.
Violin schools, 29–32.
—— Turin, 29.
—— Padua, 30.
—— Bergamo, 31.
—— London, 31.
—— Mannheim, 31.
—— Paris, 32.
Violoncello, 39.
VIOTTI, 9, 32, 37–8, 122.
VIVALDI, 29, 42, 58.

WAGENSEIL, 89, 207, 216.
WEBER, Aloysia, 28.
WEBER, Bernhard, 137.
WEBER, C. M. von, 140.
WEISS, 279.
WERNER, 207.
WESLEY, S., 177.
WILHELMJ, 32.
WOELFL, 278.
WORNUM, 56.

YRIARTE, 45, 53, 181, 225.

Zarzuela, 88, 180.
ZELTER, 330.
ZINGARELLI, 114, 143, 156.
ZMESKALL, 279.
Zopf, 6.
ZUMPE, 52.